Albert and Michel Roux

Albert

Michel

With best wishes

T·H·E
ROUX
BROTHERS
COOKING
FOR · TWO

T·H·E
ROUX
BROTHERS
COOKING
FOR·TWO

Albert and Michel Roux

Photographs by
MARTIN BRIGDALE

SIDGWICK & JACKSON
LONDON

ACKNOWLEDGEMENTS

Our deepest thanks go to Christopher Sellors, sous chef of The Waterside Inn, whose patience with us was only surpassed by his talent with testing all these recipes; Kate Whiteman for her continued sympathetic translations of our books; La Boucherie Lamartine, 229 Ebury Street, London SW1, 071-730 4175, for all our ingredients from tomatoes through wild mushrooms to every conceivable piece of meat and game used in this book; Martin Brigdale for his talent with a camera; Kelly Flynn for her art direction; Andrea Lambton for styling the photographs; Claude Grant for her ability to understand and type the manuscript and Robyn Roux who is still loyally here after four books.

First published in Great Britain in 1991
by Sidgwick & Jackson Limited
Cavaye Place, London SW10 9PG

ISBN 0-283-060751

Translated and edited by Kate Whiteman

Edited, designed and produced by Swallow Books,
260 Pentonville Road, London N1 9JY

Art director: Kelly Flynn
Managing editor: Anne Yelland
Photographer: Martin Brigdale
Stylist: Andrea Lambton
Indexer: Kathie Gill

Typeset by Servis Filmsetting, Manchester
Colour origination by Imago Publishing

Printed in Great Britain by BPCC Hazell Books, Aylesbury

CONTENTS

COOKING FOR TWO

At our own private retreats, or when one of us spends some time with our mother at one of her homes, each of us often cooks for just two people. Our children are in their twenties now, so our holiday homes are often just for a couple. All through the year, we spend hours in the kitchen, so on holiday, we yearn for rest, relaxation and simplicity in the meals we prepare. These are inspired and cooked with a natural creativity which varies according to our mood and whim. Those meals which we prepare on holiday without a kitchen brigade to help us inspire us in our cooking when we return to work.

OUR VISITS TO OUR MOTHER

Every two or three months, we take turns to spend a few pleasurable days with our mother. She adores the Vendée, where she spends the summer months, and during the winter, she lives at Vincennes, near Paris. Thus our visits to her take place in different parts of France and Albert, as the oldest child, makes it a point of honour to clock up more days with our mother during the year than Michel.

Germaine, our mother, who is now seventy-nine, clucks over us like a mother hen the moment we enter her house. In the mornings, she brings us coffee in bed as of right, and we are awoken from our sleep only by birdsong, since she will allow no other noise to disturb the slumbers of her sons, in the belief that they never have time to sleep except when they visit her.

We each like to start the day walking hand-in-hand with her to market. The first ten minutes there are devoted to inspecting the stacks of new baby vegetables and choosing the best and most attractive. From time to time, we stop to greet one of mother's stallholders 'by appointment' with a handshake and the short introduction, 'You see, Marcel, today I have one of my sons from England with me.' This brief remark sounds good to us; Mother is happy and that makes us contented too. Our basket begins to fill up with provisions: two quails, a bunch of asparagus, a skewer of frogs' legs (which are wonderful in the Vendée), some Marmande tomatoes, strawberries and other good things. At this stage, Mother never fails to remark 'That's quite enough, there are only the two of us; let's try to come back tomorrow', adding finally, 'There is nothing to beat freshly bought food which has not been kept in the fridge.'

Since Mother is a woman of experience and authority, that is the end of the day's shopping. Now she tries to discover how we propose to prepare the provisions we have just bought for lunch or dinner. She tells us exactly how she prefers this or that dish to be cooked, but in fact, whatever the method, she always takes great delight in our cooking. We make a final stop at the bakery on the way home to choose a well-baked, crusty loaf, and finally it is time to relax and prepare the meal.

OUR RELAXATION

Our great relaxation is to cook for Mother, while hers is to lay the table, to ensure that the sparkling cider which her sons adore is at the correct temperature and to pour us a glass, humming as she does this. If the weather is fine and we are in the Vendée, she sets the table in the garden. Michel likes to write out the menu for Mother; he writes it on a sheet of exercise paper and sticks it in the window: melon with Pinot de Charentes, pan-fried quails with their juices and baby vegetables, watercress salad with cream, local goat cheese and fresh strawberries. Mother spreads a little slightly salted butter on a slice of bread, pronounces herself hungry after reading the menu and offers to help in the kitchen. This offer is promptly refused; after all, until very recently she has lovingly cooked our meals for us – now it is our turn to spoil her.

Within half an hour, all is ready. First, we do the basic preparation; carefully pick off the flat parsley leaves, shred some tarragon, chop a little shallot – how hungry all this makes us. Soon, the house is filled with the aroma of the simmering quails; the baby vegetables are so tender that they need only be washed and the white onions peeled. 'To table!', we cry triumphantly, both brothers shouting as though Mother were deaf. Now mother and son sit at the table together. It is a magical moment. Each dish is a discovery, punctuated with approving comments on the choice of ingredients and the method of cooking. We always spend a good hour over our meal. Time no longer matters, and the joy we experience in sharing the pleasures is intense.

After the meal, Mother always makes a cup of delicious coffee and invites us to take an afternoon siesta on a lounger in the garden. It is a life of indulgence, a dream, or better still, a reality. This is the life which we invite you to share in our book *Cooking for Two*.

ABOUT THIS BOOK

Even if you are not accustomed to cooking, you need not be daunted by the recipes in this book. They are all designed to make entertaining your guest a pleasure, not a chore.

Recipes for two: Although the recipes are conceived for two people, just double all the ingredients to serve four.

The ingredients: All the ingredients used in the recipes can be easily obtained in any large supermarket and most are inexpensive. Of the 150 recipes in this book, only one uses caviar and two truffles, while lobster, crayfish and foie gras do not feature at all.

Preparation and cooking times: These do not include pre-preparing (peeling and chopping, for example) and measuring ingredients, which should always be done before embarking on the recipe. On average, the recipes take about 25 minutes to prepare; the shortest take only 10 minutes and the longest 40 minutes.

Preparing the meal in advance: Many of the recipes can be prepared before your guest arrives, and need only a few moments' last-minute assembling or cooking.

Simplicity of the recipes: All these recipes are easy to make, and very few need any particular culinary knowledge or skill. Thus anyone, whatever their age or aptitude, can prepare a meal from these recipes without giving themselves a headache!

The chapters in this book: They are divided into times of the year, but not really into seasons, since nowadays most foods are always available. Whatever the season, cook what appeals to you at the time.

Our suggested menus: At the beginning of each chapter, we suggest several recipes which can be combined to make a well-balanced meal.

Nutritional values: These are healthy recipes which conform to today's nutritional needs and tastes. They contain plenty of fruit, vegetables and fish, and use dairy products, such as cream, butter and eggs, sparingly.

EQUIPMENT AND INGREDIENTS

Weights and measures: We use metric measurements and suggest that you do the same; however, these have been converted as accurately as is practically possible to imperial measurements. Stick to one or the other and do not mix metric and imperial measures in one recipe. Spoon measures are for level, not heaped spoonfuls: 1 teaspoon = approximately 5 g, 1 tablespoon = approximately 15 g.

Equipment: Very little special equipment is needed for these recipes; any domestic kitchen catering for two people will be equipped with the necessary implements. Sizes and dimensions of any equipment given are approximate. Do not be put off if you do not have a mould of the precise dimensions suggested!

Ovens: We recommend that you use an oven thermometer rather than depending on the thermostat to measure temperature, since these vary from oven to oven. Microwave ovens are perfect for reheating most vegetable and sauced dishes, but we do not recommend them for cooking.

Clingfilm: Do not allow it to come into direct contact with the food: the safety of its properties with certain foods is still being investigated by health experts.

Dairy produce: We use eggs weighing 55–60 g/2 oz (size 3), and unsalted butter. To clarify butter, melt it gently in a saucepan, skim the froth, and pour through a muslin-lined strainer; do not use the milky deposit at the bottom of the pan.

Oils: Like vinegars, there are many different varieties. Olive oil is one of our favourites, and is also low in cholesterol. We dress salads with flavoured oils and keep groundnut oil (which is flavourless) for cooking.

Home-made stocks: These are used in a dozen recipes, and are often optional.

Flour: The flour we use is always plain and should be sifted.

Alcohol: All spirits and liqueurs should be of the best quality and pure.

Sorbets and ice creams: The recipes we give contain no stabilisers or preservatives. If you want to pasteurise home-made ice cream, cook the basic mixture at a constant temperature of 79.4°C/175°F for 15 seconds.

HOW TO CHOOSE AND BUY INGREDIENTS

The quality of the ingredients is the key to any successful recipe, so they must be chosen with care. Always give priority to seasonal produce and check the freshness by sight, smell and touch.

Fruit and vegetables: Nowadays, exotic fruits and vegetables are available all year round. It is worth trying them and using them in your cooking, but not to excess.

Anyone can go out and buy two carrots, one leek, three potatoes and an onion, which means that it is as easy to cook for two as for four. There was a time when shopkeepers were reluctant to weigh out small quantities for their customers, but this is no longer a problem: you can pick and weigh your own produce in most supermarkets. We recommend that you do not keep fresh produce for more than a day or two, as even in the fridge it tends to lose vital nutrients. Try to shop as often as you can for the freshest ingredients and use them as soon as possible.

CHOOSING MEAT AND FISH FOR QUALITY AND FRESHNESS

Beef: The meat should be dark red, finely grained, marbled with fat and firm to the touch. Firm white or creamy fat indicates a young animal.

Lamb: A young lamb has pale pink, finely-grained flesh with firm white or creamy fat. Reddish-brown flesh means an older, less tender animal with a coarser flavour. The leg should be compact, with a covering of pale fat.

Pork: The flesh should be finely grained and lightly marbled with moist fat. There should be a thin layer of fat between the flesh and the skin, which should be thin, smooth and elastic.

Veal: The flesh should be white or very pale pink (although this indicates that the calf has been reared in the dark) and soft and moist, but not flabby. The bones should be quite flexible and very pale pink in colour.

Poultry and game: Birds should have big feet and fat 'knees'. The beak and pinions should feel flexible and the skin should be smooth, not knobbly. The tip of the breastbone should be flexible and the spurs rounded. If the tips of the large wing feathers of pheasants and partridges are pointed, this is an indication that the bird is young.

Fish: The eyes should transfix you with their bulging, lively gaze. The gills should be difficult to open and should be a clear dark pink or red inside. The fish should be stiff, with firm flesh and a taut skin, and have a salty tang.

Shellfish: Never buy shellfish which are already open, as this indicates that they are probably dead. They should be tightly closed and heavy with sea water, and should smell of the sea.

Crustaceans: They should still be alive and very lively, ready to make their escape – should you by chance drop them – back to the seashore! They should also feel very heavy for their size.

Finally, if you are doing your shopping while on holiday in France, you should know that the best produce is on offer between 8 and 10 o'clock in the morning, and this disappears very quickly. From 10 o'clock until noon, there will be queues and you will be jostled by the crowds. From noon to 1 o'clock, there will be very little choice, but you can buy at bargain prices.

HERBS, AROMATICS AND SPICES

These will add a special flavour to sweet and savoury dishes – subtle, peppery, musky, aniseedy, sugary. They are also noted for their medicinal properties.

We use herbs at every possible opportunity, especially fresh herbs, but we do counsel you to use them in moderation, or they may overpower the flavour of the other ingredients in the dish.

Nowadays, most supermarkets and greengrocers sell little packets of many varieties of fresh herbs, which are generally of excellent quality. It is, however, very easy to create your own herb garden in a flower bed or window box; just buy the seeds from a garden centre and remember to water the herbs regularly, but not to excess! The four classic and indispensable herbs are flat-leafed or curly parsley, chervil, chives and tarragon.

A herb garden also looks delightful and smells delicious with all its different fragrances. An added advantage, if it is planted in an open area, is that it will attract butterflies, bees and even dragonflies.

You will see in the chapter on Outdoor Eating, that in many of our summer salads we use flowers, such as borage, marigold and carnation petals, geraniums and sweet violets. Do not overdo the floral additions; you should not offer your guest an entire flower-bed, but simply a flowery note.

1

2

4

5

A selection of herbs from our herb garden which you will find invaluable in cooking: 1 sage, 2 lavender, 3 thyme, 4 flat-leafed parsley, 5 chervil, 6 basil.

6

STOCKS

There is nothing to beat a home-made stock. When you are cooking for only two people, it is reasonable to wonder whether it is really worth the effort of preparing a stock when the recipe might call for only a few millilitres. The answer is always a resounding 'Yes'.

At home, we use only three types of stock: vegetable, chicken and fish. We would recommend these for a household of two people.

Stocks can be frozen for several weeks and will keep very well in the fridge for up to 1 week. Some shops now sell vacuum-packed stocks, just as they sell frozen puff pastry. We have tried these out of curiosity and found them to be almost as good as the home-made variety. This is an encouraging development, which offers you a choice, especially if you are in a hurry.

As a last resort, there are always stock cubes, but care must be taken if you are using these since they can often ruin a sauce with their strong flavour of herbs, salt, spices and concentrated aromatic essences.

FISH STOCK
Fumet de poisson

PREPARATION TIME
15 minutes

COOKING TIME
35 minutes

INGREDIENTS

1 kg/2 lb fish heads and bones (eg: sole, turbot, whiting, or any white-fleshed fish)

50 g/2 oz butter

50 g/2 oz onions, chopped

white part of 1 leek, washed and chopped

50 g/2 oz mushrooms, wiped and chopped

100 ml/4 fl oz dry white wine

1 bouquet garni

——— PREPARATION ———

Remove the gills from the fish heads (they have a bitter flavour). Soak the bones and heads in cold water for 3–4 hours, then chop them roughly.

——— COOKING ———

Melt the butter in a saucepan, add the chopped vegetables and sweat for 2–3 minutes, until soft but not coloured. Add the fish bones and heads and sweat for another 2 minutes. Pour in the wine, increase the heat and reduce by half. Add 2 litres/3½ pts water and bring slowly to the boil, skimming the surface frequently. Reduce the heat and simmer the stock for 5 minutes. Add the bouquet garni and simmer, uncovered, for 25 minutes, skimming as necessary. Strain the stock through a muslin-lined sieve and leave to cool before refrigerating.

——— NOTE ———

The stock will keep for 1 week in the fridge, or for several weeks in the freezer.

CHICKEN STOCK
Fonds de volaille

PREPARATION TIME
15 minutes

COOKING TIME
2½ hours

INGREDIENTS

1 kg/2¼ lb chicken carcasses, necks, wings and feet, or 1 boiling fowl

100 g/4 oz carrots

white part of 1 leek

½ celery stalk

100 g/4 oz mushrooms

20 g/¾ oz butter

1 onion, stuck with 1 clove

1 bouquet garni

——— PREPARATION ———

Wash and thinly slice the carrots, leek, celery and mushrooms. Melt the butter in a large saucepan and sweat the vegetables until soft. Add the chicken or the boiling fowl, cover with cold water and bring to the boil. Lower the heat and simmer gently, skimming the surface frequently. After 10 minutes, add the onion and clove and the bouquet garni.

Cook for a further 2 hours 20 minutes, then strain the stock through a muslin-lined sieve into a bowl. Leave in a cool place until it is completely cold before refrigerating.

——— NOTE ———

The stock will keep in the fridge for 1 week, or can be frozen for several weeks.

VEGETABLE STOCK
Fonds de légumes

─────────── PREPARATION ───────────

Peel, wash, and dice all the vegetables, and put them in a large saucepan with 1.5 litres/2½ pints water. Set over high heat and, as soon as the liquid comes to the boil, lower the heat and simmer the stock at about 90°C/194°F for 1 hour, skimming the surface when necessary. Strain the stock through a conical or muslin-lined sieve and leave to cool at room temperature.

When the stock is cold, it should be stored in a jar in the fridge, or put it into small containers and frozen.

─────────── NOTE ───────────

Vary the flavour of the stock by adding your favourite herb, such as tarragon or sage, but be cautious; remember that this is a vegetable, not a herb stock.

MAKES 1 litre/1¾ pints

PREPARATION TIME
20 minutes

COOKING TIME
1 hour

INGREDIENTS
250 g/9 oz celery
250 g/9 oz carrots
250 g/9 oz leeks
250 g/9 oz onions
200 g/7 oz fennel (optional)
250 g/9 oz celeriac
20 coriander seeds, crushed
20 white peppercorns, crushed
1 bouquet garni
12 fresh basil leaves (optional)
2 unpeeled garlic cloves
½ lemon
a pinch of salt

PASTRIES AND DOUGH

It is said that the job of the *tourrier*, the person responsible for making pastries and doughs, is one of the most important in pâtisserie. Certainly, a good pastry or dough base is essential to the success of many dishes. Five basic doughs are used in the recipes in this book: light, delicate shortcrust pastry is good for fish and meat dishes, and for classic flans and tarts; sweet shortcrust, which is used for fruit tarts and tartlets, and is especially suitable if you want to transport dishes, since it is not so fragile as other pasties; shortbread dough, which is fragile, but wonderfully rich and delicate; quick puff pastry, although it does not rise so much as the classic puff pastry, is quick and easy to make; and the extremely versatile choux paste, which is marvellous for all types of dishes. All these pastry doughs keep well in the fridge if wrapped to prevent drying out; they also freeze successfully.

SHORTCRUST
Pâte brisée

MAKES about 475 g/1 lb 1oz

PREPARATION TIME
15 minutes

INGREDIENTS

250 g/9 oz flour

1 egg

½ teaspoon salt

a pinch of sugar

160 g/5 oz butter, cubed and
slightly softened

1 tablespoon milk

--- PREPARATION ---

Put the flour on a marble or wooden surface and make a well in the centre. Put in the egg, salt, sugar and cubed butter and rub the ingredients together with the fingertips of your right hand, gradually drawing the flour into the well with your left hand. When everything is almost amalgamated, add the milk and knead the dough 2–3 times with the heel of your hand to make it smooth, but do not overwork it.

Wrap the dough in clingfilm or greaseproof paper and leave to rest in the fridge for several hours before using.

--- NOTE ---

Shortcrust will keep in the fridge for 3–4 days, or, if you prefer, for several weeks in the freezer.

SWEET SHORTCRUST
Pâte sucrée

MAKES about 500 g/1 lb 2 oz

PREPARATION TIME
15 minutes

INGREDIENTS

250 g/9 oz flour

100 g/4 oz butter, diced

100 g/4 oz icing sugar

a pinch of salt

2 eggs, at room temperature

--- PREPARATION ---

Put the flour on a marble or wooden work surface and make a well in the centre. Put the butter in the well and work with your fingertips until completely softened. Add the sugar and salt, mix well, then add the eggs and mix again. Gradually draw the flour into the mixture. When everything is completely amalgamated, knead the dough 2–3 times with the palm of your hand until it is very smooth.

Roll the dough into a ball, flatten the top slightly and wrap in clingfilm or a polythene bag. Leave to rest in the fridge for several hours before using.

--- NOTE ---

The dough will keep well in the fridge for 3–4 days, and can be frozen successfully for several weeks.

QUICK PUFF PASTRY
Feuilletage minute

---------- PREPARATION ----------

Heap the flour on a marble or wooden surface and make a well in the centre. Cut the butter into small cubes and put it in the well, together with the salt. Using the fingertips of your right hand, work the ingredients together, gradually drawing in the flour with your left hand. When the cubes of butter have become very small and half squashed and the mixture is turning grainy, pour in the iced water and gradually work it into the pastry. Do not knead the pastry, and stop working as soon as it becomes homogenous, but still contains some small flakes of butter.

Flour the work surface and roll the pastry away from you into a 40 × 20 cm/16 × 8 in rectangle. Fold in the ends to make 3 layers. This is the first turn. Give the pastry one-quarter turn and again roll it gently away from you into a 40 × 20 cm/16 × 8 in rectangle. Fold as above. This is the second turn. Wrap the pastry in greaseproof paper and leave to firm up in the fridge for 20 minutes.

Give the chilled pastry 2 more turns. It is now ready to use. Roll it into your desired shape, place on a dampened baking sheet and chill for 20 minutes.

---------- BAKING ----------

Bake at 240°C/450°F/gas 8 until the pastry is well risen and golden.

---------- NOTE ----------

This pastry will keep for 2 days in the fridge and 3 days in the freezer.

MAKES 2.5 kg/5 ½ lb

PREPARATION TIME
20 minutes, plus 40 minutes chilling

INGREDIENTS

1 kg/2 ¼ lb flour, plus extra for dusting

1 kg/2 ¼ lb firm but not hard butter, removed from the fridge 2–3 hours before using

20 g/¾ oz salt

500 ml/18 fl oz iced water (add ice cubes if necessary)

CHOUX PASTE

Pâte à choux

MAKES *about 24 choux buns or éclairs*

PREPARATION TIME
20 minutes

COOKING TIME
10–20 minutes, depending on the shape and size of the buns

INGREDIENTS

125 ml/4 fl oz water

125 ml/4 fl oz milk

100 g/4 oz butter, finely diced, plus extra for greasing

a good pinch of salt

½ teaspoon sugar

150 g/5 oz flour, sifted

4 eggs

PREPARATION

Put the water, milk, butter, salt and sugar in a saucepan, set over high heat and boil for 1 minute, stirring continuously. Take the pan off the heat and quickly tip in the sifted flour, all at once, stirring with a wooden spatula as you do so.

When the mixture is very smooth, return the pan to the heat and stir with a wooden spatula for 1 minute. The paste will begin to dry and some of the water will evaporate. This stage is vitally important if you want to make good choux paste. Take care not to let the paste dry out too much, or it will crack during cooking. Place in a bowl.

Immediately beat in the eggs one at a time, using a wooden spatula to beat well until the paste is very smooth. It is now ready to use. If you are not planning to use it immediately, spread a little beaten egg over the surface to prevent a crust from forming.

Using a piping bag fitted with an appropriate nozzle, pipe out your chosen shapes on to a baking sheet lined with greased baking parchment.

COOKING

Preheat the oven to 220°C/425°F/gas 7.

Bake the choux buns in the oven for 4–5 minutes, then open the oven door and leave it slightly ajar while you finish cooking the buns. They will take 10–20 minutes, depending on their size and shape.

NOTE

Cooked choux buns can be kept in the fridge in an airtight container for up to 3 days, or frozen for up to 1 week.

SHORTBREAD DOUGH
Pâte sablé

―――――――――――― PREPARATION ――――――――――――

Sift the flour on to a marble or wooden surface and make a well in the centre. Put the butter in the well and mash it with your fingertips until very soft. Sift the icing sugar and salt on to the butter and work in. Gradually, draw in the flour and mix until completely amalgamated. Add the vanilla or lemon essence if you wish and rub it into the dough with the palm of your hand 2–3 times.

Wrap the dough in a plastic bag and chill for 2 hours before using.

―――――――――――― NOTES ――――――――――――

The dough will keep well for several days in the fridge.

The flour is the last ingredient to be mixed into the shortbread so that it remains crumbly and 'short'. Once you have added the flour, do not overwork the dough or it will become too elastic. Since it is extremely fragile, you must work very fast when rolling it out. It softens very quickly, so take care not to handle it any more than is absolutely necessary.

MAKES about 680 g/1 ½ lb

PREPARATION TIME
15 minutes

INGREDIENTS

250 g/9 oz flour

200 g/7 oz butter, at room temperature and diced

100 g/4 oz icing sugar

a pinch of salt

2 egg yolks

1 drop of vanilla or lemon essence (optional)

BASIC RECIPES

These are the recipes that form the basis of several of the dishes in this book, and indeed of classic cookery. Many desserts would be poorer without a melting, delicate French or Italian meringue, or pastry cream, base, and it is difficult to make successful ice-creams and sorbets, or soak sponges, without a stock syrup. Home-made pancakes, pasta and bread are impossible to beat in terms of taste and texture, and the smell of freshly baked bread lingering in the kitchen is one of the pleasures of cooking. Fresh mayonnaise is an essential part of a summer lunch or dinner, or a picnic. With the simplicity of preparing dried tomatoes during the season, you can be well stocked all year round, for cooking, or simply spread them on toast as a snack.

DRIED TOMATOES
Tomates séchées

PREPARATION TIME
20 minutes, plus 12 hours
marinating

COOKING TIME
8 hours

INGREDIENTS
2 kg/4½ lb Roma plum tomatoes
100 ml/4 fl oz olive oil
1 garlic clove
*20 leaves each of basil, rosemary
and tarragon, snipped*
salt

—— PREPARATION ——

The herb oil: Mix the olive oil, garlic and herbs and leave to marinate for 12 hours, then strain.

The tomatoes: Peel, remove the stalks, halve lengthways and remove the seeds. Lightly salt the inside of each tomato half. Arrange them, rounded side up, on one or two oven racks. Do not pack them together too tightly.

Turn on the oven to 60°C/140°F/gas ¼, leave the door slightly ajar and dry the tomatoes for 8 hours. Remove the tomatoes from the oven and leave until cold, then pack them into sealable jars with the herb-flavoured olive oil, finishing with a little olive oil.

—— NOTES ——

If the tomatoes are very large, they may take up to another 2 hours to dry. These dried tomatoes will keep for two or three months in the fridge.

ITALIAN MERINGUE
Meringue italienne

PREPARATION TIME
7 minutes

COOKING TIME
about 15 minutes

INGREDIENTS
6 egg whites
80 ml/3 fl oz water
360 g/12 oz sugar
*30 ml/1 fl oz liquid glucose
(optional)*

—— PREPARATION AND COOKING ——

Place the egg whites in the bowl of an electric mixer. Pour the water into a copper or heavy-bottomed saucepan and add the sugar and glucose if you are using it. Set over medium heat and bring to the boil, stirring with a skimming spoon. Skim the surface and use a pastry brush dipped in cold water to wash down the sugar crystals which form on the inside of the pan. Increase the heat so that the syrup boils rapidly and put in a sugar thermometer to check the temperature.

When the temperature of the syrup reaches 110°C/230°F, beat the egg whites in the mixer until well risen and stiff. Keep an eye on the syrup and, as soon as it reaches 121°C/248°F, take the pan off the heat.

Set the mixer to its lowest speed and gently pour the syrup on to the beaten egg whites in a thin stream, taking care not to let it run on to the beaters. Continue to beat at low speed for about 15 minutes, until the meringue is almost cold. It is now ready to use.

—— NOTES ——

Store the meringue in an airtight container. Packed in this way, it will keep in the fridge for up to 1 week.

FRENCH MERINGUE
Meringue française

———————————————— PREPARATION ————————————————

Preheat the oven to 120°C/250°F/gas ½. Line 2 baking sheets with baking parchment or lightly buttered and floured greaseproof paper.

Whisk the egg whites until they form soft peaks. Whisk in the caster sugar, a spoonful at a time, and continue to beat for 10 minutes, until the mixture is very firm, smooth and shiny.

Using a large metal spoon, gradually add the sifted icing sugar, folding it in as delicately as possible; take care not to overwork the mixture. French meringue should be used as soon as it is ready.

———————————————— COOKING ————————————————

Fill a piping bag with the meringue mixture and pipe it on to the prepared baking trays, or shape it into ovals with two soup spoons. Place in the oven, lower the temperature to 100°C/200°F/gas ¼ and cook the meringues for 1¾ hours, until both the top and underside are crisp and dry. Cool on a wire rack.

———————————————— NOTES ————————————————

Store the meringues in an airtight container. They will keep for up to 2 weeks.

PREPARATION TIME
15 minutes

COOKING TIME
1¾ hours

INGREDIENTS
4 egg whites

125 g/4 oz caster sugar

125 g/4 oz icing sugar, sifted

PASTRY CREAM
Crème pâtissière

———————————— PREPARATION AND COOKING ————————————

Put the egg yolks and 30 g/1 oz sugar in a bowl and whisk until thick and frothy. Sift in the flour and mix until smooth.

Combine the milk, remaining sugar and vanilla pod in a saucepan and bring to the boil. Remove the vanilla pod and pour about one-third of the boiling milk on to the egg mixture, whisking continuously. Pour this mixture back into the pan and bring back to the boil over gentle heat, stirring all the time. Simmer for 2 minutes, then pour the pastry cream into a bowl. Dot a little butter over the surface, or, if you prefer, dust with icing sugar to prevent a skin from forming as the pastry cream cools down.

———————————————— NOTE ————————————————

The pastry cream can be kept successfully in the fridge for 24 hours.

MAKES about 750 g/1¾ lb

PREPARATION AND
COOKING TIME
15 minutes

INGREDIENTS
6 egg yolks

120 g/4 oz caster sugar

40 g/1½ oz flour

500 ml/18 fl oz milk

1 vanilla pod, split

butter or icing sugar, for coating

PANCAKES

Crêpes

MAKES 20 × 25 cm/10 in pancakes

PREPARATION TIME
10 minutes, plus 2 hours resting the batter

COOKING TIME
about 2 minutes per pancake

INGREDIENTS

250 g/9 oz flour, sifted

a pinch of salt

30 g/1 oz caster sugar (for sweet pancakes only)

4 eggs

900 ml/1 ½ pt milk

150 ml/5 fl oz double cream

flavouring of your choice

30 g/1 oz clarified butter, for cooking the pancakes

THE BATTER

Mix the flour, salt and sugar, if using, in a bowl and make a well in the centre. Break in the eggs and pour in 200 ml/7 fl oz milk. Beat together the eggs and milk, using a wooden spoon, and gradually incorporate the flour until you have a smooth thick batter. Gradually stir in the remaining milk and the cream, beat until smooth, then add any flavouring of your choice. Cover the bowl and leave the batter to rest in a cool place for 2 hours before using.

COOKING THE PANCAKES

Brush the base of a non-stick 25 cm/10 in frying pan with clarified butter and set over medium heat. Ladle in a little batter and immediately tilt the pan so that the batter covers the entire base. If there is not enough to do this, quickly add a little more batter. Cook for about $\frac{3}{4}$–1 minute, until the underside of the pancake is golden, then turn over the pancake with a palette knife, or toss it if you are feeling brave. Cook the other side for about 45 seconds, until golden brown.

Make more pancakes in the same way, stacking up the cooked ones, with a piece of greaseproof paper between each one.

NOTES

The wrapped pancakes can be kept in the fridge for 1 week. Alternatively, they can be frozen and will keep for up to 4 weeks.

MAYONNAISE

MAKES 500 ml/18 fl oz

PREPARATION TIME
10 minutes

INGREDIENTS

3 egg yolks

1 tablespoon Dijon mustard

1 teaspoon salt

freshly ground white pepper

500 ml/18 fl oz vegetable oil, at room temperature

½ tablespoon white wine vinegar or lemon juice

PREPARATION

Combine the egg yolks, mustard, salt and pepper to taste in a bowl and mix with a balloon whisk. Gradually pour in the oil in a thin, steady stream, beating all the time. Stir in the vinegar or lemon juice and adjust the seasoning to taste.

NOTES

Keep the mayonnaise at room temperature, not in the fridge. If you are not using it immediately, it will keep in the larder or a cool place for 2–3 days.

FRESH PASTA DOUGH

Pâte à nouilles

SERVES 6

PREPARATION TIME
10 minutes, plus about 1 hour resting

COOKING TIME
about 2 minutes

INGREDIENTS

250 g/9 oz plain flour, plus extra for dusting

2 eggs

3 egg yolks

1 teaspoon salt

4 teaspoons groundnut oil

PREPARATION

Heap the flour in a mound on a large work surface and make a well in the centre. Put the whole eggs and yolks into the well with the salt and 1 teaspoon oil. Work the eggs in a circular movement with your fingers, gradually drawing in the flour with one hand, while heaping up the wall of the mound with the other hand. When the mixture is no longer runny, push the remaining flour on to the dough and use your palm and fingertips to mix all the ingredients into a smooth, non-sticky dough, which pulls away cleanly from the work surface. Knead the dough for a few moments, then leave it to rest for 1 hour, covered.

Lightly flour the work surface and roll out the dough, pushing it outwards and away from you and giving it a quarter-turn between rollings to keep it in a circular shape. Continue to roll and turn until you have a 60 cm/24 in circle, about 2 mm/$\frac{1}{12}$ in thick. Lightly dust the surface of the dough with flour, cover with a clean tea towel and leave to rest for 10 minutes.

Roll the dough into a flattish roll, about 7.5 cm/3 in wide. Using a very sharp knife, cut the roll into 5 mm/$\frac{1}{4}$ in wide strips. Unroll these thin strips, wrap loosely in the tea towel and leave to rest for 3–4 minutes.

COOKING

Bring a saucepan of lightly salted water to the boil and add the remaining oil. Tip the pasta strips into the boiling water and quickly stir with a wooden spoon. Bring the water back to the boil, run a little cold water into the pan to prevent further cooking and immediately drain the pasta. It is now ready to serve.

NOTE

If you do not want to use it straightaway, the pasta can be dried (drape it over a broom handle or clothes airer) and stored in plastic bags.

STOCK SYRUP

Sirop à sorbet

MAKES 1.5 litres/2$\frac{1}{2}$ pts

COOKING TIME
3 minutes from the boil

INGREDIENTS

750 g/1 lb sugar

100 ml/4 fl oz liquid glucose

PREPARATION AND COOKING

Put the sugar and glucose in a saucepan with 650 ml/22 fl oz water. Cook gently, stirring frequently with a wooden spoon, until all the sugar has dissolved. Stop stirring, bring the syrup to the boil and boil for 3 minutes, skimming the surface from time to time, if necessary. Pass through a conical sieve into a bowl and leave to cool completely before using.

NOTE

The syrup will keep in the fridge, covered, for up to 2 weeks.

BREAD
Le pain

PREPARATION

The dough can be made by hand or in an electric mixer.

By hand: Put the flour, sugar and salt into a mixing bowl and make a well in the centre. In another bowl, mix the yeast and water and pour into the well. Mix the ingredients with your right hand until well blended, gradually drawing in the flour with your left hand. Do not overwork the mixture.

Using an electric mixer: Put the water and yeast in the bowl of the mixer and beat lightly with a whisk. Fit the dough hook, add the flour, sugar and salt and beat on the lowest speed until thoroughly amalgamated.

Rising: Cover the dough with a damp cloth or baking sheet and leave to rise in a warm place (about 24°C/75°F) for about 2 hours, until doubled in bulk. Knock back the dough by flipping it over with your fingertips not more than 2–3 times.

Shaping the loaf or rolls: Put the dough on a marble or wooden surface and shape it into a large loaf, or place in a 500 g/1 lb 2 oz loaf tin. To make rolls, using a sharp knife, cut the dough into even pieces of the size you require. Shape these into balls or pull them into long rolls and place on a baking sheet, or make a single large loaf.

Using scissors or a razor blade set into a cork so that you do not cut yourself, make shallow slashes in the top of the long rolls and cut crosses in the top of the round rolls, for decoration.

Cover loosely with clingfilm to prevent the dough from drying out and forming a crust; this will also protect it from draughts. Leave to rise again at 24°C/75°F for about 30 minutes for the rolls and 1–1½ hours for a loaf. If you want your bread to have a rich amber glaze, brush the top with beaten egg just before baking.

BAKING THE BREAD

Preheat the oven to 240°C/475°F/gas 9.

Stand several small tins of water in the bottom of the oven; the steam they give off will bake the bread to perfection. Bake the rolls for about 12 minutes and the loaf for 40–50 minutes. For a shiny finish, brush the top with a lightly moistened pastry brush as the bread comes out of the oven.

NOTES

Bread freezes very successfully. To freeze, cool on a wire rack, then immediately wrap in clingfilm and freeze. The bread will taste as good as if it were freshly baked if you use it within a few days. Warm in a moderate oven (190°C/375°F/gas 5) for 5 minutes before using.

By varying the flour used, you can make different types of bread, such as wholemeal, rye or wheat flour. For best results, use equal quantities of strong bread flour and your chosen flour.

MAKES 1 × 500 g/1 lb 2 oz loaf, or 15–20 rolls

PREPARATION TIME
35 minutes

RISING TIME
2½ hours for rolls, about 3 hours for a loaf

BAKING TIME:
about 12 minutes for rolls, 40–50 minutes for a loaf

INGREDIENTS
450 g/1 lb strong bread flour
30 g/1 oz sugar
15 g/½ oz salt
15 g/½ oz fresh yeast
250 ml/9 fl oz cool water
beaten egg, for glazing (optional)

BREAKFAST AND BRUNCH

Lazy mornings, huge appetites, a desire to make the night last longer, breakfast in bed or snatched illicitly . . . everyone's dream is different. Appetites that have been deadened by sleep or ravening hunger, unfulfilled dreams, which leave you full of longing . . . there are a thousand reasons for presenting your companion with a superb, unforgettable breakfast.

We suggest:
Salmon rillettes
Scrambled eggs with diced ratatouille surprise
Chilled melon with candied ginger
Black pudding with apple and potato
Wild strawberries on mango coulis

SALMON RILLETTES
Rillettes de saumon

*T*HIS *dish satisfies a palate looking for something more flavoursome than the traditional breakfast fare, and the hunger pangs at mid-morning. It is sophisticated, tempting and altogether perfect for a leisurely, late breakfast or brunch.*

PREPARATION

The court-bouillon: Put all the ingredients in a small saucepan, cover with plenty of cold water, add a pinch of salt and boil for 5 minutes.

COOKING THE SALMON

Rinse the salmon in cold water, and place in the boiling court-bouillon. Immediately take the pan off the heat, leave the salmon in the hot liquid for 5 minutes, then drain. With a small knife, lift off the skin and remove the backbone and all the side bones. Put the salmon flesh in a bowl, cover with dampened kitchen paper and leave at room temperature for 20 minutes until almost cold.

BUTTERING THE RILLETTES

Carefully flake the cooled salmon flesh and work in the softened butter with a spatula. Add the cream, peppercorns, lemon juice, cayenne and snipped chives, and season with salt. Pack the rillettes into a small soufflé dish or 2 ramekins, cover with clingfilm and chill in the fridge for 2 hours.

PRESENTATION

Garnish the rillettes with a small bouquet of chives and serve them straight from the dish, with grilled country bread or toast.

NOTE

The rillettes should not be served too cold. If you have prepared them the day before, be sure to take them out of the fridge a good hour before serving.

PREPARATION TIME
20 minutes, plus 2 hours chilling

COOKING TIME
5 minutes

INGREDIENTS
1 salmon steak, about 140 g/ 5 oz
50 g/2 oz softened butter
50 ml/2 fl oz whipping cream, whipped to a ribbon consistency
10 soft green peppercorns, crushed
1 tablespoon lemon juice
a pinch of cayenne pepper
1 teaspoon snipped chives
coarse cooking salt
2 or 3 whole chives tied together, for garnish

COURT-BOUILLON:
1 bouquet garni
1 onion, thinly sliced
1 leek, thinly sliced
1 carrot, cut into rounds
100 ml/4 fl oz dry white wine
5 peppercorns, crushed

BLACK PUDDING WITH APPLE AND POTATO

Boudin noir aux deux pommes

*B*LACK *pudding makes an excellent winter breakfast dish. The apple helps to make this rustic dish more digestible, while the puréed potato with garlic and parsley is full of flavour without being overpoweringly garlicky, since the garlic is pre-cooked.*

PREPARATION TIME
20 minutes

COOKING TIME
6 minutes

INGREDIENTS

2 pieces of black pudding, each about 100 g/4 oz

1 garlic clove

1 potato, about 200 g/7 oz

100 g/4 oz butter

100 ml/4 fl oz lukewarm milk

a small pinch of nutmeg

1 dessert apple (preferably a Cox), about 150 g/5 oz

20 g/¾ oz caster sugar

1 tablespoon flat-leafed parsley, snipped

coarse and fine salt

freshly ground pepper

PREPARATION

Preheat the oven to 200°C/400°F/gas 6 for 10 minutes.

The garlic: Put the garlic clove in a small frying pan or gratin dish with a small handful of coarse salt and cook in the preheated oven for 10 minutes. Remove from the oven and peel the garlic. Leave the oven turned on.

The potato: Peel, cut into 6 pieces and place in a small saucepan. Cover with cold water, add a pinch of salt and boil for 15–20 minutes, until the potato is soft all through. Drain the potato pieces and place in the oven with the peeled garlic to dry for 1 minute.

Rub the dried potato and garlic through a vegetable mouli or coarse sieve into the saucepan. Use a spatula to work in 50 g/2 oz butter, a little at a time, and mix until smooth. Finally, stir in the warm milk. Season with the nutmeg and salt to taste. Cover the pan and stand it in a bain-marie.

The apple: Peel, cut into 6 or 8 segments and remove the core. Heat 30 g/1 oz butter in a frying pan, put in the apple segments and fry until golden. Sprinkle with sugar and cook until the apple segments are lightly caramelised, then place on a plate.

The black pudding: Melt the remaining butter in a frying pan and heat the black pudding over a very low flame for 3 minutes on each side.

PRESENTATION

Add the parsley to the potato purée. Divide the purée between two hot plates, place the black pudding on the purée and arrange the apple segments around the edge. This dish should be served very hot.

SCRAMBLED EGG AND DICED RATATOUILLE SURPRISE

Oeufs brouillés et dés de ratatouille en surprise

*S*URPRISE *your beloved with the original presentation of this elegant and delicious dish. He or she will be amazed by your talent in producing this classy breakfast.*

PREPARATION

The ratatouille: Heat the olive oil in a thick-bottomed casserole or saucepan. Add the onion and sweat for 1 minute, then add the garlic and bouquet garni. After another minute, put in the peppers and aubergine, cook for 2 minutes, then add the courgette and tomato. Season with a little salt and pepper and cook for another 2 minutes. Remove the bouquet garni and keep the ratatouille warm.

The croutons: Trim the edges of the bread to make 9×7 cm/$3\frac{1}{2} \times 2\frac{3}{4}$ in rectangles, and cut 1 cm/$\frac{1}{2}$ in off each corner. With the point of a knife, cut a 5×3 cm/$2 \times 1\frac{1}{4}$ in oval out of the centre of each crouton and lift them out to leave egg-shaped cavities.

Heat the clarified butter in a frying pan and fry the croutons over medium heat until golden on both sides. Place on a wire rack.

The eggs: Carefully wash them in cold water and dry with a tea towel. Lay an egg on its side on a tea towel and, with a soft pencil, trace a fine line round the contour of the egg, about two-thirds of the way up its long side.

Using a very sharp serrated knife, gently cut round the pencil mark at least twice, without applying pressure, until you have cut through the eggshell. Empty the egg into a bowl. Rinse the deeper part of the shell in cold water, gently pat dry and set aside. Prepare the other 3 eggs in the same way.

COOKING THE EGGS

Keep 2 of the eggs for another use. Beat the remaining 2 with a fork for 30 seconds, then season lightly with salt and pepper. In a saucepan, melt the butter over low heat, pour in the eggs and scramble gently with a wooden spatula, still over low heat. When the eggs are almost done to your taste, stir in the cream, cook for another 30 seconds, and keep warm.

PRESENTATION

Lay an eggshell in each of the cavities in the croutons. Half-fill each shell with ratatouille, fill up with scrambled egg and decorate with a sprig of chervil. Slide the croutons with their cargo of egg on to one or two plates and serve at once.

NOTE

You will find that you have made too much ratatouille to use in the 4 eggshells, but it is difficult to make a smaller quantity. The solution is simple: just spread the surplus on a slice of toast and enjoy it!

PREPARATION TIME
40 minutes

COOKING TIME
9–11 minutes

INGREDIENTS

4 fresh free-range eggs

1 tablespoon olive oil

1 small onion, about 30 g/1 oz, finely diced

1 garlic clove, crushed

1 small bouquet garni

$\frac{1}{2}$ small red pepper, about 30 g/ 1 oz, finely diced

$\frac{1}{2}$ small green pepper, about 30 g/1 oz finely diced

$\frac{1}{4}$ small aubergine, about 40 g/ 1$\frac{1}{2}$ oz, finely diced

$\frac{1}{3}$ small courgette, about 40 g/ 1$\frac{1}{2}$ oz, finely diced

1 small tomato, about 50 g/ 2 oz, peeled, deseeded and finely diced

4 slices of white bread

30 g/1 oz clarified butter

30 g/1 oz butter

50 ml/2 fl oz double cream

4 sprigs of chervil

salt and freshly ground pepper

SURPRISE OMELETTE WITH SORREL

Omelette en surprise à l'oseille

*T*HE *surprise element of this omelette comes as you cut into it to serve; the hidden soft-boiled egg in the centre adds a childish, unexpected pleasure to your breakfast.*

PREPARATION TIME
15 minutes

COOKING TIME
1–2 minutes

INGREDIENTS

3 eggs

40 g/1 ½ oz sorrel

2 tablespoons double cream

20 g/ ¾ oz finely grated parmesan

20 g/ ¾ oz butter

1 tablespoon groundnut oil

1 egg, soft-boiled for 4 minutes, shelled

salt and freshly ground pepper

PREPARATION

Wash the sorrel in cold water and remove the stalks. Pile up 4 or 5 leaves, roll them up like a cigar and snip finely. Snip all the sorrel in this way.

Preheat the grill.

COOKING THE OMELETTE

Break the eggs into a bowl, add the cream and half the parmesan, and beat with a fork for 30 seconds. Season to taste.

Heat the butter and oil in an omelette pan, add the sorrel and sweat gently for 30 seconds. Turn up the heat as high as possible and pour the eggs into the pan. Cook until the omelette is done to your taste, stirring with a fork. Place the soft-boiled egg in the centre, roll over the omelette, and immediately lift it on to a heatproof serving plate. Sprinkle over the remaining parmesan and place the omelette under the grill for a few seconds, until the cheese melts.

PRESENTATION

Serve the omelette hot, or, as a delicious alternative, leave it to cool at room temperature, then serve when it is almost cold.

SMOKED SALMON ROULADES WITH FROMAGE BLANC AND MINT
Roulade de saumon fumé au fromage blanc

*C*REAMY, *refreshing and very easy to eat, this delicious dish will tempt you even when you are not very hungry. It is one of our favourite breakfasts.*

PREPARATION

The lemon: With a flexible knife, remove the peel and pith, cut out the segments and reserve them, keeping the best 4 for decoration.

The mint-flavoured cheese coulis: In a mortar or blender, blend 30 g/1 oz fromage blanc with the milk and mint leaves. Season to taste. Strain the coulis through a fine or muslin-lined conical sieve and refrigerate.

ASSEMBLING THE PAPILLOTES

Trim the edges of the smoked salmon with a sharp knife to make neat rectangles. Finely dice the trimmings and mix into the remaining cheese. Season with salt and pepper. Spread the cheese over the centre of each smoked salmon rectangle and top with the lemon segments, reserving 4 for decoration. Roll the smoked salmon over to make neat cigar shapes. Cover with clingfilm and place in the fridge.

PRESENTATION

Place a roulade on each plate. Pour the coulis over one side of the plate and scatter the diced cucumber over the coulis. Arrange a mint sprig decoratively, with a lemon segment on either side. Serve cold but not chilled.

NOTE

An added advantage of this dish is that the separate elements can be prepared the previous evening and assembled in 5 minutes on the morning.

PREPARATION TIME
15 minutes

INGREDIENTS

2 thin slices of smoked salmon, about 12 × 8 cm/5 × 3¼ in, each weighing about 40 g/1½ oz

1 lemon

120 g/4 oz fromage blanc, either high or low fat

3 tablespoons milk

16 mint leaves

50 g/2 oz cucumber, peeled, deseeded and finely diced

2 small sprigs of mint

salt and freshly ground pepper

Illustrated on page 45

CHILLED MELON WITH CANDIED GINGER

Melon glacé au confit de gingembre

*T*HE *interesting marriage of the half-candied ginger with the soft flesh of the iced melon makes a most delicious breakfast for a hot summer's morning.*

PREPARATION TIME
15 minutes

COOKING TIME
20 minutes, plus 1 hour draining the ginger

INGREDIENTS

1 melon, about 600 g/1¼ lb

1 large fresh ginger root, about 60 g/2 oz

100 g/4 oz caster sugar

4 small ice cubes

—————— PREPARATION ——————

The ginger: Peel with a small, sharp knife and cut the flesh lengthways into wafer-thin slices. Blanch in boiling water for 5 minutes. Put the sugar with 200 ml/7 fl oz water in a saucepan and bring to the boil. Reduce the heat to about 95–100°C/203–212°F, add the ginger and cook for 20 minutes, until it becomes translucent. Take the pan off the heat and leave the ginger to cool in the syrup.

Drain the cooled ginger, arrange the slivers on a wire rack and leave to drain off the syrup for at least 1 hour.

The melon: Using a knife with a long, flexible blade, cut the melon in sharply angled zig-zags round the middle. Remove the seeds and use a soup spoon to scoop out about two-thirds of the flesh, leaving enough to keep the border intact. Put the flesh in a blender with 2 ginger slivers and blend to a smooth coulis. Transfer to a bowl and place in the fridge.

—————— PRESENTATION ——————

Crush the ice cubes and mix the crushed ice into the melon coulis. Pour into the two melon halves. Arrange the slivers of ginger on the zig-zags. Place the melon halves in bowls or deep dishes filled with crushed ice. Suck the melon coulis through a straw, or, if you prefer, eat it with a dessert spoon.

Top: Smoked salmon roulades with fromage blanc and mint (recipe, page 43);
Bottom: Chilled melon with candied ginger.

MARINATED ESCALOPES OF SALMON WITH A TANGY CUCUMBER SAUCE

Escalopes de saumon cru au jus de citrus sur frisson de concombre

*T*HE *success of this dish depends entirely on the absolute freshness of the salmon and the thinness of the escalopes. A simple dish with warm, glowing colours and a fresh, fruity flavour, it makes the perfect breakfast for spring or summer!*

PREPARATION

The cucumber: Peel and keep one-fifth of the peel. Cut this lengthways into very thin strips and place in the fridge. Cut the cucumber into chunks and scoop out the seeds with the end of a spoon handle. Slice each chunk as thinly as possible and sprinkle with a pinch of salt. Stir the lightly salted cucumber with a spoon and place in the fridge to disgorge for 30 minutes. Meanwhile, make the marinade.
The marinade: Put the orange and lemon juice and the sugar in a saucepan and bring to the boil over low heat. Skim if necessary and add the julienne of orange zest. Reduce the liquid by half and season to taste with salt and pepper. Leave to cool, then add the olive oil.
The salmon: Lay the escalopes in a deep dish, taking care that they do not overlap. Pour over the marinade and orange zest, cover with clingfilm and marinate in the fridge for 20 minutes, turning the salmon after 10 minutes.
Seasoning the cucumber: Take the cucumber slices from the fridge, and squeeze them in a piece of muslin or a cloth in order to extract all the liquid. Mix the cucumber into the yoghurt, then add the snipped chives and season to taste.

PRESENTATION

Arrange a salmon escalope in the centre of each plate. Spread the cucumber mixture over each slice, trying to keep most of it on the salmon, but letting it spill on to the plate on one side. Cover the cucumber with a second salmon escalope and pour over any remaining marinade. Arrange the strips of cucumber skin in a decorative manner around the salmon, grind a turn of pepper over the fish itself and serve immediately, spanking fresh.

PREPARATION TIME
20 minutes, plus 20 minutes marinating

INGREDIENTS
4 small, extremely thin slices of very fresh raw salmon, each about 25 g/1 oz

½ cucumber, about 250 g/9 oz

juice of ½ orange

juice of ½ lemon

a pinch of caster sugar

zest of ½ orange, cut into julienne and blanched

1 tablespoon olive oil

75 g/3 oz plain yoghurt

1 tablespoon snipped chives

salt and freshly ground pepper

CHICKEN BREASTS STUFFED WITH LEEKS IN ASPIC

Suprême de volaille aux moelleux de poireaux en aspic

A great advantage of this dish is that it can be prepared a day or two in advance. It is very simple to make, and is pleasing to the eye and palate – a real feast for breakfast.

PREPARATION TIME
40 minutes

COOKING TIME
20 minutes for the chicken, plus 45 minutes for the stock and 6 hours chilling

INGREDIENTS
1 chicken, about 1.6 kg/3 lb

600 g/1 ¼ lb medium leeks, washed and trimmed

120 g/4 oz carrots

1 medium bouquet garni

10 peppercorns, crushed

1 onion, about 80 g/3 oz, stuck with a clove

40 g/1 ½ oz butter

2 tablespoons double cream

2 eggs, separated

a pinch of curry powder

1 gelatine leaf, soaked in cold water

1 small tomato, peeled, deseeded and cut into diamond shapes

8 sprigs of chervil

salt and freshly ground pepper

PREPARATION

The chicken: Cut off the legs and breast fillets from the carcass and keep the legs for a lunch or dinner dish another time. Chop the carcass with a chef's knife and wash in cold water. Remove the skin from the breast fillets.

The stock: Put the chopped carcass in a saucepan and cover with 1.5 litres/2½ pts water. Bring to the boil, then lower the heat to 80°C/176°F. Skim, then add the carrots, bouquet garni, peppercorns, a pinch of salt and the onion. Slice the greenest parts of the leeks, add them to the stock and cook for 45 minutes. Strain through a conical sieve into a medium saucepan, and keep at room temperature.

POACHING THE CHICKEN BREASTS

Slice the green heart of the leeks as thinly as possible, to within about 5 cm/2 in of the root ends. Leave the white ends in chunks. Sweat the sliced leeks in the butter in a medium saucepan for 30 minutes. Leave to cool at room temperature.

Add the cream, egg yolks and curry powder to the cooled leeks. Using a knife with a thin blade, make an incision in each chicken breast to form a small pocket. Season the pockets with salt and pepper, then fill with the cooked leek mixture. Roll them up in clingfilm like a ballotine and tie the ends with kitchen string.

Heat the stock to just simmering (80–90°C/176–194°F) and put in the wrapped chicken breasts and the chunks of leek. Poach for 20 minutes, then leave to cool in the stock. When the chicken breasts and leeks are cold, remove them from the stock and refrigerate for at least 4 hours.

CLARIFYING THE ASPIC

Lightly beat the egg whites, whisk into the cold stock and bring to the boil, whisking continuously. As soon as the stock reaches boiling point, reduce the heat to 80°C/176°F, gently stir in the gelatine and carefully strain the aspic through a muslin-lined conical sieve. Keep in a cool place.

PRESENTATION

Remove the clingfilm from the chicken breasts, cut each one into 6 or 8 slices, and arrange them on one or two deep plates. Halve the leeks lengthways and place them round the chicken. Scatter the tomato diamonds over the leeks, garnish with chervil, then carefully pour the cold, half-set aspic over the chicken and garnish. Leave in the fridge for about 2 hours, until the aspic has set to a jelly. Serve the dish by itself or with a salad of rocket or lamb's lettuce.

COURGETTE CHARLOTTES
Charlottes de courgettes

SERVE this pleasant vegetable dish as an hors d'oeuvre, or just on its own for breakfast. It can be served cold or hot, straight from the oven, or is ideal at any time of year.

--------- PREPARATION ---------

The courgettes: Wash in cold water and trim off the ends. Do not peel. Cut the largest courgette on the diagonal to make elongated rounds 3 mm/$\frac{1}{8}$ in thick. Season these lightly with salt and pepper. Heat the olive oil in a frying pan and cook the courgette rounds over high heat until pale golden on both sides. Drain on kitchen paper for a few moments, then place on a plate.

Cut the 3 remaining courgettes into 1 cm/$\frac{1}{2}$ in cubes. Bring a pan of lightly salted water to the boil, drop in the diced courgettes and cook for 7–8 minutes, until very soft and tender. Drain the courgettes and press lightly with the back of a ladle to extract as much water as possible.

Pour the cream into a saucepan and boil until reduced by half. Add the boiled courgettes and boil for 3 minutes, stirring continuously with a spatula. Pour into a blender or food processor and blend for about 3 minutes, to make a very smooth purée. Add the egg yolks, gruyère and nutmeg, season to taste and mix well.

Preheat the oven to 150°C/300°F/gas 2 for 20 minutes.

--------- ASSEMBLING THE CHARLOTTES ---------

Line two dariole moulds or ramekins, 8 cm/3 in diameter, 4 cm/1$\frac{1}{2}$ in deep, with overlapping rounds of courgette, starting from the bases and working up the sides so that they are completely covered. Fill with courgette purée, arrange the remaining courgette rounds on top and cover the moulds with clingfilm. Line a deep dish with a sheet of greaseproof paper and put in the moulds. Pour a little boiling water between the moulds and cook in the preheated oven for 25 minutes.

Remove the clingfilm from the cooked charlottes and leave at room temperature until cold, then refrigerate.

--------- PRESENTATION ---------

To unmould the charlottes, dip the base of the moulds in boiling water for about 20 seconds, then invert the charlottes on to individual serving plates. Serve the charlottes cold, but not chilled.

--------- NOTE ---------

Running the fine point of a knife between the edge of the moulds and the courgette rounds will loosen the charlottes and make them easier to unmould.

PREPARATION TIME
25 minutes

COOKING TIME
25 minutes

INGREDIENTS

4 courgettes, each about 150 g/ 5 oz

3 tablespoons olive oil

100 ml/4 fl oz double cream

2 egg yolks

20 g/$\frac{3}{4}$ oz gruyère, finely grated

a pinch of nutmeg

salt and freshly ground pepper

COUSCOUS WITH GRAPEFRUIT SEGMENTS

Couscous aux segments de pamplemousse

*M*ICHEL *adores this refreshing, fruity dish for breakfast, especially in the summer. The combination of the couscous and grapefruit is particularly delicious.*

PREPARATION TIME
15 minutes, plus 45 minutes marinating the couscous

INGREDIENTS

2 grapefruit, preferably pink

100 g/4 oz couscous

1 teaspoon orange zest, finely chopped

1 small shallot, finely chopped

1 tablespoon chopped parsley

20 mint leaves, snipped

a pinch of sugar

juice of ½ lemon

juice of ½ orange

1 small tomato, peeled, deseeded and finely diced

3 radishes, cut into rounds

salt and freshly ground pepper

2 sprigs of mint, for decoration

PREPARATION

The grapefruit: With a flexible knife, remove the peel and pith from one of the grapefruit, cut out the segments and reserve them. Squeeze the pulp to extract all the juice into a bowl.

Run the point of a knife round the edge of the second grapefruit to make a light incision. Slide the handle of a soup spoon between the peel and the flesh and use it to scrape out the flesh without damaging the peel. Place the empty grapefruit shells in the fridge. Squeeze the juice from the flesh and pulp of the second grapefruit into the bowl.

The couscous: Place in a bowl, add the chopped orange zest, shallot, parsley, mint leaves, sugar and finally the grapefruit, lemon and orange juices. Mix with a spatula, cover with clingfilm and refrigerate for 45 minutes. The couscous is now ready to serve. Mix in the tomato and season to taste.

PRESENTATION

Heap the chilled couscous mixture into the two grapefruit shells. Arrange the grapefruit segments and radish rounds like a flower on top, and finally top each mound of couscous with a small sprig of mint.

NOTE

The couscous can be prepared the night before and kept in the fridge. Fill the grapefruit halves only at the last minute.

MUSHROOM CAPS FILLED WITH GRILLED LAMB'S KIDNEYS

Têtes de champignons farcies aux rognons d'agneau grillés

*T*HIS *dish fills the kitchen with a glorious aroma as it cooks. It has a wonderful velvety, musky flavour, and is perfect for a winter's morning.*

PREPARATION

The kidneys: Cut in half lengthways. Remove the fat and membrane surrounding them, then cut out the fatty central cores. Place 2 kidney halves in the fridge, and cut the other 2 halves into neat 1 cm/½ in dice.

The mushrooms: Trim the gritty parts of the stalks, then gently wipe the whole surface of the mushrooms with a damp cloth. Separate the caps and stalks. Place the caps in the fridge and finely chop the stalks.

COOKING

The sauce: Melt one-third of the butter in a small saucepan and sweat the shallot for 1 minute. Add the chopped mushroom stalks, bouquet garni, crushed peppercorns and the red wine, cover the pan and simmer for 15 minutes. Take the pan off the heat and leave the sauce in the pan.

The mushroom caps: Season lightly with salt and pepper. Heat 2 tablespoons of the oil in a frying pan and fry the mushrooms over high heat for 1 minute on each side, until golden brown. Place the mushrooms on a plate. Add the last spoonful of oil to the same pan and fry the diced kidneys over very high heat for 30 seconds, then drain in a colander. Heat the grill and a grill pan.

STUFFING THE MUSHROOMS

Gently heat the sauce. Lift out the bouquet garni, press to squeeze out any sauce from inside, then discard it. Add the diced kidneys to the sauce, taking care not to let it boil. Take the pan off the heat, stir the sauce with a wooden spatula, whisk in the remaining butter and pour the sauce and diced kidneys over the mushroom caps. Sprinkle with the breadcrumbs.

FINAL COOKING

Brush the kidney halves with a very little oil. Season with salt and pepper, and cook in the hot grill pan for 1½ minutes on each side (for pink kidneys), giving them a quarter-turn as they cook, to make attractive lattice markings.

Meanwhile, place the mushroom caps under the medium hot grill for 3–5 minutes, until they are very hot and the breadcrumbs have turned light brown.

PRESENTATION

Put a mushroom cap on each plate. Top with a kidney half and arrange the parsley sprigs around the edge. Serve piping hot.

PREPARATION TIME
20 minutes

COOKING TIME
15 minutes for the sauce, plus 7 minutes for the mushrooms and kidneys

INGREDIENTS

2 lamb's kidneys

2 large field mushrooms, 10 cm/ 4 in diameter, each about 80 g/ 3 oz

30 g/1 oz butter

1 small shallot, finely chopped

1 small bouquet garni

6 peppercorns, crushed

100 ml/4 fl oz red wine

3 tablespoons groundnut oil

1 tablespoon breadcrumbs

2 sprigs of curly parsley

salt and freshly ground pepper

STRAWBERRIES WITH FRESH CURDS
Lait caillé aux fraises

*T*HE *delicious flavour and soft colours of this light, refreshing dish make it ideal for breakfast, particularly during summer when soft fruits are at their peak of perfection.*

PREPARATION TIME
10 minutes, plus several hours curdling and chilling

INGREDIENTS
250 ml/9 fl oz milk
½ teaspoon rennet
150 g/5 oz strawberries
25 g/1 oz sugar

PREPARATION

The milk: Heat in a saucepan to a temperature of no more than 37–40°C/ 98.6–104°F. Take the pan off the heat, add the rennet and leave in a warm place for 30 minutes until the curds have solidified.

Pour the curds into a muslin-lined colander. Stand the colander in a dish and refrigerate the curds for at least 2 hours. If you prefer a firmer consistency to your curds, then leave them longer.

Put the drained curds into a blender with 120 g/4 oz strawberries and the sugar. Blend for 1 minute until you have a delicate, creamy mixture of curds and strawberries, then rub through a conical sieve.

PRESENTATION

Slice the remaining strawberries and mix them into the curds. Pour into a bowl or deep dish and chill in the fridge for several hours before serving.

NOTE

You can substitute raspberries or wild strawberries for the strawberries, in which case, leave the last 50 g/2 oz fruit whole when you mix them into the curds.

COMPOTE OF RHUBARB AND PINK CHAMPAGNE

Compôte de rhubarbe au champagne rosé

*T*HIS *delectable, easy to prepare compote should be served cold, but not iced. A warm, freshly baked brioche (recipe, page 60) served on the side complements the compote perfectly, and gives your morning tastebuds a real treat.*

―――――――――― PREPARATION ――――――――――

Wash the rhubarb in cold water and cut into 4 cm/1½ in chunks. Place in a saucepan with all the other ingredients and slowly bring to the boil. Poach at about 80°C/176°F for 6 minutes, then leave to cool at room temperature. When the compote is cold, chill in the fridge for 2 hours.

―――――――――― PRESENTATION ――――――――――

Serve the compote in a bowl or glass fruit dish. Don't remove the vanilla pod, but leave it floating amidst the rhubarb.

―――――――――― NOTE ――――――――――

A less extravagant sparkling rosé wine can be used instead of the pink champagne.

PREPARATION TIME
5 minutes

COOKING TIME
6 minutes, plus 2 hours chilling

INGREDIENTS

200 g/7 oz pink rhubarb, as young and tender as possible

100 ml/4 fl oz pink champagne

50 g/2 oz caster sugar

1 vanilla pod, split

juice of 1 lemon

WILD STRAWBERRIES WITH MANGO COULIS

Fraises des bois sur coulis de mangue

*T*HE marriage of the flavours of these fruits, with their bright, jewel-like colours, is
sublime. It is the perfect summer breakfast for all lovers of fruit.

PREPARATION TIME
10 minutes

INGREDIENTS

50 g/2 oz wild strawberries

*1 very ripe mango, about 250 g/
9 oz*

*100 ml/4 fl oz Stock syrup
(recipe, page 32)*

2 teaspoons flaked almonds

2 pinches of icing sugar

PREPARATION

The mango: Using a thin, very sharp knife, peel the mango and cut 2 good slices,
about 8 mm/$\frac{1}{3}$ in thick, keeping the attractive rounded edges. Place in the fridge.
   Cut all the flesh from the stone and put it in a blender with the syrup. Blend for
2 minutes to make a coulis, and place in the fridge.
The almonds: Heat the grill. Spread the almonds on a baking tray, sprinkle over the
icing sugar and glaze under the hot grill for a few seconds. Keep in a dry place.

PRESENTATION

Lay each slice of mango in the centre of a plate. Pour the mango coulis in a ribbon
along one side. Arrange the wild strawberries on the other side and stick the
almonds into the mango slices to give a hedgehog effect. Sprinkle each plate with a
pinch of icing sugar and serve immediately.

BRIOCHE

PREPARATION TIME
20 minutes in an electric mixer,
or 35 minutes by hand, plus 6
hours rising and resting

COOKING TIME
8 minutes for a small brioche,
40–45 minutes for a large
brioche

INGREDIENTS

70 ml/3 fl oz milk, warmed to
blood heat

15 g/½ oz fresh yeast

2 teaspoons salt

500 g/1 lb 2 oz plain flour, plus
extra for dusting

6 eggs

350 g/12 oz butter, softened

30 g/1 oz sugar

eggwash (1 egg yolk lightly
beaten with 1 tablespoon milk)

PREPARATION

Pour the warmed milk into the mixer bowl, crumble in the yeast and beat lightly with a wire whisk until the yeast has dissolved. Add the salt, then the flour and eggs, and knead with the dough hook of the mixer, or by hand with a wooden spatula until the dough is smooth and elastic; this will take about 10 minutes in a mixer, or 20 minutes by hand.

In another bowl, beat together the softened butter and sugar, and with the mixer on low speed, add it to the dough, a little at a time, making sure each addition is completely amalgamated before adding the next. Continue to beat for about 5 minutes in the mixer or 15 minutes by hand, until the dough is perfectly smooth, glossy and fairly elastic. Cover the bowl with a tea towel and leave to prove in a warm place (about 24°C/75°F) for about 2 hours, until the dough has risen and doubled in bulk.

Knock back the dough by flipping it over quickly with your fingers not more than 3 times. Cover and refrigerate for several hours, but not more than 24 hours.

Place the dough on a lightly floured work surface and shape it into a large ball. If you are using a saucepan, line it with buttered greaseproof paper to twice the height of the pan. Place the dough in the pan. If you have a brioche mould, cut off one-third of the dough to make a 'head'. Shape the larger piece into a ball, place it in the mould and press a hollow in the centre with your fingertips. Roll the 'head' into an elongated egg shape. Lightly flour your fingers and gently press the narrow end of the 'head' into the hollow. Lightly glaze the top of the brioche with eggwash, working from the outside inwards and taking care not to let any run into the cracks in the dough or on to the edges of the mould, as this will prevent the dough from rising properly.

Leave the dough to rise in a warm draught-free place until almost doubled in bulk (about 20 minutes for small brioches and 1 hour for a large one).

COOKING

Preheat the oven to 220°C/425°F/gas 7. Lightly glaze the top of the brioche again, then, if you are making a large brioche, snip all round the edges with scissors or a razor blade dipped in cold water. Do not snip small brioches.

Bake the brioche immediately in the preheated oven, 8 minutes for small ones and 40–45 minutes for a large one. Take out of the oven, unmould immediately and turn out on to a wire rack to cool.

NOTES

The dough can be divided into 3 or 6 and plaited to make 1 or 2 plaits, which are perfect for breakfast. As an extra treat, slice the brioche, sprinkle the slices with icing sugar and glaze under a very hot grill.

The dough can also be frozen. Wrap it in polythene and freeze after the knocking back stage. Leave it to thaw gradually in the fridge for about 4–5 hours, then mould and bake as described above.

SUMMER LUNCHES

Summer is a wonderful time. The new vegetables are in full season and bursting with bright colours. Fish and shellfish are delicious, light and full of flavour; you will find plenty of recipes for these in this chapter.

All these recipes make for a simple life, and many make use of fresh herbs. We sing as we cook; why not join in with us?

Our favourite dishes for a light summer menu are:
Tomato and courgette tart with olives
Grilled squid with a light tarragon sauce
Caramelised melon filled with melon cubes and
    a light syrup

TOMATO AND COURGETTE TART
WITH OLIVES

Tarte fine de tomates et courgettes aux olives

*S*INCE *it is made with a pastry, rather than bread, base, this rustic but elegant tart is lighter than a pizza, and makes an excellent summer dish, which really constitutes a meal in itself. You could also serve thin slices as an amuse-gueule or with an aperitif.*

PREPARATION TIME
20 minutes, plus 20 minutes chilling

COOKING TIME
30 minutes

INGREDIENTS

8 small tomatoes, about 80 g/ 3 oz each

3 tablespoons olive oil

1 garlic clove, crushed

1 bouquet garni

1 courgette, about 200 g/7 oz

a pinch of flour

200 g/7 oz Shortcrust pastry (recipe, page 22)

30 g/1 oz black olives, stoned and finely diced

1 tablespoon snipped basil

salt and freshly ground pepper

PREPARATION

The tomatoes: Peel and cut into 3 mm/$\frac{1}{8}$ in thick rounds. Keep enough of the best slices to top the tart, and roughly chop the rest (about one-third). Put the chopped tomatoes in a saucepan with 1 tablespoon olive oil, the garlic and bouquet garni, and simmer for 10 minutes, stirring every few minutes. Remove the bouquet garni, tip the tomato coulis into a bowl, season with salt and pepper and keep in a cool place.

The courgette: Cannelise it along its length, then cut into very fine (2 mm/$\frac{1}{12}$ in) slices. Blanch in boiling salted water for 30 seconds, refresh, drain and pat dry.

Rolling out the pastry: On a lightly floured surface, roll out the pastry into a circle about 3 mm/$\frac{1}{8}$ in thick. Roll it on to the rolling pin, then unroll it on to a baking sheet. Leave to rest in the fridge for 20 minutes.

Preheat the oven to 220°C/425°F/gas 7.

BAKING THE TART

Prick the pastry base with the point of a knife in about a dozen places. Generously spread over the tomato coulis, then arrange the tomato and courgette slices alternately on top, to look like a rosette. Bake the tart in the preheated oven for 30 minutes. As soon as it comes out of the oven, slide it on to a wire rack and keep at room temperature. Brush the tart all over with the remaining 2 tablespoons of oil and scatter on the diced olives.

PRESENTATION

Serve the tart on the baking sheet or a bread board. Sprinkle the top with basil and add a grinding of pepper just before serving.

NOTE

The tart is at its best if eaten within 12 hours of cooking.

SPRING VEGETABLES A LA GRECQUE

Légumes angevins à la grecque

*T*HIS *dish will tempt you even if you are not hungry. The region around Angers produces the most exceptional primeurs (baby vegetables), and this is a superb way to serve them. It is essential to use small vegetables to ensure that they are young, tender and very fresh.*

PREPARATION

Peel all the vegetables and wash in cold water. Cut the carrot into 8 batons, or trim into 8 elongated olive shapes. Separate the cauliflower and broccoli into florets. Bring a saucepan of water to the boil, put in the onions and cauliflower and blanch for 30 seconds. Refresh, drain and keep with the other vegetables.

COOKING

Put all the sauce ingredients in a saucepan, bring to the boil and simmer for 10 minutes. Put all the vegetables except the chopped shallot and basil into the sauce and cook gently for about 7 minutes. Taste the vegetables to check that they are still slightly crunchy. Transfer to a bowl and leave at room temperature – see Note, below – until completely cold.

PRESENTATION

Remove the bouquet garni, stir the chopped shallot and basil into the vegetables, and serve on a deep pottery dish or plate.

NOTE

It is best not to refrigerate the vegetables. If you must, take them out of the fridge at least an hour before serving, since chilling numbs their subtle flavours.

PREPARATION TIME
20 minutes

COOKING TIME
about 7 minutes

INGREDIENTS

1 carrot, about 100 g/4 oz

75 g/3 oz cauliflower

75 g/3 oz broccoli

75 g/3 oz small new onions

120 g/4 oz small button mushrooms

30 g/1 oz shallot, finely chopped

6 basil leaves, snipped

FOR THE SAUCE:

2 tablespoons white wine vinegar

100 ml/4 fl oz water

100 ml/4 fl oz olive oil

30 coriander seeds, crushed

30 white peppercorns, crushed

1 medium bouquet garni

2 garlic cloves, crushed

40 g/1 ½ oz tomato purée

juice of 1 lemon

½ teaspoon caster sugar

½ teaspoon coarse salt

STILTON TARTS

Goyères au stilton

*T*HESE *delicious tarts, or 'goyères', originate in northern France, where they are, traditionally, made with maroilles cheese. We both love this type of cheese flan or tart; Michel has adapted this recipe using blue stilton, which he adores.*

PREPARATION TIME
15 minutes, plus 1 hour rising time

COOKING TIME
14 minutes

INGREDIENTS

100 g/4 oz flour

2 eggs

a pinch of soft brown sugar

1 teaspoon fresh yeast

2 tablespoons lukewarm milk

35 g/1¼ oz butter, melted and cooled

50 g/2 oz stilton or fourme d'Ambert

50 ml/2 fl oz double cream

8 walnut kernels, skinned

salt and freshly ground pepper

PREPARATION

The dough: Put the flour in a bowl. Make a well in the centre and put in 1 egg, a pinch of salt and the sugar. Whisk the yeast into the milk and put the mixture in the well, together with the melted butter. With your fingertips, mix until you have a supple, homogenous dough, taking care not to overwork it.

SHAPING THE GOYERES

Divide the dough into two equal parts, and with your fingertips, press them on to a baking sheet into the roundest possible shapes, 10 cm/4 in diameter and about 5 mm/¼ in thick. Leave in a warm place (about 22–24°C/70–75°F) for about 1 hour, until the dough has almost doubled in thickness.

As soon as the dough has risen, preheat the oven to 200°C/400°F/gas 6.

FILLING AND COOKING THE GOYERES

Remove the rind from the stilton and crush the cheese into a bowl. Add the remaining egg and the cream and season with a little pepper. With your fingertips, lightly press down the centre of the goyères, leaving a 1.5 cm/⅝ in raised border. Starting from the centre of the dough, spread the cheese mixture with a spoon to fill the middle of the goyères, leaving the borders unfilled. Arrange 4 walnut kernels on top of each goyère and cook in the preheated oven for 14 minutes. As soon as they come out of the oven, slide a palette knife under each goyère and transfer them to a wire rack to cool.

PRESENTATION

The goyères are best served just warm. They can either be eaten on their own, or served with a small salad of lamb's lettuce.

FRIED EGGS ON AUBERGINE ROUNDS

Oeufs frits sur rouelles d'aubergine

*W*E love this dish for its simple flavours and textures. The whites of the fried eggs are crisp, in contrast to the soft and creamy yolks. As for the aubergine, it tastes divine.

PREPARATION

The aubergine: Rinse in cold water and dry, then cut two long, diagonal slices, 1 cm/$\frac{1}{2}$ in thick, from the middle. Salt the slices very lightly, place on a plate and refrigerate for about 20 minutes. Keep the ends of the aubergine for another dish (eg: a ratatouille or aubergine purée).

The treviso lettuce and parsley: Cut off the lettuce stalk and pull off the leaves, keeping them whole. Pick off the parsley leaves. Wash them with the treviso in cold water, drain and pat dry very thoroughly. Keep at room temperature.

DEEP-FRYING

In a deep-frying pan or small saucepan, heat the groundnut oil until a very light heat haze rises from the surface. Drop in a few treviso leaves and stir with a skimmer. When the leaves have turned a beautiful light brownish-red, and are crisp, lift them out with the skimmer and lay on kitchen paper to drain.

Reheat the oil and continue to fry the treviso in batches. Fry the parsley in the same way and place it on the kitchen paper with the treviso.

COOKING THE AUBERGINE

In a medium frying pan, heat the olive oil until very hot. Pat the aubergine slices dry with kitchen paper and fry them in the hot oil for 1$\frac{1}{2}$ minutes, until the undersides are golden, then turn them over and fry for 1$\frac{1}{2}$ minutes on the other side. Lay them on kitchen paper for 1 minute to drain a little, then place a slice on each plate and keep warm.

FRYING THE EGGS

Break each egg into a separate cup. Reheat the oil in which you fried the treviso and parsley. As soon as a light heat haze begins to rise, drop in one egg and use two wooden spatulas to push in the straggly ends of white, taking care not to break the yolk. After about 1 minute, the egg will be cooked and will turn the colour of old gold. Lift it out of the oil with the skimmer and place on kitchen paper. Immediately, fry the second egg in the same way.

PRESENTATION

Lightly salt the parsley, treviso and eggs. Place the eggs on the aubergine slices, top with parsley and arrange the treviso leaves around the edge of the plate. Serve straight away – this dish tastes best very hot.

PREPARATION TIME
30 minutes

COOKING TIME
3 minutes for the aubergine, plus 2 minutes for the eggs

INGREDIENTS

1 aubergine, about 300 g/11 oz

1 small treviso lettuce or radicchio, about 100 g/4 oz

30 g/1 oz curly parsley

250 ml/9 fl oz groundnut oil, for deep-frying

2 tablespoons olive oil

2 eggs

salt and freshly ground pepper

GARLIC AND SORREL SOUP
Potage à l'ail et à l'oseille

*T*HIS *soup is surprisingly delicate in flavour. The sweetness of the garlic is perfectly balanced with the slight bitterness of the sorrel, and the tapioca gives a gentle texture.*

PREPARATION TIME
10 minutes

COOKING TIME
20 minutes

INGREDIENTS

3 garlic cloves, total weight about 20 g/$\frac{3}{4}$ oz

20 g/$\frac{3}{4}$ oz butter

30 g/1 oz sorrel, snipped

600 ml/1 pt Chicken stock (recipe, page 18) or Vegetable stock (recipe, page 19)

20 g/$\frac{3}{4}$ oz tapioca

3 tablespoons double cream

1 egg yolk

salt and freshly ground pepper

PREPARATION AND COOKING

Peel and grate the garlic.

In a saucepan, melt the butter, put in the garlic and sweat very gently for 1 minute. Add the sorrel, then the chicken or vegetable stock, increase the heat and bring quickly to the boil. Scatter in the tapioca like rain, stir with a spatula and cook gently for 20 minutes.

PRESENTATION

In a bowl, mix the cream and egg yolk. Ladle a little soup into the cream mixture, stirring as you do so. Pour the contents of the bowl into the soup and stir, taking care that the soup does not boil. Season to taste and serve immediately in bowls or soup plates.

NOTES

It is best to use new season's garlic for this summer soup, as its delicate, subtle flavour is not too powerful. Chicken stock makes the soup richer, while vegetable stock gives it a lighter, fresher flavour. Choose whichever you prefer.

The soup is also delicious served cold; add 100 ml/4 fl oz milk straight from the fridge just before serving.

LIGHTLY JELLIED LANGOUSTINE CONSOMME

Demi-tasse de consommé de langoustine tremblotant

*T*HIS *is a most refined dish, pleasing to both the eye and palate, and full of good and delicate things. Serve in chilled clear glass bowls for maximum effect.*

--------------------- PREPARATION ---------------------

The langoustines: Bring a pan of lightly salted water to the boil, drop in the langoustines and simmer for 3 minutes. Drain and keep at room temperature.
The mussels: Scrub them, wash in several changes of water, then place in a saucepan with one-third of the white wine. Cover and cook over high heat for 2 minutes, until all the mussels have opened. Immediately, take them out of their shells, debeard them if you prefer and keep in a bowl with their cooking juice.

--------------------- COOKING THE CONSOMME ---------------------

Take the heads off all but two of the langoustines, and reserve these two for the garnish. Keep them in a cool place, together with the tails.

With a heavy knife, chop the ten langoustine heads and place in a saucepan with the bouquet garni, garlic, onion, carrot, peppercorns, the mussel juice, the rest of the wine, the tomatoes and 300 ml/$\frac{1}{2}$ pt water. Set over medium heat, and when the liquid becomes lukewarm (about 30°C/86°F), add the egg whites and bring the mixture to the boil, stirring continuously with a wooden spatula, and constantly scraping the residue from the bottom of the pan. At the very first sign that it is boiling, reduce the heat, and simmer the consommé at about 80°C/175°F for 45 minutes. Add the soaked gelatine and beetroot, simmer for another 2 minutes, then take the pan off the heat.

Using a ladle, strain the stock through a muslin-lined sieve into a scrupulously clean saucepan, being extremely careful not to disturb it and make it cloudy. Set the pan over medium heat and reduce the stock to not more than 200 ml/7 fl oz. Season with salt. Leave the clear stock or consommé at room temperature until cold, then chill in the fridge for at least 2 hours. At the same time, chill the bowls you intend to use for serving.

--------------------- PRESENTATION ---------------------

The consommé should now be half-jellified and trembling. Ladle it into the chilled bowls and decorate with the asparagus tips, mussels and cold langoustine tails. Lay a whole langoustine with its tail resting on the edge of the glass, scatter with chervil or parsley and serve very cold.

--------------------- NOTE ---------------------

If your fishmonger can let you have 150 g/5 oz sole or turbot bones, add them to the consommé with the langoustine heads for an even richer taste.

PREPARATION TIME
45 minutes, plus 2 hours chilling

COOKING TIME
45 minutes

INGREDIENTS

12 fresh or frozen raw langoustines, about 80 g/3 oz each

12 mussels

200 ml/7 fl oz dry white wine

1 small bouquet garni

1 small garlic clove, crushed

1 medium onion, chopped

1 carrot, about 60 g/2 oz, roughly chopped

10 peppercorns, crushed

2 tomatoes, about 80 g/3 oz each, peeled and roughly chopped

2 egg whites, lightly broken with a fork

2 gelatine leaves, soaked in cold water

1 teaspoon grated raw beetroot

10 small green asparagus tips, cooked 'al dente'

salt

1 tablespoon chervil or flat parsley leaves, for garnish

LEEKS ON A BASIL-FLAVOURED TOMATO COULIS

Poireaux tièdes sur coulis de tomates au basilic

*T*HIS *simple dish tastes all the better if you prepare it three or four hours in advance, so that the tomatoes have time to absorb the wonderful flavour of the basil.*

PREPARATION TIME
10 minutes

COOKING TIME
15–25 minutes

INGREDIENTS

8 leeks, about 1 kg/2¼ lb

1 ripe beef tomato, preferably marmande, about 300 g/11 oz

3 tablespoons olive oil

juice of ½ lemon

6 basil leaves, snipped

1 hard-boiled egg, coarsely chopped

salt and freshly ground pepper

PREPARATION

The leeks: Cut off the roots and the greenest part of the tops with a sharp knife, leaving on the tender green parts. Cut each leek lengthways into 4, stopping one-third of the way up the white part. Cut a small cross in the base to ensure even cooking. Wash thoroughly in cold water.

Cooking the leeks: Bundle the leeks and tie with string. Bring a pan of lightly salted water to the boil, put in the leeks and cook for 15–25 minutes, depending on their size and how well cooked you like them. To check if they are ready, insert the point of a knife into the white part.

As soon as the leeks are cooked to your taste, refresh them under cold running water, drain and untie the bundle. Keep at room temperature.

The tomato coulis: Peel the tomato, chop roughly with a knife and rub the flesh through a coarse sieve or mouli set over a bowl to catch the pulpy liquid. Using a spoon, stir in the olive oil, lemon juice and basil and keep at room temperature.

PRESENTATION

Pour the tomato coulis over the bottom of two plates and arrange 4 leeks on each plate, folding the tender green parts over the white. Scatter the chopped egg over the leeks and serve at room temperature.

NOTE

On no account should you purée the tomatoes in a blender or food processor, as this will completely alter the colour and texture of the coulis, and produce exactly the opposite result from that which is intended.

COLD CRAB WITH RAW VEGETABLE STICKS
Tourteau froid au naturel

*W*HAT *could be more natural than this delicious, very simple dish? It can also be served with decoratively carved lemon halves, if you like.*

--- PREPARATION ---

The crab: Rinse and scrub carefully under cold running water to remove any mud from the shell. Bring a pan of lightly salted water to the boil, drop in the crab and simmer for 15 minutes. Leave to cool in the cooking water for 30 minutes, then drain in a colander and leave at room temperature for 2 hours.

The vegetables: Peel the carrots, wash and cut into thick matchsticks. Peel the cucumber, halve lengthways, scoop out the seeds and cut into matchsticks, about the same size as the carrots. Shell the broad beans, scrape off the outer skins with your fingernail and keep in a bowl.

The crab shell: Turn the crab on its back and twist off the legs and claws, one at a time. Crack the claws lightly with the flat side of a chopping knife. Use your thumbs to push the central part of the body out of the shell. Remove the feathery gills surrounding the central body and, with a heavy knife, chop the body section into 4. Place on a plate with the legs and claws. Scrape out the brown meat from inside the shell.

The sauce: Rub the brown meat through a sieve, or mash it to a fine consistency with a fork, then whisk in the cream, lemon juice and cognac, and season to taste with salt and cayenne pepper.

--- PRESENTATION ---

Rinse the crab shell inside and out with cold water and wipe dry. Lay the shell on its back and heap the sauce in a mound in the centre. Arrange the vegetable sticks all round the sauce and dot the raw broad beans and cherry tomatoes among them. Put the shell on an oval dish, arrange the watercress all around the shell and place the claws, body and legs on top. Serve at room temperature, providing lobster picks to help extract the white meat from the body and legs. Dip the vegetables into the sea-scented sauce.

--- NOTE ---

Do not refrigerate the crab once it is cooked, or it will lose its flavour.

PREPARATION TIME
30 minutes

COOKING TIME
15 minutes, plus 2½ hours cooling

INGREDIENTS

1 live crab, about 750 g/1½ lb

2 carrots, each about 100 g/4 oz

½ cucumber, about 200 g/7 oz

250 g/9 oz small tender broad beans in the pod

6 tablespoons double cream

juice of ½ lemon

1 tablespoon cognac

a small pinch of cayenne pepper

10–12 cherry tomatoes, about 50 g/2 oz, washed in cold water

a small bunch of watercress, for garnish

salt

GRILLED SQUID WITH A LIGHT TARRAGON SAUCE

Calmars grillés, petite nage à l'estragon

NEVER *be concerned about the cleaning of this wonderful seafood. It is relatively quick and worth the effort for the praise you will receive from your guest. The sesame oil offers a nutty addition to the flavours of the tarragon sauce and the sharp, clean spinach salad.*

PREPARATION TIME
30 minutes

COOKING TIME
5 minutes

INGREDIENTS

2 or 3 squid, about 250 g/9 oz

5 tablespoons sesame oil

100 g/4 oz young spinach leaves

20 g/$\frac{3}{4}$ oz tarragon, half on the stalk, one-quarter whole leaves and one-quarter snipped

200 ml/7 fl oz Vegetable stock (recipe, page 19)

40 g/1$\frac{1}{2}$ oz butter

1 tablespoon lemon juice

1 tablespoon white wine vinegar

1 teaspoon Dijon mustard

salt and freshly ground pepper

PREPARATION

The squid: Squeeze out the ink and quills from the sacs. Pull off the thin membrane from the sacs and wash the squid very thoroughly in cold water. Drain and pat dry with kitchen paper. Cut the sacs, flaps, fins and tentacles into 2–3 cm/$\frac{3}{4}$–1$\frac{1}{4}$ in lozenge shapes. Place in a bowl with 2 tablespoons sesame oil, season lightly with salt and pepper and keep in the fridge until ready to cook.

The spinach: Separate and discard the stalks, wash the leaves, allow to drain thoroughly and place in the fridge.

The tarragon sauce: Put the tarragon stalk in a small pan with the vegetable stock and reduce over low heat until two-thirds of the liquid has evaporated. Take the pan off the heat and whisk in the butter, a small piece at a time. Pass the sauce through a conical sieve, season to taste, cover and keep hot.

The vinaigrette: Put the lemon juice, wine vinegar, mustard, the remaining oil, a pinch of salt and a little pepper in a bowl and whisk until smooth.

GRILLING THE SQUID

Heat a grill pan until very hot, then put in the squid pieces and cook for 1 minute. Give them a quarter-turn so that the ridges of the pan make attractive lattice markings, and cook for another minute. Turn the squid over and repeat on the other side.

PRESENTATION

Mix the spinach into the vinaigrette and arrange in loose piles in the centre of the serving plates. Place the grilled squid on top and scatter on the whole tarragon leaves. Reheat the sauce if necessary, but do not let it boil, then whisk in the snipped tarragon, pour the sauce in a ribbon around the spinach and serve at once.

NOTES

The squid are equally delicious barbecued, but take care not to overcook them; they should be tender inside, and slightly crunchy outside.

All the elements of this dish can be prepared several hours in advance, if you prefer. It will then take only a few minutes to grill the squid and assemble the rest of the ingredients on the plates.

POACHED RIVER TROUT ON A BED OF SAMPHIRE

Truite de rivière pochée sur croquants d'asperges de mer

*T*HIS *light dish is perfect for a summer meal, particularly on a very hot day. The deliciously crisp samphire contrasts wonderfully with the soft flesh of the trout.*

PREPARATION TIME
20 minutes

COOKING TIME
3–5 minutes

INGREDIENTS
2 absolutely fresh river or farmed trout, each about 250 g/9 oz

60 g/2 oz carrot, peeled and thinly sliced

80 g/3 oz onion, peeled and thinly sliced

2 tablespoons white wine vinegar

10 black peppercorns, crushed

1 bouquet garni containing a stem of lemon grass

1 tablespoon very thinly sliced celery

40 g/1½ oz butter

80 g/3 oz samphire

salt and freshly ground pepper

PREPARATION

The trout: Cut off the fins with scissors. Use the point of the scissors to snip open the gills, and clean the trout by pulling out the guts through the gill openings. Snip a small opening at the base of the stomach and, holding the fish under cold running water, wash the insides. Rinse the outsides and put the trout on a plate, cover with another plate and refrigerate.

The court-bouillon: In a small saucepan, put the sliced carrot and onion, the vinegar, crushed peppercorns, bouquet garni, a small pinch of salt and 1 litre/1¾ pints water. Bring to the boil, then simmer for 30 minutes.

POACHING THE TROUT

Put the trout side by side in a lidded flameproof dish and pour over the boiling court-bouillon. Bring to the boil over high heat, then take the pan off the heat, cover the dish, and leave for 3 minutes if you like your trout cooked pink, or 5 minutes for medium. Drain the trout and wrap them carefully in foil. Keep warm while you make the sauce.

The nage: Strain one-third of the court-bouillon into a shallow pan and reduce over very high heat to about 70 ml/2½ fl oz. Add the celery, take the pan off the heat and whisk in the butter. Season to taste.

PRESENTATION

Drop the samphire into boiling water for 30 seconds, drain and spread in the bottom of a warmed oval platter. Unwrap the trout and use a small knife to remove the skin from both sides, starting at the heads and working down to within 5 cm/2 in of the tails. Arrange the fish on the samphire and pour over plenty of hot nage with celery. Serve the rest of the sauce in a sauce boat.

NOTE

If you ask nicely, your fishmonger might be persuaded to clean the trout for you.

COLD FLAKED COD WITH CAPERS AND FRENCH BEANS

Effeuillé froid de cabillaud aux câpres et haricots verts fins

*T*HIS *pleasing dish takes very little time to prepare, but is refreshing and most attractive. Try to choose fresh young cod, if you can, since this poaches very successfully.*

PREPARATION

Poaching the cod: Put the fish in a saucepan with the bouquet garni, onion, vinegar, a little salt and enough water to cover the fish copiously. Bring to the boil over high heat, reduce to about 95°C/203°F and poach for 3 minutes. Take the pan off the heat and leave the cod to cool in the cooking liquid.

The French beans: Top and tail and snap in half if they are too long. Cook in a pan of boiling salted water until still firm but not crunchy. Refresh and drain well.

PRESENTATION

Mix the drained beans with the mayonnaise. Check the seasoning and spread the beans in the bottom of an oval dish. Drain the cod, remove the skin and bone and flake the fish over the beans. Scatter on the tarragon leaves and capers.

Quarter the lemon, cannelise it decoratively and arrange in the dish. Scatter the borage flowers over the white flesh of the fish. Serve cold but not chilled.

PREPARATION TIME
20 minutes

COOKING TIME
about 3 minutes

INGREDIENTS

1 cod steak, about 350 g/12 oz

1 small bouquet garni

1 onion, thinly sliced

1 tablespoon white wine vinegar

250 g/9 oz fine French beans

8 tablespoons Mayonnaise (recipe, page 30)

leaves from 1 stem of tarragon

20 g/$\frac{3}{4}$ oz capers

1 lemon

10 borage flowers (optional)

salt and freshly ground pepper

SKATE WINGS FLAVOURED WITH OLIVES

Ailerons de raie aux senteurs d'olives

*M*ICHEL *often cooks this dish at his cottage in Provence, where it fills the kitchen with its wonderful Mediterranean aroma of olive oil, basil and tomatoes.*

PREPARATION TIME
20 minutes

COOKING TIME
6 minutes

INGREDIENTS

2 skate wings, about 220 g/8 oz each

¼ cucumber, about 100 g/4 oz

100 g/4 oz black olives

4 tomatoes, each about 75 g/ 3 oz

1 bouquet garni

50 ml/2 fl oz olive oil

8 basil leaves

salt and freshly ground pepper

PREPARATION

The cucumber: Peel, deseed and cut the flesh into long strips.
The olives: Stone, then chop 75 g/3 oz very finely and keep in a bowl. Halve the remainder lengthways and keep separately.
The tomatoes: Peel, deseed and cut into 1 cm/½ in lozenges.

PRE-COOKING THE SKATE

Trim off the non-fleshy parts with scissors and rinse the wings in cold water. Fill a shallow pan with salted water, add the bouquet garni and bring to the boil. Plunge in the skate wings, skin-side down and immediately turn off the heat. Leave the skate for 30 seconds to infuse in the liquid, then drain the wings with a skimmer. Reserve the bouquet garni.

With a small, sharp knife, remove the skin, which will come away easily. Pat the wings dry with kitchen paper and season to taste. Using your fingertips, lightly press the chopped olives on to both sides of the fish.

COOKING THE SKATE

In a large shallow pan, gently heat the olive oil. Put in the olive-covered skate wings and the bouquet garni and cover the pan. Cook gently for 3 minutes, then turn the wings and scatter over the tomato lozenges and olive halves. Replace the lid and cook for another 3 minutes. The skate is now ready to serve; and the bouquet garni may be discarded.

PRESENTATION

Place a skate wing on each plate. Make sure that the fish is partly covered with tomato and the olives are evenly distributed. Arrange the strips of cucumber and the basil leaves around the edge of the plates and serve at once.

On plates: Skate wings flavoured with olives;
On dessert stand: Timbale of berry fruits in Beaumes de Venise jelly (recipe, page 91).

GRILLED SARDINES ON SPINACH SALAD
Sardines grillées sur pousses d'épinards en salade

*T*HIS *light, refreshing dish will tempt you to eat even on a hot summer's day. All the ingredients can be prepared several hours in advance, so your only task just before the meal will be to grill the sardines – a job that takes only a few minutes.*

PREPARATION TIME
20 minutes

COOKING TIME
4 minutes

INGREDIENTS
6 very fresh sardines, 80–100 g/ 3–4 oz each

60 ml/2 fl oz olive oil

100 g/4 oz young spinach shoots

a pinch of caster sugar

1 tablespoon balsamic vinegar

1 teaspoon strong Dijon mustard

1 tablespoon double cream

zest and juice of ½ lemon

salt and freshly ground pepper

PREPARATION

The sardines: Scrape off the scales with the back of a knife, then rinse the sardines in very cold water and sponge dry. With a very sharp filleting knife, cut off the heads and, starting from the back, lift the fillets off the backbones, without separating them at the belly. Pull out the backbones and guts. Carefully sponge the insides of the boned sardines, making sure you have removed all the bones; pull out any that remain with tweezers. Open the sardines out flat, lay them in a deep dish, season lightly with salt and pepper and pour over 40 ml/1½ fl oz olive oil.

Preheat a grill pan, and the grill or the oven to 160°C/310°F/gas 2.
The spinach: Wash in cold water, drain and gently pat dry. In a bowl, whisk together the sugar, a little salt and pepper, the vinegar, mustard, cream and lemon zest and juice. Keep this vinaigrette at room temperature.

COOKING THE SARDINES

Place the sardines in the very hot grill pan, skin-side down, and grill for 1 minute, then give them a quarter-turn to make an attractive lattice pattern and cook for another minute. Transfer the sardines to a heatproof plate and place under the grill or in the preheated oven for 2 minutes to finish cooking.

PRESENTATION

Mix the spinach into the vinaigrette and place on a large plate or oval dish. Arrange the sardines like sunrays, with their tails pointing inwards and the fattest part of the fillets towards the edge of the plate. Serve immediately.

NOTE

To avoid any smell or smoke as you grill the sardines spoiling the effect, switch on the cooker hood a few minutes before starting to cook.

GRILLED CUTLETS AND SHOULDER OF YOUNG RABBIT WITH WATERCRESS SALAD

Côtelettes de lapereau et ses épaules grillées sur salade de cresson

*W*E *adore this recipe for rabbit, which you can also cook very successfully on the barbecue. It is quite permissible – even advisable – to use your fingers to eat the rabbit; sucking the bones is a real treat, so put a couple of finger bowls on the table.*

PREPARATION

The rabbit: Use a boning knife to cut off the front legs. With a chef's knife or very sharp scissors, split the rib cage lengthways. Cut 4 double cutlets from the front of the rib cage. Put all the rabbit pieces in a dish, brush with 3 tablespoons olive oil, then sprinkle with thyme and crushed peppercorns and leave to marinate for at least 30 minutes before cooking.

The watercress: Pick off the leaves, wash in cold water and pat dry.

The vinaigrette: Mix the vinegar with the remaining olive oil and add a pinch of salt and pepper and the chopped shallot.

Heat a grill pan until very hot.

COOKING THE RABBIT

Put the shoulders and cutlets in the very hot grill pan and cook for 2 minutes. Give them a quarter-turn to make an attractive lattice pattern, and cook for another 1–2 minutes. Turn the rabbit pieces over and cook the other side in the same way. The cutlets will need a total of 5 minutes, and the shoulders 8 minutes.

Add the front of the rib cage and cook for only 3–4 minutes, so that it does not dry out. As soon as the rabbit pieces are cooked, sprinkle with the mustard seeds and season to taste with salt and pepper.

PRESENTATION

Mix the watercress with the vinaigrette and arrange on an oval platter. Put the rabbit pieces on the watercress and scatter over the pine kernels. Serve very hot.

NOTE

An experienced butcher can joint the rabbit for you in 5 minutes, so – if you have such a butcher locally – you might prefer to leave that job to him.

PREPARATION TIME
20 minutes, plus 30 minutes marinating

COOKING TIME
3–8 minutes, depending on the size of the rabbit pieces

INGREDIENTS
front half of a young rabbit, including the head, heart and lungs, about 600 g/1 $\frac{1}{4}$ lb, skinned

6 tablespoons olive oil

a sprig of lemon thyme, or thyme, chopped

10 peppercorns, crushed

1 small bunch of watercress

1 tablespoon red wine vinegar

40 g/1 $\frac{1}{2}$ oz shallot, finely chopped

1 teaspoon mustard seeds

20 g/ $\frac{3}{4}$ oz pine kernels, grilled until golden

salt and freshly ground pepper

GRILLED FILLET OF VEAL WITH REDCURRANT PEARLS

Filet mignon de veau aux perles de groseille

*T*HE *redcurrants give this refreshing dish its sharp flavour and glowing colours. It is very easy to make, since the redcurrants and cucumber can be prepared in advance.*

PREPARATION

The cucumber: Peel, deseed and use a sharp knife to trim the flesh into small olive-shaped pieces. Blanch in a pan of lightly salted boiling water for 30 seconds, refresh and drain.

The currants: Pull the currants off their stalks with the prongs of a fork. Reserve the white currants and an equal quantity of redcurrants. Carefully press the rest of the redcurrants through a fine wire sieve to extract a very clear juice. Mix in 30 g/ 1 oz sugar and keep in a sauceboat.

Preheat the grill pan for 10 minutes before starting to cook the veal. At the same time, warm two serving plates.

COOKING

The veal: Sprinkle the fillets with salt, oil them lightly and grill for about 5 minutes, turning them over so that they are well-patterned on both sides. Leave to rest for 1 minute before slicing.

The cucumber: Put the pieces in a small saucepan with the butter and 1 tablespoon water, and sweat for 2–3 minutes, until the liquid has evaporated. Add the remaining sugar and heat for 30 seconds to glaze the cucumber.

PRESENTATION

Slice the veal fillets slightly on the diagonal. Fan out each one on a warmed plate, decorate with a few watercress leaves and arrange the cucumber 'olives' and red and white currants on the plates. Pour the unheated redcurrant sauce around the edge and serve at once.

PREPARATION TIME
20 minutes

COOKING TIME
5 minutes

INGREDIENTS

2 small centre cut fillets of veal, each about 150 g/5 oz

½ cucumber, about 150 g/5 oz

300 g/11 oz redcurrants

20 g/¾ oz white currants (optional)

1 tablespoon groundnut oil

20 g/¾ oz butter

40 g/1½ oz caster sugar

salt

1 small bunch of watercress, washed and trimmed, for the garnish

PLATTER OF EARLY SUMMER VEGETABLES
L'Assiette de légumes mois de juin

*T**HE first baby vegetables of the season are so deliciously tender and delicate, and full of flavour, that we always try to treat ourselves to a plateful at this time of year.*

PREPARATION TIME
20 minutes

COOKING TIME
depends on the size of the vegetables

INGREDIENTS

8 small new carrots with their tops

6 small blue turnips with their tops

8 small new onions

250 g/9 oz peas or broad beans in the pod

150 g/5 oz small new potatoes

2 sprigs and stalks of parsley

1 teaspoon snipped fresh mint

40 g/1 ½ oz butter

salt and freshly ground pepper

PREPARATION

Peel or shell the vegetables as appropriate. Rinse them separately in cold water.

Bring a pan of water to the boil, add a very little salt and cook each variety of vegetable separately, using the same cooking water. Test them with the point of a knife or, in the case of the peas or broad beans, your teeth; the vegetables should still be firm – neither crunchy nor soft. Only the potatoes should be tender. As each type of vegetable is cooked, remove them from the cooking water with a slotted spoon and place in a bowl of very cold water to which you have added a few ice cubes. When all the vegetables have been cooked and refreshed, drain them well and immediately put them in a dish. Cover with clingfilm and keep in a cool place. Do not cook them more than 2–3 hours in advance.

Pour half the cooking water through a conical sieve into a saucepan and reduce to only 75 ml/3 fl oz. Add the parsley, then leave the liquid in a cool place to infuse.

PRESENTATION

Just before serving, reheat the vegetables in a steamer. Start by steaming the potatoes for 4 minutes, then add all the remaining vegetables and steam for another 2 minutes. Alternatively, drop the potatoes into a pan of boiling water and, when the water comes back to the boil, add the other vegetables and reheat them for 2 minutes.

In a small saucepan, heat the reduced cooking liquid and whisk in the butter. Discard the parsley and season the sauce to taste with pepper and salt if necessary. Take the pan off the heat and stir in the mint.

Arrange the vegetables in a serving bowl or terrine. Pour over the warm sauce and serve immediately.

NOTES

When vegetables are cooked in water, many of the vitamins they contain are dispersed in the water, and much of the flavour is lost. By using the cooking water for the sauce, at least the flavour is saved.

You may prefer to steam the vegetables. If so, begin with the potatoes and add the other vegetables every 3–5 minutes, in the following order: onions, carrots, turnips and finally the peas or broad beans.

SWEETCORN WITH GREEN PEPPER
AND PARMESAN FLAKES

Grains de maïs au poivron doux et copeaux de parmesan

*I*F *you have an Italian cheesemonger, ask him to cut the parmesan into flakes for you. You can also use thin slivers of fromage de Comté, although it will not taste as good.*

PREPARATION TIME
10 minutes

INGREDIENTS

1 × 340 g/12 oz tin of sweetcorn (drained weight 300 g/11 oz)

1 small pepper, preferably green

6 tablespoons Mayonnaise (recipe, page 30)

a pinch of sweet paprika

1 piece of parmesan, about 60 g/ 2 oz, cut into thin slivers or flakes

8 small cherry tomatoes, washed in cold water

salt and freshly ground pepper

PREPARATION

The sweetcorn: Tip into a colander, rinse in cold water and leave to drain.
The pepper: Cut off the stalk and the hard flesh around it. Halve the pepper lengthways and remove all of the seeds and white membrane from around the inside. Rinse the two halves in cold water and dice finely.

PRESENTATION

Mix the sweetcorn and diced pepper into the mayonnaise and season to taste. Place in a small salad bowl and sprinkle on a light veil of paprika through a strainer. Arrange the flakes of parmesan interspersed with the tomatoes on top and serve as cold as possible.

NOTE

If you are intending to take this delicious salad on a picnic, it is best to use a thermal container to keep it really cool.

TIMBALE OF BERRY FRUITS IN BEAUMES DE VENISE JELLY

Timbale de fruits au vin de Beaumes de Venise

*Y*OUR *guest will be entranced by this sparkling, jewel-like dessert, which is bursting with sweet, juicy flavours. An advantage is that it can be made a day or two in advance.*

--------------------------------- PREPARATION ---------------------------------

Chill a 10 cm/4 in soufflé dish, 6.5 cm/2½ in deep, or two 9 cm/3½ in ramekins, 4 cm/1½ in deep, in the fridge.

The orange: With a flexible knife, peel the orange and cut the segments between the membrane. Keep the segments and squeeze the pulp into a separate bowl. Scoop out the passion fruit juice and seeds and mix with the orange juice. Place the two bowls in the fridge.

The berries: Carefully hull or destalk them, as appropriate. Do not wash, it is important that they are as dry as possible.

--------------------------- ASSEMBLING THE TIMBALE ---------------------------

Heat about 30 ml/1 fl oz of the wine in a small pan until lukewarm. Take off the heat and stir in the soaked gelatine. Add this mixture to the remaining wine, stir gently with a spoon and place in the fridge for about 30 minutes, until the wine is cold but not set.

Pour about 5 mm/¼ in wine into the soufflé dish or ramekins and replace in the fridge until the wine sets to a jelly. Scatter some of the fruits over this layer of jelly, pour over a little more wine and replace in the fridge until set. Carry on making layers of fruit and jelly until the dish or ramekins are full. Leave in the fridge for at least 3 hours before serving.

--------------------------------- PRESENTATION ---------------------------------

Dip the base of the dish or ramekins into a bowl filled with very hot water for 2 seconds, then carefully invert the dish or ramekins on to one or two plates. Pour the orange and passion fruit juice around the edge and arrange the remaining fruits in little mounds on the juice. Add the mint sprigs and serve at once.

PREPARATION TIME
15 minutes, plus at least 4 hours chilling

INGREDIENTS

1 small orange

1 passion fruit (optional)

25 g/1 oz small strawberries

25 g/1 oz redcurrants

25 g/1 oz blackberries

25 g/1 oz small black grapes

15 g/½ oz raspberries

15 g/½ oz blueberries

250 ml/9 fl oz Beaumes de Venise

1 gelatine leaf, soaked in cold water

4 small sprigs of mint

Illustrated on page 83

RED FRUITS WITH LEMON-FLAVOURED CUSTARD
Soupe de fruits rouges

*T*HIS *is a particular favourite of Michel in the South of France, where he finds the sun brings the full sweetness to the red fruits. Choose your fruits with love – their succulence is the key to the success of this very simple, delicious dessert.*

PREPARATION

The lemon-flavoured custard: In a saucepan, bring the cream to the boil with 30 g/1 oz sugar and the lemon juice. In a bowl, whisk the egg yolks with 40 g/1½ oz sugar to a ribbon consistency. Pour the boiling cream on to the egg yolks, whisking constantly. Pour the mixture back into the pan and poach very gently at 85°C/185°F for 2 minutes, stirring continuously with a wooden spatula. On no account let the custard boil. Pass it through a conical sieve into a bowl and keep in a cool place, stirring the custard occasionally to prevent a skin from forming. Once the custard is cold, cover the bowl with clingfilm and refrigerate.

The lemon julienne: Put the zest in a small saucepan with a little water and bring to the boil. As soon as the water boils, refresh and drain. Return the zest to the same pan with the remaining sugar, 2 tablespoons water and the mint syrup. Bring slowly to the boil and poach gently until all the liquid has evaporated. Use a fork to lift the candied zest into a small, fine strainer and spread it out evenly. When it has cooled, transfer it to a cup or saucer and keep at room temperature.

The fruits: Gently rinse in cold water, hull or stone as appropriate, but leave the redcurrants on their stalks. Chill until needed.

PRESENTATION

Place the well-chilled fruits in two deep plates. Pour over the chilled custard, scatter with lemon julienne and eat with soup spoons.

NOTES

It is essential to use very ripe, sweet fruits to contrast with the wonderfully sharp lemony custard. Some can even be so ripe that their juices are running. You need not use all the suggested fruits, but remember that you will need at least three different varieties.

All the separate elements of this dish can be prepared the day before; it will take you only 2 minutes to assemble the dessert on the plates at the last moment.

PREPARATION TIME
25 minutes

COOKING TIME
2 minutes

INGREDIENTS

400 g/14 oz mixed red fruits (raspberries, strawberries, bilberries, redcurrants, cherries)

120 ml/4 fl oz single cream

100 g/4 oz caster sugar

120 ml/4 fl oz lemon juice (from about 3 lemons)

3 egg yolks

zest of ½ lemon, cut into fine julienne strips

1 tablespoon crème de menthe

CARAMELISED MELON FILLED WITH MELON CUBES AND LIGHT SYRUP

Rouelle de melon caramelisée

A refreshing and imaginative dish. The warm caramelised melon has an intense flavour, which makes a delightful contrast with the well-chilled melon cubes.

PREPARATION TIME
15 minutes

COOKING TIME
2 minutes

INGREDIENTS

1 melon, about 700 g/1½ lb

80 g/3 oz caster sugar

juice of ½ lemon

a pinch of cinnamon (optional)

2 sprigs of fresh mint

PREPARATION

The syrup: Put 50 ml/2 fl oz water and 50 g/2 oz sugar in a saucepan, bring to the boil and simmer gently for 1–2 minutes. Keep this syrup in a cool place.

The melon: Wash the melon in cold water. Halve it horizontally and remove the seeds. Cut off the bottom of each melon half about 4 cm/1½ in from the base. Place the two large melon circles in the fridge. Peel the two bases with a sharp knife and cut the flesh into neat 5 mm/¼ in dice. Place in a bowl, add the syrup, lemon juice and cinnamon, if you are using it, and chill in the fridge.

PRESENTATION

Ten minutes before serving, heat a salamander or grill until red hot. At this point, arrange the two melon circles on a baking sheet, sprinkle with the remaining sugar and place under the salamander or grill to caramelise. This will take about 2 minutes, depending on the intensity of the heat. As soon as the sugar caramelises, put each melon circle on a chilled plate. Pour the well-chilled diced melon into the centre, decorate each circle with a sprig of mint and serve at once.

NOTES

If the melon is full of flavour, juicy and sweet, the cinnamon will not be necessary.

A scoop of melon sorbet placed on top of the diced melon at the last minute will add a third delectable dimension to your dessert.

SUMMER DINNERS

At this time of year, there is an abundance of fruit, young vegetables and fish. Market stalls, laden with produce, offer a palette of attractive colours, glowing and full of life. Pleasure begins with buying, so why resist temptation!

The air becomes fresh and cool at around 10 o'clock in the evening. Until then, give your eyes and tastebuds a holiday. Lay the table with flowers and candles and serve fine wines in sparkling crystal glasses to complement the elegant food. Perhaps even dress for dinner; all this creates an atmosphere of summer romance.

This is the menu we have selected:
Cream of asparagus soup with curry
Salmon brawn with a tangy aigrelette sauce
Roast rack of lamb with a herb crust
Pastry cigars filled with red fruits and fruit coulis

ASPARAGUS AND MANGE-TOUT WITH SAUCE MALTAISE

Asperges et pois mange-tout, sauce maltaise

*A*N extremely easy dish, whose delicate flavour and soft colours inspire romance. The maltaise sauce should not be made more than one hour in advance, or it will lose its lightness, and the characteristic delicate orange flavour will be diffused.

PREPARATION

The asparagus: Peel the stalks with a potato peeler and cut them 5 cm/2 in from the tips. Cut the most tender part of the lower stalk into 5 mm/$\frac{1}{4}$ in rounds, discarding the fibrous bases. Wash tips and rounds in cold water, and cook in boiling salted water for 3 minutes; the asparagus should be neither crunchy nor soft, but firm to the bite. Refresh, drain, cover with a damp cloth and keep at room temperature.
The mange-tout: Top and tail, and cut diagonally into 5 cm/2 in lengths. Wash in cold water, and cook in boiling salted water for about 3 minutes, until slightly crunchy. Refresh, drain and put with the asparagus.
The oranges: Wash in cold water. Grate the whole surface of one orange, using the fine side of a grater. Put the resulting fine pulp into a cup.

Using a potato peeler, remove the zest of the other orange, then use a chef's knife to cut it into fine julienne. Blanch in boiling water for 30 seconds, refresh, drain and place in another cup. Using a knife with a fine blade, pare off all the pith from one orange, cut out the segments, removing all the membrane and reserve. Squeeze the core and membranes into a bowl to extract all the juice, and squeeze the juice of the second orange into the same bowl.

THE SAUCE MALTAISE

Put the orange juice into a small saucepan and reduce to 2 tablespoons liquid. Take the pan off the heat and leave the juice for a few minutes, until cold. Add the pulpy grated orange zest, the egg yolk and a soup spoon of cold water.

Set the pan over the lowest possible heat (50–55°C/122–131°F) and whisk the sauce to a ribbon consistency. You may prefer to stand the pan in a bain-marie, to avoid the risk of curdling the sauce. Skim the melted butter and pour it gently into the sauce, whisking continuously. Be careful not to pour the white milky liquids at the bottom of the butter into the sauce. Season to taste, cover the pan and keep in a warm place. Heat two plates.

PRESENTATION

Plunge asparagus tips and mange-tout into a pan of boiling water for 20 seconds, then drain. Warm the orange segments and asparagus rounds in separate pans.

Place the asparagus rounds in the centre of the warmed plates and heap the mange-tout, asparagus tips and orange segments on top. Spoon over a generous amount of sauce maltaise, scatter on the blanched orange zests and serve at once.

PREPARATION TIME
20 minutes

COOKING TIME
4–5 minutes for the sauce

INGREDIENTS

12 small asparagus spears, each about 30–40 g/1–1 $\frac{1}{2}$ oz

50 g/2 oz tender mange-tout

2 small oranges, preferably blood oranges

1 egg yolk

100 g/4 oz butter, melted and cooled

salt and freshly ground white pepper

PANCAKE PURSES FILLED WITH COLD SOFT-BOILED EGGS AND PIQUANT MAYONNAISE
Petite bourse froide d'oeuf mollet

*D*O *not be deterred from serving these pancakes by the slightly childish presentation of the dish — the pancakes hide a fresh-tasting and elegant filling.*

PREPARATION TIME
35 minutes, plus 30 minutes resting the batter

COOKING TIME
1 ½ minutes per pancake

INGREDIENTS
50 g/2 oz broccoli

2 eggs, preferably free range, soft-boiled for 4–5 minutes

1 teaspoon snipped chives

1 small shallot, finely chopped

30 g/1 oz pickled gherkins, cut into small julienne

½ quantity Mayonnaise (about 6 tablespoons) (recipe, page 30)

4 long chives, blanched for 20 seconds and refreshed

2 cupped lettuce or iceberg lettuce leaves, washed and dried

8 fronds of fennel or dill

THE PANCAKE BATTER:
30 g/1 oz flour

1 egg

100 ml/4 fl oz milk

1 teaspoon snipped chives and tarragon

1 tablespoon groundnut oil

salt and freshly ground pepper

PREPARATION

The pancake batter: Put the flour, egg and half the milk in a bowl and whisk with a small balloon whisk until smooth and homogenous. Add the rest of the milk, a little salt and pepper and the snipped herbs. Leave to rest in a cool place for 30 minutes. You will have enough batter to make four 25 cm/10 in pancakes.

Cooking the pancakes: Heat a non-stick frying pan, 25 cm/10 in diameter if possible, add a drop of oil for each pancake, and cook 4 pancakes for about 45 seconds on each side, taking care that they do not become dry. They should be lightly browned, but still moist and malleable. Stack the pancakes on a plate, with a piece of greaseproof paper between each one, and keep at room temperature.

The broccoli: Trim into small florets and wash in cold water. Cook in a pan of lightly salted boiling water until still firm and slightly crunchy to the bite. Refresh, drain and place on kitchen paper.

ASSEMBLING THE PURSES

Carefully shell the boiled eggs, taking care not to break them. Mix the snipped chives, shallot, gherkins and the broccoli florets into the mayonnaise.

Lay a pancake on the work surface. Spread one-third of the mayonnaise mixture over the centre and place an egg on top. Carefully, gather up the edges of the pancake to make a little purse and tie it not too tightly with a long chive. Make a second purse in the same way.

PRESENTATION

Put the lettuce leaves on two plates and fill them with the remaining mayonnaise mixture. Stand the purses on top. Arrange the fennel or dill fronds on the mayonnaise at the base of the purses and serve cold, but not chilled.

NOTES

It is worth taking the precaution of making 4 pancakes, just in case you should tear one while assembling the purses.

The purses can be prepared up to 2 hours before dinner. Cover them loosely with clingfilm, so that it does not touch the purses, and keep in a cool place.

PASTRY CASES WITH ASPARAGUS TIPS AND MUSHROOMS

Feuilleté de pointes d'asperges et champignons de Paris

*T*HE *perfect dish for a romantic summer dinner, when asparagus is available at its freshest. It takes a little effort to prepare, but is deeply satisfying.*

PREPARATION

The pastry cases: On a lightly floured surface, roll out the pastry into a 13 cm/5¼ in square, about 5 mm/¼ in thick. With a heavy knife, cut two 10 × 6 cm/4 × 2¼ in rectangles from the pastry. Place on a lightly dampened baking sheet and leave to rest in the fridge for 30 minutes.

Preheat the oven to 240°C/475°F/gas 9.

COOKING THE PASTRY CASES

Brush the tops with eggwash. With the point of a knife, lightly score around the inside edges of the rectangles, leaving a 5 mm/¼ in border. Without actually cutting through the pastry, score criss-cross lines on the inner rectangles.

Bake in the preheated oven for 3 minutes, then lower the temperature to 200°C/400°F/gas 6 and bake for another 4 minutes. Remove the cases from the oven and immediately run the point of a knife around the incisions in the rectangles. Slide the knife blade into the pastry and lift out these 'lids'. Place the cases and lids on a pastry rack.

The asparagus: Peel the stalks with a vegetable peeler. Wash and cook in lightly salted water until tender. Refresh and drain. Starting at the tip, cut each spear into 4 cm/1½ in lengths. Reserve the tips and chop the stalks to use in the sauce.

The mushrooms: Peel, if necessary, and wipe with a damp cloth. Cut off the stalks and keep them for the sauce. Heat 20 g/¾ oz butter in a frying pan, add the mushroom caps, a few drops of lemon juice and a pinch of salt, and sauté over medium heat for 2 minutes. Transfer both caps and juices to a bowl and keep warm.

The sauce: Heat 20 g/¾ oz butter in a small saucepan, add the mushroom stalks, chopped asparagus, half the celery and the peppercorns and sweat for 5 minutes. Add 6 tablespoons water, the juice from the mushrooms and the remaining lemon juice and cook gently for another 3 minutes. Purée in a food processor for 1 minute, then rub the sauce through a conical sieve into a small saucepan. Whisk in the remaining butter and season with salt and pepper.

PRESENTATION

Place the empty pastry cases in the oven at 180°C/350°F/gas 4 for a few minutes to reheat lightly. Heat the asparagus tips in boiling water for 30 seconds. Mix them gently with the mushrooms and spoon into the pastry cases. Arrange the feuilletés on plates, scatter over the remaining snipped celery leaves and pour the sauce around the edge of the feuilletés. Arrange 4 cherry tomatoes at the edge of each plate and serve at once.

PREPARATION TIME
35 minutes, plus 30 minutes chilling

COOKING TIME
7 minutes

INGREDIENTS
12 small asparagus spears
100 g/4 oz button mushrooms
a pinch of flour
100 g/4 oz Quick puff pastry (recipe, page 23)
eggwash (1 egg yolk, lightly beaten with 1 teaspoon milk)
80 g/3 oz butter
juice of ½ small lemon
1 tablespoon tender green celery leaves, snipped
5 peppercorns, crushed
salt and freshly ground pepper
8 cherry tomatoes, for the garnish

SCRAMBLED EGGS IN A SMOKED SALMON COAT

Oeufs brouillés en habit de saumon fumé

*O*N *a hot summer's evening, this dish can also be served cold. The great advantage of this is that it can be prepared during the day, leaving you nothing to do before the meal.*

PREPARATION TIME
15 minutes

COOKING TIME
3–5 minutes

INGREDIENTS

2 long thin slices of smoked salmon, each about 80 g/3 oz

2 eggs, preferably free range

40 g/1½ oz butter

2 tablespoons double cream

1 tablespoon snipped chives

1 lemon

salt and freshly ground pepper

PREPARATION

Scrambling the eggs: Break the eggs into a bowl and beat with a fork for 30 seconds, then season with a very little salt and plenty of pepper. Melt 30 g/1 oz butter in a small saucepan, pour in the eggs and cook very gently, scrambling them with a wooden spatula, until done to your liking. Take the pan off the heat, stir in the cream, transfer the eggs to a bowl and keep at room temperature.

Assembling the smoked salmon parcels: Spread the smoked salmon slices on the work surface and trim the edges if necessary to make two more or less regular rectangles. Finely dice the salmon trimmings and delicately mix them into the eggs, together with two-thirds of the chives. Spread the egg mixture over the middle of the smoked salmon and fold over the four sides to make neat parcels. Put on a plate, cover with foil and place in the fridge.

HEATING THE PARCELS

Melt the remaining butter and brush it over the top of the parcels. Fill the bottom of a steamer with boiling water, put the parcels in the top, cover and steam for 5 minutes. Alternatively, microwave the parcels on their plate for 2 minutes.

PRESENTATION

Use a palette knife to transfer the salmon parcels to two heated plates, squeeze half a lemon over each one, sprinkle on the remaining chives and serve.

NOTE

If you prefer to serve the parcels hot, they will have a somewhat creamier texture if reheated in a steamer, rather than the microwave.

CREAM OF ASPARAGUS SOUP WITH CURRY
Velouté d'asperges au curry

*T*HE *mild Madras curry powder used in this dish brings out the flavour of the asparagus and gives the delicate cream soup a wonderful aroma and taste.*

─────────────── PREPARATION ───────────────

The asparagus: Peel the stalks with a vegetable peeler, wash in cold water and cut off all the tips to the same length. Cook the tips in salted boiling water for 2 minutes, refresh, drain and place in a bowl. Cover with clingfilm and refrigerate. Chop the stalks, discarding the woody and stringy ends.
The potato, onions and leek: Peel, wash in cold water and chop.

─────────────── COOKING THE SOUP ───────────────

Melt the butter in a saucepan, put in the chopped vegetables and asparagus stalks, the bouquet garni and curry powder, and sweat gently for 4 minutes, stirring continuously. Add the chicken stock or water and cook at just below boiling point for 15 minutes. Add the cream, bubble for 2 minutes, then discard the bouquet garni and pour the contents of the pan into a blender. Purée for 3 minutes, then pass the soup through a conical sieve. Season to taste.

─────────────── PRESENTATION ───────────────

Divide the reserved aparagus tips between two deep plates or soup bowls, pour over the hot soup and serve immediately.

─────────────── NOTES ───────────────

If you cannot find small asparagus, simply halve the tips lengthways for the garnish. Some croûtons, fried in clarified butter, drained and served separately make a good additional garnish for this dish.

PREPARATION TIME
15 minutes

COOKING TIME
20 minutes

INGREDIENTS

300 g/11 oz small asparagus spears

30 g/1 oz butter

60 g/2 oz potato

80 g/3 oz onions

60 g/2 oz white of leeks

1 small bouquet garni

½ teaspoon mild Madras curry powder

500 ml/18 fl oz Chicken stock (recipe, page 18), or water

100 ml/4 fl oz double cream

salt and freshly ground pepper

TIMBALE OF SCALLOPS WITH FRESH HERBS
Timbale de coquilles Saint-Jacques aux fines herbes

*T*HIS *delicate dish is not as rich as you might suppose, and simple to prepare. It should be served hot, but not too hot, or the fragile, light texture of the mousse will disintegrate.*

PREPARATION TIME
35 minutes

COOKING TIME
15 minutes

INGREDIENTS

2 large scallops, fresh if possible, about 60 g/2 oz each

2 tablespoons fresh herbs, about $\frac{1}{2}$ tablespoon/$\frac{1}{4}$ oz each of tarragon, chives, flat-leafed parsley and dill

1 egg

100 ml/4 fl oz double cream, plus 1 tablespoon for the sauce

1 small celery stalk

1 small carrot, about 40 g/ $1\frac{1}{2}$ oz

$\frac{1}{2}$ leek, about 30 g/1 oz

1 small shallot, finely snipped

1 small bouquet garni

100 ml/4 fl oz dry white wine

50 g/2 oz butter, plus extra for greasing

20 chervil or flat-leafed parsley leaves

salt and freshly ground pepper

PREPARATION

The herbs: Wash in cold water and gently pat dry. Reserve one-third of the best tarragon and parsley leaves, dill fronds and chives for the moulds, and refrigerate. Keep the remaining leaves and the stalks for the sauce.

The scallop mousse: Debeard the scallops, remove the membrane which covers them and any sand. If they have corals, keep these for the sauce. Gently wipe the scallops with a cloth and place them in a blender with the egg, cream (keeping 1 tablespoon for the sauce), a pinch of salt and a little pepper. Blend for 45 seconds, transfer the mousse to a bowl, cover and refrigerate.

The sauce: Scrape the vegetables, wash, slice thinly and place in a saucepan with the shallot, bouquet garni, wine, 200 ml/7 fl oz water and the reserved herb leaves and stalks. Cook over medium heat for 30 minutes, until the liquid is reduced by about two-thirds.

Take the pan off the heat and add the corals if you have any, and the reserved spoonful of cream. Discard the bouquet garni and pour the sauce into the blender. Blend for 1 minute, then strain through a fine or muslin-lined conical sieve into a saucepan or bowl. Still off the heat, whisk the butter into the sauce, season to taste and keep the sauce in a bain-marie.

Preheat the oven to 160°C/315°F/gas 2–3. Heat two deep plates.

COOKING THE MOUSSES

Generously butter the insides of two timbale moulds, about 7.5 cm/3 in diameter, 4 cm/$1\frac{1}{2}$ in high. Sprinkle the buttered surface with the reserved herb leaves and divide the mousse mixture between the moulds. Cover the moulds with clingfilm.

Line the bottom of a deep ovenproof dish with foil and put in the moulds. Pour in enough almost boiling water to come half-way up the sides of the moulds. Cook in the preheated oven for 15 minutes. Remove from the oven and keep warm.

PRESENTATION

Remove the clingfilm and invert the mousses on to the warmed plates. Pour the sauce around the mousses and scatter on the chervil or parsley leaves to garnish. Serve immediately.

WARM FILLETS OF SMOKED EEL ON A FRISEE SALAD

Filets d'anguille fumeé tièdes sur salade de frisée

M ICHEL *Roux Junior created this recipe, which he serves as an hors d'oeuvre on the set menu at Le Gavroche, where it is much enjoyed by his uncle and the customers. It is a sure-fire winner even with those who have never tasted smoked eel before.*

PREPARATION

The frisée: Trim with a sharp knife, discard the greenest and tough parts, wash in cold water and drain.

The croûtons: Toast the bread under the grill until golden on both sides. Leave until cold, then rub lightly with the garlic.

The dressing: Into the mayonnaise, stir the lemon juice, 2 tablespoons cold water, the snipped herbs, and salt and pepper to taste.

The eel: Cut off the skin from the two pieces and take the fillets off the backbone. Place in the top of a steamer, and steam the eel fillets for 3 minutes.

PRESENTATION

While you are steaming the eel, mix half the mayonnaise dressing with the frisée. Heap it into the centre of two serving plates, and pour the remainder of the dressing all round the frisée.

Heat the oil in a frying pan and fry the lardons over high heat for 1 minute. Drain and immediately scatter them over the salad. Arrange the eel fillets on top and make an attractive border of croutons at the base of the frisée. Scatter the whole chives haphazardly on to the plates and serve at once.

NOTES

This dish has the advantage that all the ingredients can be prepared in advance and assembled in just a few minutes when you are ready to eat.

PREPARATION TIME
20 minutes

COOKING TIME
1 minute for the lardons, plus 3 minutes for the smoked eel

INGREDIENTS

150 g/5 oz medium-thick piece of smoked eel, halved

1 small frisée endive

8 thin slices of French bread, cut from a baguette

½ garlic clove

4 tablespoons Mayonnaise (recipe, page 30)

juice of ½ lemon

2 tablespoons snipped mixed herbs, including at least 3 of the following: chives, chervil, parsley, tarragon and dill

80 g/3 oz smoked streaky bacon, cut into small, even lardons, blanched, refreshed and drained

1 tablespoon groundnut oil

10 young, tender whole chives

salt and freshly ground pepper

SALMON BRAWN WITH A TANGY AIGRELETTE SAUCE

Hure de saumon, sauce aigrelette

*T*HIS *wonderfully refreshing hors d'oeuvre is unusual, in terms of both its flavour and its presentation. It needs very little attention once it has been assembled.*

PREPARATION TIME
40 minutes

COOKING TIME
1 hour 5 minutes, plus 30–60 seconds for cooking the salmon cubes and 1 hour chilling

INGREDIENTS

1 piece of salmon tail, about 300 g/11 oz

1 salmon head, gills removed, or 300 g/11 oz salmon bones

1 carrot, about 50 g/2 oz

1 leek

1 celery stalk

½ onion, about 40 g/1 ½ oz

100 ml/4 fl oz dry white wine

juice of 2 limes

1 tablespoon green peppercorns

1 garlic clove

1 large bouquet garni

1 tablespoon tarragon

2 egg whites

2 gelatine leaves, soaked in cold water

1 tablespoon olive oil

1 tablespoon capers

salt and freshly ground pepper

THE AIGRELETTE SAUCE:
½ orange

2 small pickled gherkins, cut into fine julienne

1 tablespoon balsamic vinegar

40 ml/1 ½ fl oz groundnut oil

salt and freshly ground pepper

PREPARATION

The moulds: Use a piece of cardboard to make two 10 cm/4 in circles, 2 cm/¾ in deep, secure with sellotape and cover with foil. Alternatively, use two 8 cm/3¼ in ramekins, 4 cm/1½ in deep.

The salmon: Use a filleting knife to lift the two salmon fillets off the bone. Remove the skin and cut the flesh into 1 cm/½ in cubes. Place in the fridge. Chop the backbone into 4 or 5 pieces, and place with the salmon head or other bones.

The fish stock: Peel the carrot and leek. Wash them, the celery and unpeeled onion, then slice finely. Reserve about one-quarter of each vegetable for clarifying the stock later.

Split the salmon head in half and meticulously wash it and the bones in cold water. Place in a saucepan and add the wine, lime juice, green peppercorns, garlic, chopped vegetables and bouquet garni. Strip off about 20 of the best tarragon leaves and reserve them, then add the rest of the tarragon on its stalk to the pan. Pour in 500 ml/18 fl oz cold water.

Bring the stock to the boil, then lower the heat and barely simmer at about 95°C/203°F. Cook for 30 minutes, skimming the surface when necessary. Strain through a conical sieve into a clean saucepan, lightly pressing the salmon head, bones and vegetables with the back of a ladle to push through as much stock as possible. Set the pan over low heat and reduce the stock to half its quantity (this will take about 20 minutes). Skim as necessary. Leave the reduced stock at room temperature until almost cold.

CLARIFICATION

Beat the egg whites with a fork for 30 seconds, then mix them into the reserved vegetables. Add the mixture to the nearly cold stock, stir with a wooden spatula, then set over gentle heat and heat until the stock begins to bubble, stirring continuously. As soon as the bubbles begin to rise, lower the heat even further and simmer for 15 minutes. Season to taste, add the well-drained gelatine leaves to the stock and very carefully pass the clarified stock through a fine or muslin-lined conical sieve, and leave until cold and half-set.

COOKING THE SALMON

Heat the olive oil in a frying pan. Season the salmon cubes with salt and pepper and fry for 30 seconds, or a fraction longer if you like your salmon less pink in the middle. Lay the salmon cubes on kitchen paper until cold.

ASSEMBLING THE SALMON BRAWN

Place a circle in the middle of each plate. Divide the salmon cubes, reserved tarragon leaves and capers between the circles, then refrigerate for 20 minutes. Fill the circles with the half-set jelly and refrigerate for at least 1 hour.

THE AIGRELETTE SAUCE

Peel and segment the orange, remove all the pith, then finely dice the segments. Mix together all the sauce ingredients.

PRESENTATION

Take the plates out of the fridge. Dip the point of a knife into boiling water and slide it round between the circle and the jelly. Lift off the circles and pour the sauce around the salmon brawn. Serve immediately.

NOTES

The brawn can be prepared and assembled the previous day. Cover with clingfilm and keep in the fridge until ready to serve.

FILLET OF SALMON WITH CRISP ASPARAGUS TIPS

Dos de saumon aux croquants d'asperges

*S*ALMON and asparagus are the most delicious and harmonious summertime partnership. The sauce in this dish is somewhere between a light sauce and a vegetable nage, as such it makes the perfect foil for the rich texture of the fish.

PREPARATION

The asparagus: Peel the stalks with a potato peeler, wash in cold water and cut the stalks 5 cm/2 in from the tips. Cut the tips lengthways into 8. Chop the lower part of the stalks and keep them for the sauce.

The sauce: Melt 1 tablespoon butter in a saucepan and sweat the shallots, mushrooms and chopped asparagus stalks, making sure that they do not colour at all. After 3 minutes, add the bouquet garni, then the fish or vegetable stock. Simmer gently for 5 minutes, then add the cream and let the sauce bubble for 2 minutes. Pour it into a blender and blend for 2 minutes. Strain through a fine or muslin-lined conical sieve and keep warm.

Preheat the oven to 220°C/425°F/gas 7.

POACHING THE SALMON

With a filleting knife, remove the salmon skin, then cut the fillet in half, across the middle. Lightly butter a deep dish and put in the two pieces of salmon. Cover with water, season with a little salt, arrange the lemon slices round the fish and cover the dish with foil.

Cook the salmon in the preheated oven for 6–8 minutes, depending on whether you prefer it to be rosy in the middle or cooked right through. Remove from the oven and immediately take the salmon out of the cooking liquid. Reserve the liquid. Meanwhile, heat two plates.

PRESENTATION

As soon as the salmon is cooked, place a fillet on each warm plate. Heat the sauce until it comes to the boil, take the pan off the heat and whisk in the remaining butter. Season to taste.

Put the asparagus spears in a small saucepan with 1 tablespoon of the poaching liquid from the salmon and heat for 1 minute.

Scatter the hot asparagus spears over and around the salmon and pour the sauce around the edge. Sprinkle with the chives and serve at once.

NOTE

Do not begin to poach the salmon until you and your guest are already at the table, and have finished your first course.

PREPARATION TIME
20 minutes

COOKING TIME
10 minutes for the sauce, plus 6–8 minutes for the salmon

INGREDIENTS

300 g/11 oz salmon fillet, preferably from the back

8 small asparagus spears, about 30 g/1 oz each

50 g/2 oz butter

2 shallots, finely sliced

2 small mushrooms, thinly sliced

1 small bouquet garni

250 ml/9 fl oz Fish stock (recipe, page 18) or Vegetable stock (recipe, page 19)

100 ml/4 fl oz double cream

½ lemon, cut into rounds

1 tablespoon snipped chives

salt and freshly ground pepper

MARINATED SCALLOPS AND TUNA WITH FRESH HERBS

Noix de coquilles Saint-Jacques et thon marinés aux fines herbes

*T*HIS *refreshing dish is quick and easy to make, and has the added advantage that it can be prepared well in advance, leaving you free to enjoy the company of your guest.*

PREPARATION TIME
20 minutes

INGREDIENTS

3 very fresh scallops, total weight about 120 g/4 oz in all

120 g/4 oz very fresh tuna, cut into the thinnest possible escalopes (about 2 mm/ $\frac{1}{12}$ in)

1 tablespoon lemon juice

70 ml/3 fl oz olive oil

15 g/ $\frac{1}{2}$ oz mixed fresh herbs (equal quantities of dill, chives, chervil and tarragon)

35 g/1 $\frac{1}{4}$ oz onion, finely chopped

3 tablespoons balsamic vinegar

salt and freshly ground pepper

PREPARATION

The scallops: Debeard them and remove the membrane which partially covers them. Wash in cold water and pat dry. Cut each scallop horizontally into 6 slices and arrange in a deep dish large enough to hold the tuna slices alongside the scallops.

In a bowl, mix together the lemon juice and 20 ml/$\frac{3}{4}$ fl oz olive oil, and season with a little salt and plenty of pepper. Brush the scallops and tuna with this marinade. Cover with clingfilm and refrigerate for 10 minutes.

The herb marinade: Wash the herbs in cold water and dry carefully. Reserve about 10% of each kind of herb for the garnish. Strip the leaves off the best ones, leave the chives whole, and refrigerate.

Roughly chop the remaining herbs and their stalks, place in a blender with the onion, the remaining olive oil and the vinegar. Season lightly, then blend until smooth and well amalgamated. Strain through a muslin-lined or fine sieve, pressing hard to extract as much marinade as possible.

PRESENTATION

Arrange the scallops like a rosette in the centre of each plate, then lay the tuna slices around them. Pour a zigzag of marinade over the plates, so as not to mask the beautiful colours of the fish completely. Scatter over the reserved herbs and serve the dish well-chilled. Serve the rest of the marinade in a sauceboat.

NOTES

If you make the marinade in a mortar, crush the onion and vinegar to a smooth purée, then drip in the oil, working the mixture as for an aïoli. Finally, pass through a sieve as above.

If the scallops have corals, blanch these for 10 seconds, split them lengthways and use them to decorate the centre of each dish.

GRILLED HALIBUT STEAKS WITH CORIANDER-FLAVOURED TOMATO COULIS
Darnes de fletan grillées et coulis de tomates au coriandre

*T*HE *best way to enjoy the perfect simplicity of this dish is to eat the grilled halibut unadorned, or dip it into the tomato coulis inside its circle of sweet pepper.*

PREPARATION

The tomato coulis: In a small saucepan, sweat the shallot with 2 tablespoons olive oil for 30 seconds. Add the tomatoes and bouquet garni, season lightly with salt and pepper and cook gently for 30 minutes. Remove the bouquet garni and purée the tomatoes in a blender for 1 minute. Strain through a conical sieve into a small saucepan, whisk in the butter and add the snipped coriander. Cover the coulis and keep warm.

The sweet pepper: Wash in cold water, then cut 2 rounds, 3 cm/1¼ in thick from the widest part of the pepper. With a sharp knife, cut out the white membrane and seeds from inside the pepper. Blanch the rounds in lightly salted boiling water for 1 minute, refresh and drain. Cover with clingfilm and keep at room temperature.

Cut the two ends of the pepper into small lozenge shapes, taking care to remove any white pith and seeds. Heat 2 tablespoons olive oil in a small frying pan, add the pepper lozenges and garlic and sweat for 10 minutes. Discard the garlic and keep the lozenges warm.

COOKING THE HALIBUT

Heat a grill pan until searingly hot. With a filleting knife, cut off the halibut skin, rinse the steaks in cold water and pat dry. Sprinkle with crushed peppercorns and salt lightly. Brush the fish steaks with a little oil and put them into the hot pan. Cook for 1 minute, then give the steaks a quarter-turn. After 1 more minute, turn the fish over and cook the other side in the same way. Thus the total cooking time is 4 minutes.

PRESENTATION

Put the halibut steaks on two warmed plates, place a pepper round on each plate and fill it with tomato coulis. Arrange the pepper lozenges on the fish, put 3 coriander leaves in the centre of each steak and serve at once.

NOTE

We like our fish to be moist and lightly cooked, so a total cooking time of 4 minutes is just right for a 2 cm/¾ in thick steak. If you prefer your fish better cooked and slightly drier, grill it for a fraction longer.

PREPARATION TIME
20 minutes

COOKING TIME
4 minutes for the halibut, 30 minutes for the tomato coulis

INGREDIENTS

2 halibut steaks, about 2 cm/¾ in thick, 180–200 g/6–7 oz each

6 tablespoons olive oil

1 shallot, finely chopped

300 g/11 oz tomatoes, peeled, deseeded and chopped

1 small bouquet garni

50 g/2 oz butter

1 small yellow or orange pepper

1 garlic clove

10 peppercorns, crushed

10 coriander leaves, snipped, plus 6 whole leaves

salt and freshly ground pepper

MELTING COMPOTE OF RABBIT IN ASPIC
Fondant de compôte de lapereau en aspic

*I*N this recipe, the rabbit is cooked until the meat falls off the bones, which is why we call it a compote. We two brothers adore this dish served with a salad of frisée, escarole or lamb's lettuce and some delicious, fresh country bread.

PREPARATION TIME
30 minutes

COOKING TIME
2 hours, plus about 1 ½ hours cooling and setting

INGREDIENTS

front part of a young rabbit, about 450 g/1 lb

80 g/3 oz small button mushrooms

8 small button onions

8 small round carrots, or new carrots, preferably with their tops

2 tablespoons groundnut oil

1 bouquet garni

1 garlic clove, unpeeled

1 teaspoon tomato paste, or 2 fresh tomatoes, peeled, deseeded and chopped

300 ml/½ pt dry white wine

10 peppercorns, crushed

2 egg whites

1 tablespoon chopped mixed herbs (tarragon, chervil and chives)

1 gelatine leaf, soaked in cold water

1 tablespoon flat-leafed parsley leaves

salt and freshly ground pepper

PREPARATION

The rabbit: Using a boning knife, cut off the front legs and sever them at the joint. Discard the lungs and heart, split the rib cage in half, then cut into 4 equal pieces. Lightly salt all the pieces.
The vegetables: Peel and wash in cold water. Halve the mushrooms.

COOKING THE RABBIT

Heat the oil in a casserole or saucepan, put in the rabbit pieces and cook over high heat until lightly golden all over. Add the bouquet garni, garlic clove, tomato paste or fresh tomatoes, wine, crushed peppercorns and 450 ml/16 fl oz cold water. Bring to the boil, skim, then cover and simmer gently at a temperature of 90°C/194°F for 30 minutes.

Add the carrots and onions and simmer at the same temperature for another 1¼ hours. Finally, add the mushrooms and cook for another 15 minutes.

Leave at room temperature for about 1 hour, until almost cold. Carefully drain the rabbit pieces and vegetables, and keep the cooking stock. Discard the bouquet garni, cover the rabbit and vegetables with a very damp cloth and refrigerate.

CLARIFYING THE STOCK

Skim off any fat from the surface with a spoon. Lightly beat the egg whites, add the snipped herbs and pour into the almost cold stock. Bring to the boil over medium heat, whisking continuously. At the first sign of boiling, turn off the heat, add the drained gelatine and gently strain the stock through a fine, muslin-lined conical sieve to give the clearest possible aspic. Season to taste and leave in a cool place until cold but not set.

PRESENTATION

Put the rabbit pieces in a gratin or deep dish, then arrange the vegetables attractively round the edge of the dish. Scatter over the parsley leaves and pour on two-thirds of the still slightly runny aspic. Refrigerate for 30 minutes, until the aspic has set, then pour on the rest of the aspic. Serve cold but not chilled.

NOTE

Ideally, you should aim to serve this dish approximately 2 or 3 hours after pouring on the aspic, so that it is not too cold.

CASSOULET OF CHICKEN LEGS WITH GARLIC
Jambonneau de poulet et gousses d'ail à l'étouffée

*T*RY *to find some fresh new season's haricot beans for this dish, since they have a more delicate flavour and need less soaking and cooking time than ordinary haricot beans.*

—— PREPARATION ——

The beans: Drain, rinse in cold water and place in a large saucepan with the chicken stock, bouquet garni, carrots and onion. Set over low heat and cook gently for 1 hour, skimming the surface whenever necessary. After an hour, turn off the heat and leave the beans in the pan at room temperature. At this stage they will need another 45 minutes–1 hour cooking.

Preheat the oven to 180°C/350°F/gas 4 if you are using it to cook the chicken.

—— COOKING THE CHICKEN ——

Sprinkle the chicken with plenty of paprika and a little salt. Heat the olive oil in a cast iron or heavy flameproof casserole, put in the chicken and unpeeled garlic and fry until the chicken is a deep brick colour.

Pour off the fat from the pan and pour in the wine. Reduce the wine by half, then add the beans with their cooking liquid and the aromatics. Bring to the boil, immediately skim the surface, put on the lid and cook very gently on the hob at about 90°C/185°F, or in the preheated oven for 1 hour.

Discard the onion and bouquet garni, season with salt and pepper if necessary, stir in the dried tomatoes and sprinkle the chopped parsley on top. Replace the lid and keep the chicken warm.

—— PRESENTATION ——

Heat two deep plates. Bring the casserole to the table and lift the lid just before serving – out will waft the scents of a good old-fashioned family dish.

—— NOTES ——

New season's lingot beans will need only 30 minutes' soaking, and the cooking time can be reduced by at least one-third.

Any leftovers can be kept for up to 2 days and reheated in a bain-marie.

PREPARATION TIME
20 minutes

COOKING TIME
2 hours

INGREDIENTS

4 chicken drumsticks

120 g/4 oz dried white haricot beans, preferably lingot, soaked in cold water for 4 hours

750 ml/1 ¼ pt Chicken stock (recipe, page 18)

1 bouquet garni

2 carrots, total weight about 120 g/4 oz, peeled and cut into thick rounds

1 small onion, stuck with 1 clove

1 teaspoon paprika

4 tablespoons olive oil

8 unpeeled garlic cloves

150 ml/5 fl oz dry white wine

40 g/1 ½ oz Dried tomatoes, home-preserved (recipe, page 28) or bottled

1 tablespoon chopped parsley

salt and freshly ground pepper

VEAL CHOPS WITH PEAS AND BROAD BEANS

Côtes de veau parées à la verdure

*T*HIS *simple, yet most appetising dish will appeal to everyone. The succulent, white flesh of the veal contrasts beautifully in both colour and texture with the crisp, green vegetables.*

PREPARATION TIME
20 minutes

COOKING TIME
6–8 minutes for the chops, plus 1½ hours for the sauce

INGREDIENTS

2 veal chops, each about 250 g/ 9 oz

60 g/2 oz veal trimmings (ask your butcher for these)

a pinch of caster sugar

50 ml/2 fl oz white wine vinegar

250 ml/9 fl oz dry white wine

2 shallots, each about 40 g/ 1½ oz, thinly sliced

1 garlic clove

10 black peppercorns, crushed

10 juniper berries, crushed

1 small bouquet garni

60 g/2 oz button mushrooms, wiped and thinly sliced

80 g/3 oz butter

60 g/2 oz small petits pois, fresh or frozen

60 g/2 oz young tender broad beans, fresh or frozen

3 or 4 sorrel leaves

salt and freshly ground pepper

PREPARATION

The veal chops: Using a boning knife, cut away the sinews and fat from around the chops, and scrape the ends of the bones to leave them uncovered. Put the resulting trimmings with those you bought from the butcher and keep them for the sauce.
The sauce: Preheat the oven to 220°C/425°F/gas 7.

Put all the veal trimmings in a roasting tin and roast in the preheated oven for 20 minutes, until golden brown. Take the pan out of the oven and tip off the small amount of fat from the bottom. Sprinkle the trimmings with sugar and set the pan over medium heat until the trimmings are caramelised. Deglaze with the vinegar, then add the wine and cook gently for 5 minutes. Pour in 500 ml/18 fl oz water, then tip the entire contents of the roasting tin into a saucepan.

Add the shallots, garlic, peppercorns, juniper berries, bouquet garni and mushrooms, and simmer for 1 hour. Strain the sauce through a conical sieve into a small saucepan and reduce until it is thick enough to coat the back of a spoon lightly. Beat in 50 g/2 oz butter, cover the pan and keep the sauce hot without letting it boil.
The peas and broad beans: Bring a saucepan of salted water to the boil, drop in the peas and cook for 3 minutes. Refresh and drain. Cook the broad beans in the boiling water for 2 minutes, drain, refresh and skin. Place in a bowl with the peas.

COOKING THE VEAL CHOPS

Season lightly with salt and pepper. Heat the remaining butter in a shallow pan, put in the chops and cook over medium heat for 3–4 minutes on each side, depending on how you like them cooked. Remove from the pan and keep warm. Roughly snip the sorrel leaves into the pan and cook for 30 seconds. Pour the sauce over the sorrel in the pan and add the peas and broad beans.

PRESENTATION

Put the chops on two warmed plates, pour over the mixture of sauce and green vegetables and serve at once, piping hot.

ROAST RACK OF LAMB WITH A HERB CRUST

Carré d'agneau rôti aux herbes

*L*AMB *cooked in this way is so tender and full of flavour that it needs no sauce or gravy.*
An aubergine galette (recipe, page 124) makes the ideal accompaniment for this dish.

──────────────── PREPARATION ────────────────

Trim off two-thirds of the fat from the lamb, or all of it if you prefer your meat without fat. Cut off the meat and fat from the top of the bones and scrape the ends with the point of a knife. Cut off part of the bones with a cleaver or chef's knife to shorten them so that they stand about 5–6 cm/2–$2\frac{1}{2}$ in above the meat.

──────────────── PRECOOKING THE LAMB ────────────────

Lightly salt the meat. Heat the oil in a frying pan, put in the lamb and sear it over low heat for 4–5 minutes, until it is golden all over. Place on a wire rack and leave to cool at room temperature.

──────────── COOKING THE LAMB IN ITS HERB CRUST ────────────

Preheat the oven to $230°C/450°F/$gas 8.

When the rack of lamb is cold, brush it all over with the mustard. Mix the breadcrumbs with the herbs and roll the lamb in this mixture, pressing it lightly against the meat, so that it sticks to it all over. Oil a roasting pan very lightly, put in the lamb and roast in the hot oven for 5 minutes. Baste with the melted butter and roast for another 5 minutes if you like your lamb pink, or 8 minutes if you prefer it medium. Remove it from the oven and leave to rest for 1–2 minutes before carving the rack into cutlets.

──────────────── PRESENTATION ────────────────

Carve the lamb in the kitchen and serve the cutlets on individual plates, simply garnished with a bouquet of watercress, or, equally good, put the whole rack on a small carving board and carve it at the table.

──────────────── NOTES ────────────────

The lamb can be pre-cooked and coated in its herb crust several hours in advance. Keep it in the fridge until ready to cook; this will leave you with practically no last-minute preparation.

Fresh home-made breadcrumbs are very quick and easy to make, and taste infinitely better than the dried, shop-bought variety.

PREPARATION TIME
12 minutes

COOKING TIME
about 15 minutes

INGREDIENTS

*1 rack of lamb, about 800 g/
1¾ lb*

*2 tablespoons groundnut oil, plus
a little for greasing*

*1 tablespoon strong Dijon
mustard*

*3 tablespoons breadcrumbs,
preferably fresh, but dried will do*

*1 tablespoon mixed fresh herbs,
including at least 3 of the
following: thyme, tarragon,
parsley, chives, sage, rosemary,
marjoram*

30 g/1 oz butter, melted

1 small bunch of watercress

salt and freshly ground pepper

Illustrated on page 125

AUBERGINE AND CHICKEN LIVER GALETTES WITH TOMATO COULIS
Galettes d'aubergine et de foies de volaille au coulis de tomates

*T*HIS *summer dish, which can be eaten as an hors d'oeuvre or as a vegetable accompaniment, will fill your kitchen with good smells as it cooks, and will satisfy the greediest guest.*

PREPARATION TIME
20 minutes

COOKING TIME
30 minutes for the coulis, plus 10 minutes for the livers and aubergines

INGREDIENTS

1 aubergine, about 250 g/9 oz

80 g/3 oz fresh chicken livers, soaked in a little milk for 1 hour

9 tablespoons olive oil

1 teaspoon lemon juice

300 g/11 oz very ripe tomatoes, peeled, deseeded and chopped

2 shallots, each about 30 g/1 oz, finely chopped

1 small garlic clove, finely chopped

2 branches of thyme

2 stalks of curly parsley, 1 of them chopped

salt and freshly ground pepper

PREPARATION

The aubergine: Wash in cold water and wipe dry. Cut 4 rounds, 1 cm/$\frac{1}{2}$ in thick, out of the fattest part. Place them on a plate, season lightly with salt and pepper and pour over 2 tablespoons olive oil and the lemon juice. Cut the rest of the aubergine into 1 cm/$\frac{1}{2}$ in cubes, place them on the plate with the slices, cover with clingfilm and leave at room temperature for 30 minutes.

The tomatoes: Heat 2 tablespoons oil in a small saucepan, put in 1 chopped shallot, the garlic and thyme and sweat very gently for 1 minute. Add the chopped tomatoes, season lightly, cover the pan and simmer very gently for 30 minutes, stirring every 10 minutes. Remove the thyme, add the chopped parsley, cover the pan and keep the coulis warm.

COOKING

The aubergines: Heat 3 tablespoons olive oil in a frying pan and fry the aubergine rounds over medium heat until deep golden on both sides. Drain on kitchen paper and leave in a warm place. Better k grill, oiled each side.

Add another spoonful of oil to the same pan and sauté the aubergine cubes until deep golden brown all over. what a lot of oil!

The chicken livers: Drain, carefully pat dry and cut each one into 2–3 pieces, depending on their size. Heat the rest of the oil in the pan in which you fried the aubergines, put in the livers and sauté briskly for 30 seconds. Add the second chopped shallot and cook for another 30 seconds. Season lightly with salt and pepper, and put the livers in a bowl. Gently mix in 1 spoonful of tomato coulis.

In the meantime, heat two plates.

PRESENTATION

Place an aubergine round in the centre of each plate and pile on the chicken livers and diced aubergine. Top with another aubergine round and decorate with a sprig of parsley. Pour the tomato coulis all round the galettes, or serve it separately in a sauce boat.

NOTE

If you are serving galettes as the vegetable, leave out the livers and use more cubes of aubergine to fill the galettes.

Top: Roast rack of lamb with a herb crust (recipe, page 123);
On plates: Aubergine and chicken liver galettes with tomato coulis.

CLAFOUTIS OF SPINACH BEET
Clafoutis de bettes

*T*HIS *very pleasant summer main course also makes a delicious and successful starter. Served with a tomato coulis and a green salad, it will satisfy even a non-vegetarian. It is, however, essential to have a non-stick loose-bottomed tart or flan dish, approximately 18 cm/7 in diameter and 2 cm/¾ in deep for this recipe.*

—————— PREPARATION ——————

The clafoutis batter: Separate one of the eggs and place the white in a bowl. Put the yolk in a larger bowl, add the other egg, flour and milk and whisk until amalgamated, but do not overwork. Add the cream, season with a little salt and pepper, cover with clingfilm and keep at room temperature.

The spinach beet: Trim off the ends of the stalks. If the stems are stringy, pare off the fibrous parts with a sharp knife. Halve the entire branches lengthways and wash thoroughly in cold water.

Drop the spinach beet into lightly salted boiling water and cook for 5 minutes. Refresh and drain well. With a sharp knife, cut away the leaves from the stems, then use a chef's knife to shred the leaves very finely.

Melt 40 g/1½ oz butter in a saucepan and sweat the shallots until they begin to colour. Add the garlic and shredded spinach beet leaves, cook gently for 2 minutes, stirring with a spatula, then pour in the white wine and cook until all the liquid has evaporated. Season with a little salt and plenty of pepper, remove from the heat, and keep in a cool place.

Cut the central stems of the spinach beet into 5 cm/2 in lengths, shred them lengthways into fine julienne and place in the fridge.

—————— COOKING THE CLAFOUTIS ——————

Preheat the oven to 180°C/350°F/gas 4.

Use the remaining butter to grease the loose-bottomed mould generously. Mix one-third of the clafoutis batter into the cooked spinach beet leaves and pour into the bottom of the mould. Scatter the shredded stems evenly over the surface. Lightly beat the egg white until just risen, mix it into the remaining clafoutis mixture and pour it into the mould. Sprinkle the top with a little nutmeg and cook in the preheated oven for 45 minutes.

Leave the cooked clafoutis in the tin for 2 minutes, then turn it out on to a heated plate and serve very hot.

—————— PRESENTATION ——————

Serve the clafoutis hot by itself, or eat it cold, although if it is served cold, the flavour will be less delicate and the texture more robust.

PREPARATION TIME
30 minutes

COOKING TIME
45 minutes

INGREDIENTS

300 g/11 oz spinach beet

2 eggs

40 g/1½ oz flour

100 ml/4 fl oz milk

100 ml/4 fl oz double cream

60 g/2 oz butter

2 shallots, about 30 g/1 oz each, finely chopped

1 garlic clove, finely chopped

50 ml/2 fl oz dry white wine

a pinch of freshly grated nutmeg

salt and freshly ground pepper

FRESH PASTA WITH LEMON, OLIVES AND PARMA HAM

Pâtes fraîches aux citron, olives et jambon cru

*T*HE *white wine, lemon and cream make a marvellous combination in this light, refreshing pasta dish, perfect for a summer evening. If you are fond of olives, you can double the quantity, particularly if you are using the small black niçois variety.*

PREPARATION TIME
15 minutes

COOKING TIME
3–5 minutes

INGREDIENTS

150 g/5 oz fresh pasta, home-made (recipe, page 32) or bought

100 ml/4 oz dry white wine

100 ml/4 fl oz double cream

1 tablespoon groundnut oil

finely grated zest of 1 lemon, and its juice

10 black olives, stoned and quartered

50 g/2 oz Parma or raw ham, very thinly sliced and cut into thin strips

salt and freshly ground pepper

PREPARATION

The sauce: Put the wine into a saucepan and reduce by half. Add the cream and cook gently for 5 minutes. Meanwhile, cook the pasta.

COOKING THE PASTA

Bring a pan of lightly salted water to the boil, add the groundnut oil, drop in the pasta and cook for 3–5 minutes, until done to your taste – it should not be soft, but retain a little firmness to the bite. Immediately run a little cold water into the pan to prevent further cooking, then drain the pasta in a colander.

PRESENTATION

Add the lemon zest and juice to the sauce and cook until it is thick enough to coat the back of a spoon lightly. Put in the pasta and bubble for 2 minutes, stirring gently. Add the olives and ham and immediately take the pan off the heat. Divide the pasta between two preheated plates and serve at once.

LIGHT POTATO PUREE
WITH OLIVE OIL AND BASIL
Pommes mousseline l'huile d'olive et au basilic

*T*HIS *potato purée makes the perfect accompaniment for Veal chops with peas and broad beans (recipe, page 122), as well as many other meat dishes. It can be prepared several hours in advance and reheated very satisfactorily in the oven or microwave.*

PREPARATION

Peel the potatoes, wash in cold water and cut into approximately 1 cm/½ in slices. Lay them in a sauté dish or shallow pan, add 500 ml/18 fl oz water, the butter, olive oil and basil, season lightly and cook over high heat for about 20 minutes, until all the water has evaporated.

Rub the potatoes through a vegetable mouli or a coarse sieve into a saucepan. Stir in enough of the lukewarm milk to give a purée of the consistency you like, working the milk in gradually; the precise quantity will depend on the variety of potato you use (some absorb more liquid than others) and on whether you prefer a soft or firm purée. Season to taste, cover the pan with a plate and keep the purée hot, in a bain-marie if possible.

PRESENTATION

Serve the purée very hot in a small vegetable dish, and help yourselves.

PREPARATION TIME
10 minutes

COOKING TIME
about 20 minutes

INGREDIENTS
400 g/14 oz potatoes
30 g/1 oz butter
50 ml/2 fl oz olive oil
12 basil leaves, snipped
100–150 ml/4–5 fl oz lukewarm milk
salt and freshly ground pepper

PASTRY CIGARS FILLED WITH RED FRUITS AND FRUIT COULIS

Cigares de fruits rouges et son coulis

*A*LL *the elements of this dessert can be prepared in advance, although it should be assembled at the last minute so that the pastry cigars remain crisp. Serve with a sauternes. You will need to have to hand a cylindrical object 4 cm/1 ½ in diameter.*

PREPARATION TIME
30 minutes, plus 20 minutes resting the pastry

COOKING TIME
5–6 minutes

INGREDIENTS
180 g/6 oz strawberries

180 g/6 oz raspberries

20 g/¾ oz caster sugar

juice of ½ lemon

100 ml/4 fl oz double cream, whipped to a ribbon consistency

100 g/4 oz Pastry cream (recipe, page 29)

a few drops of double cream

2 sprigs of mint

a pinch of icing sugar

THE CIGAR PASTRY
(FOR 4 CIGARS):
25 g/1 oz butter, softened, plus 1 teaspoon for greasing

30 g/1 oz icing sugar, sifted

½ egg white

20 g/¾ oz flour

1 drop of vanilla essence

PREPARATION

The cigar pastry: Using a spatula, mix the softened butter into the icing sugar. Work well, then add the egg white. Work for 1 minute, and finally add the flour and vanilla essence. Mix until smooth and well amalgamated. Leave the pastry to rest at room temperature for 20 minutes.

COOKING THE CIGARS

Preheat the oven to 200°C/400°F/gas 6.

Lightly grease a baking sheet. Using a piping bag with a 5–8 mm/¼–⅓ in nozzle, pipe 4 large bun shapes spaced well apart , then use a palette knife to spread the shapes thinly into 15 cm/6 in circles. Bake for 5–6 minutes, until the pastry is a pale nutty brown. As soon as the circles are cooked, lift them off the baking sheet with a palette knife, one by one, and roll them round your cylindrical object. Leave to cool slightly, then carefully slide the cigars off the cylinder.

THE STRAWBERRIES AND RASPBERRIES

Wash, drain and hull the strawberries. Hull but do not wash the raspberries.

Pick out 50 g/2 oz of the least good specimens of each fruit and put in a blender with the caster sugar, 2 tablespoons water and the lemon juice. Blend for 1 minute, then strain this coulis through a conical sieve and refrigerate.

PRESENTATION

Mix the whipped double cream with the pastry cream. Using a piping bag with the same nozzle as before, pipe the cream mixture into the two best cigars. Place a cigar on each plate and generously fill both ends of the cavities with strawberries and raspberries, letting some spill out on to the plate like a horn of plenty. Pour the fruit coulis round the cigars and trickle on a few drops of cream. With a cocktail stick, flick it into a heart shape. Place a mint sprig to one side of the cigars and sprinkle lightly with icing sugar. Serve the cigars as soon as they are filled.

NOTES

To make a successful cigar pastry mixture, you need to make more than is necessary for this recipe. Once you have made your two cigars, roll the rest of the pastry into cigarettes, 8 or 10 times smaller than the original cigars. These will make the most delicious petits fours to serve with coffee.

MILLE-FEUILLES OF NOUGATINE WITH MELON
Mille-feuilles de nougatine au melon

*T*HIS *dessert is a delight. It is delicate, subtle, crunchy, light and altogether quite delectable. You will need to hand a 7 cm $\left(2\frac{3}{4} in\right)$ pastry cutter.*

PREPARATION

The nougatine: Put the fondant and glucose in a small copper or heavy-bottomed saucepan and heat gently, stirring continuously. As soon as the mixture shows signs of caramelising, add the almonds and continue to cook, still stirring, until the nougatine is a pale caramel colour.

Lightly oil a baking sheet or marble slab and a rolling pin. Pour the nougatine on to the surface and, as soon as it has cooled, roll it out as thinly as possible to make a crisp, delicate sheet. Nougatine cools very quickly and becomes brittle, so try to hurry the rolling process. If necessary, soften the mass in the oven for 1 minute at 120°C/230°F/gas 1.

When the nougatine sheet is 1–2 mm/about $\frac{1}{12}$ in thick, use a 7.5 cm/3 in pastry cutter to cut out 6 rounds. Place on a wire rack and leave at room temperature.
The melon: Cut in half, remove the seeds, then use a melon baller to scoop out as many balls as possible. Scrape out the rest of the flesh with a spoon and purée in a blender for 1 minute.

Put the caster sugar, 2 tablespoons water and the cinnamon in a small saucepan and bubble for 1 minute. Leave to cool at room temperature. When the syrup is cold, mix it into the melon purée. Place in the fridge.
The cream: Whip to a ribbon consistency with the icing sugar and kirsch.

PRESENTATION

Place a nougatine round on each of two chilled plates. Arrange the melon balls all round the inside edge of the nougatine and fill the middle with a little cream. Place a second nougatine round on top and repeat the operation. Finish with a third nougatine round. Use a piping bag with a 5 mm/$\frac{1}{4}$ in nozzle to pipe a rosette of cream on the top. Spike the rosettes with a sprig of mint, pour the melon coulis all round the mille-feuilles and serve immediately.

NOTES

All the separate elements of this dessert can be prepared several hours in advance, but the mille-feuilles should only be assembled at the last minute before serving, or the nougatine will tend to lose its crunch.

PREPARATION TIME
40 minutes

COOKING TIME
about 10 minutes

INGREDIENTS

1 canteloupe, Ogen or Cavaillon melon, 600–700 g/1 $\frac{1}{4}$–1 $\frac{1}{2}$ lb

60 g/2 oz fondant

40 g/1 $\frac{1}{2}$ oz glucose

50 g/2 oz almonds, toasted lightly in the oven for 10 minutes and chopped

1 tablespoon groundnut oil

50 g/2 oz caster sugar

a pinch of ground cinnamon

100 ml/4 fl oz double cream

10 g/1 tablespoon icing sugar

1 teaspoon kirsch

2 small sprigs of mint

RASPBERRY PANCAKES WITH KIRSCH SABAYON

Crêpes aux framboises, sabayon au kirsch

*W*E adore pancakes, and this exquisite recipe is particularly appetising. The combination of raspberries, kirsch and pancakes is so divine that we sometimes think it might be prudent to allow more than four pancakes per person! A sprig of mint is often used to decorate summer desserts, but we do not recommend it in this case.

PREPARATION TIME
20 minutes

COOKING TIME
about 2 minutes per pancake, plus 3–4 minutes for the sabayon

INGREDIENTS
¼ quantity Pancake batter (recipe, page 30)
40 g/1½ oz butter
150 g/5 oz raspberries
75 g/3 oz caster sugar
50 ml/2 fl oz kirsch
2 egg yolks

--- PREPARATION ---

Cooking the pancakes: Very lightly grease an 18–20 cm/7–8 in non-stick frying pan with butter before cooking each pancake. Cook 8 pancakes and stack on a plate, with a small piece of greaseproof paper between each one to prevent them from sticking together.

The raspberries: Reserve the ten best in a bowl for decoration. Put 20 g/¾ oz butter in a small saucepan with 35 g/1¼ oz sugar and cook over low heat, stirring with a wooden spatula until you have a pale caramel. Add all the raspberries except those you reserved, and one-third of the kirsch. Bring just to the boil for a few seconds, then transfer to a bowl.

--- ASSEMBLING THE PANCAKES ---

Preheat the oven to 120°C/230°F/gas 1.

Spread the caramelised raspberries over the centre of the pancakes, and fold each pancake into four. Very lightly butter the bottom of two plates and lay the pancakes on the plates, with the pointed ends facing into the centre. Arrange 5 of the reserved raspberries in the middle of each plate and place in the preheated oven for 3–4 minutes to warm the pancakes while you make the sabayon.

The sabayon: Preheat the grill to hot.

Put the egg yolks, the remaining sugar and kirsch and 1 tablespoon water in a small bowl. Put the bowl in a bain-marie of almost boiling water, with the bottom of the bowl just above the water. Whisk continuously for 3 minutes until the mixture has a ribbon consistency. The sabayon will begin to thicken when the temperature reaches about 50°C/122°F.

--- PRESENTATION ---

Spoon the sabayon over the pancakes and place under the grill to brown. As soon as the sabayon becomes light nutty brown, serve the pancakes.

BAVAROISE OF GREEN OLIVES WITH AVOCADO COULIS
Bavaroise d'olives vertes et coulis d'avocat

*T*HIS dish, which, served cold from the fridge, is perfect for a hot summer's day, will surprise your guest with its originality and Provençal overtones.

PREPARATION

The olives: In a saucepan, combine 300 ml/½ pint water with 30 g/1 oz sugar and bring to the boil. Add the stoned olives and poach for 5 minutes, then leave the olives to cool slightly in the syrup. Drain the olives and reserve 50 ml/2 fl oz syrup. Finely dice half the olives and keep at room temperature. Leave the remainder whole for the bavaroise.

The bavaroise: Put the egg yolks and 15 g/½ oz sugar in a bowl and mix with a balloon whisk for 2–3 minutes. Boil the milk in a small saucepan and pour it on to the egg mixture, stirring continuously. Pour the mixture back into the pan and cook very gently for a few seconds to make a custard, stirring with a wooden spatula and taking great care not to let the custard boil. Take the pan off the heat, add the remaining 30 g/1 oz olives and transfer to a blender. Purée for 3 minutes, then pass the custard through a fine conical sieve into a bowl and keep in a cool place, stirring with a wooden spatula from time to time.

Gently heat the gin to lukewarm in a small saucepan, take the pan off the heat and stir in the well-drained gelatine until dissolved. Pour this mixture into the bavaroise custard, stirring continuously. As soon as the bavaroise is almost cold, add the lightly whipped cream, sprinkle the chopped olives into the bavaroise and pour into two bowls, about 8 cm/3¼ in in diameter, 5 cm/2 in deep, or two teacups. Chill in the fridge for 1½ hours.

The coulis: Put the avocado flesh in the blender with the reserved poaching syrup, 50 ml/2 fl oz water and the lime juice and purée for 2 minutes. Pour into a cup and refrigerate.

PRESENTATION

Dip the bottom of the bowl or teacups in boiling water for 15 seconds, then invert the bavaroises on to two chilled plates and unmould them. Pour a narrow ribbon of coulis around the bavaroises and top each with a sprig of mint. Serve at once.

PREPARATION TIME
30 minutes, plus 30 minutes chilling

COOKING TIME
5 minutes, plus 2 minutes for the bavaroise custard

INGREDIENTS
60 g/2 oz green olives, stoned and blanched

30 g/1 oz caster sugar

2 sprigs of fresh mint

FOR THE BAVAROISE:
2 egg yolks

15 g/½ oz sugar

70 ml/3 fl oz milk

30 ml/1 fl oz gin

1 leaf of gelatine, soaked in cold water

120 ml/4 fl oz whipping cream, whipped to a ribbon consistency

FOR THE COULIS:
¼ of the flesh from a 200 g/7 oz avocado

juice of ½ lime

WINTER LUNCHES

This is the time of year when cold weather and shortening days draw us to our kitchens. It is also the time, however, when there is an abundant choice of fine game and shellfish. Most of the recipes in this chapter take very little time to prepare, but a fragrant dish cooked with love will make you forget the cold grey days of winter and bring a little sunshine to your table. For a light meal, we suggest that you serve only two dishes, omitting either the hors d'oeuvre or pudding, as you prefer.

This is the kind of meal we enjoy:
Mussel flan flavoured with thyme
Two-peppered entrecôte steaks
Baked apples with honey and pistachios

PIZZA WITH MORTADELLA AND BAKED EGGS
Pizza à la mortadelle, oeuf miroir

*T*HIS *pizza is a real treat, very satisfying to make, and the perfect dish for a winter's day. Michel loves to indulge in a little winter sport when he is at his cottage, by going to San Remo to buy the mortadella. You can imagine what happens next . . .*

PREPARATION TIME
25 minutes, plus 1 hour 10 minutes rising

COOKING TIME
about 15 minutes

INGREDIENTS
300 g/11 oz tomatoes, preferably Roma, peeled, deseeded and sliced into 5 mm/¼ in thick rounds

2 tablespoons olive oil

a pinch of oregano

50 g/2 oz mortadella, sliced as thinly as possible, then cut into long thin strips

4 black olives, finely diced

2 eggs

1 teaspoon grated parmesan

30 g/1 oz butter

1 teaspoon chopped parsley

salt and freshly ground pepper

FOR THE PIZZA DOUGH:
1 teaspoon fresh yeast

a very small pinch of sugar

2 tablespoons lukewarm water

120 g/4 oz flour, plus extra for dusting

2 tablespoons olive oil

a pinch of salt

PREPARATION

The pizza dough: Put the yeast, sugar and lukewarm water in a small bowl, stir and leave at room temperature for 15 minutes.

In another bowl, put the flour, olive oil, 50 ml/2 fl oz cold water and a pinch of salt, and pour in the liquid yeast mixture. Mix all the ingredients with your fingertips to make a completely homogenous dough.

Put the dough on a lightly floured marble or wooden surface and work it with the palm of your hand for 2–3 minutes, until the dough is very smooth and holds together. Shape it into a ball, place in a bowl and cover with a damp cloth. Leave to rise in a warm place (about 25°C/77°F) for approximately 1 hour, until doubled in bulk.

The tomatoes: Heat the grill. Lay the tomato rounds side by side on a baking sheet or in a grill pan, brush them with olive oil, season with a little salt and pepper and sprinkle with oregano. Place under the grill for 2 minutes, until the moisture starts to run out of the tomatoes. Tip the sheet or pan at a slight angle so that the liquid runs off to one side.

ROLLING OUT AND ASSEMBLING THE PIZZAS

Knock back the dough with the palm of your hand to its original volume, then divide it in two. On the lightly floured work surface, roll out half the dough into a 18 cm/7 in circle. Place on a baking sheet and prepare another pizza base in the same way. Arrange the sliced tomatoes on the bases, leaving a 1 cm/½ in empty border around the edge. Sprinkle generously with strips of mortadella, then with the olives and leave at room temperature for 10 minutes.

Meanwhile, preheat the oven to 220°C/425°F/gas 7.

BAKING THE PIZZAS

Bake in the preheated oven for 15 minutes. Break the eggs into a bowl, one at a time, and put an egg in the centre of each pizza. Cook in the oven for another 2–3 minutes, until the eggs are done to your liking.

PRESENTATION

Transfer the pizzas on to two plates or a wooden board. Sprinkle the eggs with parmesan. In a small saucepan, heat the butter until nutty brown, add the chopped parsley, pour over the eggs and serve at once.

SEAFOOD SOUP WITH PEARL BARLEY AND SAFFRON
Soupe de fruits de mer aux pistils de safran

*T*HIS *soup is one of our favourite dishes and we never tire of it. It is very simple to prepare and the saffron-scented steam which rises from it and the smooth, melting textures of the fish and barley are a source of great delight. It is as much fun to make as it is to eat, and is so substantial that it can make a meal on its own – depending on the size of your appetites.*

PREPARATION

The nage: In a saucepan, put half the chopped vegetables, the garlic, bouquet garni, white peppercorns, wine, 1 litre/1¾ pints water and a pinch of coarse salt. Bring to the boil, lower the heat and cook gently for 5 minutes.

The mussels: Drop into the nage for about 2–3 minutes, until they open. Remove with a slotted spoon, shell them, place in a bowl and cover with clingfilm.

The langoustines: Drop them whole into the boiling nage and poach for 3 minutes. Lift out with a slotted spoon and drain. Separate the heads from the tails, shell the tails and put them with the mussels. Chop the heads and add to the nage.

The sole: Using a flexible knife, fillet the sole and skin the fillets. Rinse the fillets and bone in cold water. Chop the bone and add it to the nage. Cut the fillets into 1 cm/½ in diamond shapes and place in a bowl in the fridge.

The scallops: Slide a rigid knife blade between the two halves of the shell, pushing the sharp edge in towards the top shell, and lever the shells apart. Debeard the scallops, rinse the beards in cold water to remove any sand, and add to the nage.

Wash the scallops and corals, if they have them, in cold water. Cut the scallops into 6 or 8 even pieces and place them and the corals in the bowl with the sole.

COOKING THE SOUP

Melt the butter in a saucepan, put in the remaining chopped vegetables and sweat until soft. Drain the pearl barley and add it to the vegetables, together with the saffron. Cook for 2 minutes, then strain the nage through a conical sieve into the saucepan. Bring to the boil, reduce the heat to 95°C/203°F and simmer for 1 hour.

Rinse the mushrooms in cold water, cut them into large batons, add to the soup and cook for 20–30 minutes, until the pearl barley is tender and creamy.

PRESENTATION

Just before serving, add the mussels, langoustine tails, scallops and sole diamonds to the soup, boil for 10 seconds, then immediately take the pan off the heat. Season to taste with sea salt and pepper. Pour the soup into a bowl or soup tureen, or straight into two deep soup plates, and serve the soup at once, piping hot.

NOTE

Ask your fishmonger to fillet and skin the sole for you and to open the scallops.

PREPARATION TIME
25 minutes

COOKING TIME
about 1½ hours

INGREDIENTS

6 raw langoustines (Dublin Bay prawns), very fresh or top-quality frozen, about 30 g/1 oz each

10 medium mussels, scrubbed, debearded and washed in cold water

2 scallops, about 50 g/2 oz each, in the shell if possible

1 Torbay or lemon sole, about 250 g/9 oz

50 g/2 oz carrots, coarsely chopped

50 g/2 oz celery, coarsely chopped

50 g/2 oz onion coarsely chopped

50 g/2 oz leek

1 garlic clove

1 small bouquet garni

15 white peppercorns, crushed

200 ml/7 fl oz dry white wine

coarse cooking salt

30 g/1 oz butter

30 g/1 oz pearl barley, soaked in lukewarm water for 1 hour

20 saffron threads, or a pinch of powdered saffron

40 g/1½ oz pleurotte mushrooms

sea salt and freshly ground pepper

RAMEKINS OF WARM SMOKED SALMON WITH CHIVE CREAM AND SOFT-BOILED QUAIL'S EGGS

Ramequins de saumon fumé tiède à la crème de ciboulette et aux oeufs de caille mollets

*W*E usually prefer to serve this simple, delicate hors d'oeuvre with a slice of country bread, which tastes even better if it is toasted just before serving.

PREPARATION TIME
15 minutes

COOKING TIME
8 minutes

INGREDIENTS

150 g/5 oz smoked salmon, thinly sliced

200 ml/7 fl oz double cream

2 bunches of chives, about 40 g/1 $\frac{1}{2}$ oz

1 tablespoon butter, softened

2 quail's eggs, soft-boiled and shelled

salt and freshly ground pepper

PREPARATION

The chive cream: Coarsely chop two-thirds of the chives and finely snip the remaining third for the garnish. Put the cream and coarsely chopped chives in a small saucepan, bring to the boil, then simmer gently for 5 minutes. Purée in a blender for 2 minutes, then strain through a conical sieve into a bowl.
The smoked salmon: Cut into 5 mm/$\frac{1}{4}$ in wide strips and mix into the chive cream. Add a very little salt, and pepper to taste.

Preheat the oven to 200°C/400°F/gas 6.

BAKING THE RAMEKINS

Generously butter two 8 cm/3$\frac{1}{4}$ in ramekins, 4 cm/1$\frac{1}{2}$ in deep, and divide the salmon and chive cream mixture between them. Lay a sheet of foil in the bottom of a deep ovenproof dish, put in the ramekins and pour in enough boiling water to come halfway up the sides of the ramekins. Bake in the preheated oven for 8 minutes. Top each ramekin with a soft-boiled quail's egg.

PRESENTATION

Place a ramekin on each plate, sprinkle with the snipped chives and serve at once.

SCRAMBLED EGGS WITH PRAWNS ON ARTICHOKE BOTTOMS

Oeufs brouillés aux crevettes roses sur fonds d'artichauts

A dream of a dish for autumn or winter, with its soft lemon, pink and green colours and simple and delicate flavours. This is a favourite with everyone.

PREPARATION

The artichokes: Snap off the stalks. Pare the artichokes with a sharp knife, cutting off the leaves to leave neatly-shaped bottoms. Rub these with the lemon.

In a bowl, whisk the flour with the vinegar and pour into a saucepan containing 1.5 litre/2½ pts lightly salted water. Bring to the boil, stirring occasionally with a balloon whisk. When the water boils, put in the artichoke bottoms and cook gently for 25–35 minutes, depending on their size. Leave in the cooking water at room temperature.

The prawns: Peel, reserve 2 whole prawns for decoration and remove the heads from the rest.

The eggs: Break into a bowl, season lightly with salt and pepper and beat lightly with a fork. In a small shallow pan, melt the butter and pour in the eggs. Scramble over low heat, preferably indirect, stirring with a wooden spatula until they are creamy. Take the pan off the heat, gently stir in the cream, prawn tails and chives and keep in a warm place.

PRESENTATION

Preheat the grill. Remove the chokes from the artichoke bottoms. Place the bottoms in a small pan under the grill to warm them slightly. Place one on each warmed plate and pile the scrambled eggs in the middle of the artichoke bottoms. Place a whole prawn in the centre of each mound of egg and serve immediately.

PREPARATION TIME
25 minutes

COOKING TIME
25–30 minutes for the artichoke bottoms

INGREDIENTS

2 artichokes, preferably from Brittany

12 good-sized prawns

½ lemon

1 tablespoon flour

2 tablespoons white wine vinegar

3 eggs

30 g/1 oz butter

1 tablespoon double cream

½ teaspoon snipped chives

salt and freshly ground pepper

MUSSEL FLAN FLAVOURED WITH THYME

Flan aux moules au parfum de thym

THIS *simple dish will enchant you with its velvety texture and scents of the sea and thyme.*
The breadcrumbs add an especially appetising colour, but are not essential.

PREPARATION TIME
40 minutes, plus 30 minutes
chilling

COOKING TIME
14 minutes baking blind, plus 20
minutes

INGREDIENTS

1.5 kg/3¼ lb mussels

70 g/3 oz butter

a pinch of flour

150 g/5 oz Shortcrust pastry
(recipe, page 22)

1 small bouquet garni

20 white peppercorns, crushed

1 garlic clove, crushed

100 g/4 oz leeks, washed and
shredded

100 g/4 oz onions, finely chopped

100 ml/4 fl oz dry white wine

100 g/4 oz spinach

a pinch of nutmeg

50 ml/2 fl oz double cream

1 egg

2 stalks of thyme, very finely
snipped

1 tablespoon breadcrumbs,
preferably fresh

salt and freshly ground pepper

PREPARATION

The pastry case: Lightly grease a loose-bottomed flan dish or a flan ring, 18 cm/7 in diameter, 2 cm/¾ in deep. On a lightly floured wooden or marble surface, roll out the pastry into a circle about 2 mm/1/12 in thick. Roll the pastry on to the rolling pin, then unroll it into the flan tin or ring. Pinch up the edges of the pastry and crimp them with your thumb and forefinger. Leave the pastry case to rest in the fridge for 30 minutes.

Preheat the oven to 190°C/375°F/gas 5.

Blind baking the pastry case: Prick the base of the pastry in about 10 different places with the prongs of a fork or the point of a knife. Line it with greaseproof paper and fill with baking beans or dried pulses. Bake in the preheated oven for 14 minutes, remove from the oven, and leave the pastry case in the tin for a few minutes at room temperature. Spoon out the baking beans or pulses and carefully remove the paper. Leave at room temperature.

Reduce the oven temperature to 160°C/310°F/gas 2.

The mussels: Scrub, debeard with a sharp knife and wash in plenty of cold water. In a large saucepan, heat 30 g/1 oz butter, add the bouquet garni, crushed peppercorns, garlic, leeks and onions, and sweat gently for 2 minutes. Add the mussels and white wine, cover the pan with a lid and cook over high heat for 3–4 minutes, stirring the mussels every 2 minutes so that those on the bottom come up to the top. All the mussels should have opened after 4–5 minutes. Discard any which have not.

Tip the mussels and their cooking broth into a colander set over a saucepan. Reduce the cooking broth to 50 ml/2 fl oz , strain through a fine or muslin-lined sieve and keep at room temperature. Take the mussels out of their shells and roll them very gently in a tea towel to dry them without crushing the delicate flesh. Keep in a bowl.

The spinach: Remove the stalks, wash in cold water and drain. In a frying pan, quickly heat 20 g/¾ oz butter, put in the spinach, season with nutmeg and cook for 1 minute, stirring continuously. Drain the spinach in a colander and press lightly to extract as much water as possible. Leave to cool at room temperature.

BAKING THE MUSSEL FLAN

Whisk the cream, egg and thyme into the mussel broth and season with salt and pepper. Line the part-baked pastry case with the spinach, which should now be almost cold. Arrange the mussels tightly packed on the spinach and pour over the custard mixture.

Bake in the preheated oven at 160°C/310°F/gas 2 for 20 minutes, until the custard filling has set. Heat the remaining butter in a saucepan, add the breadcrumbs and cook until pale nutty brown. Spread over the top of the flan.

─────────────────── PRESENTATION ───────────────────

Place the flan on a plate and serve it whole and piping hot to slice at the table.

─────────────────── NOTE ───────────────────

All the elements of the flan can be prepared individually several hours in advance, then all you have to do is bake it 20 minutes before the meal.

SCALLOPS BAKED IN THE SHELL WITH VEGETABLES AND TRUFFLE
Coquilles Saint-Jacques à la coque

*I*T is important not to open the scallop shells before serving them at the table. Firstly, you would deny your guest the pleasure of discovering the beautiful rosette of scallops and truffle contained inside, and secondly, you would both miss the wonderfully subtle aroma, a combination of sweet and salty, which wafts out as you open the shells.

PREPARATION TIME
40 minutes

COOKING TIME
15 minutes

INGREDIENTS

4 large scallops in the shell, each containing a 60 g/2 oz scallop

80 g/3 oz butter

40 g/1 ½ oz carrots, cut into fine julienne

40 g/1 ½ oz leeks, cut into fine julienne

1 tablespoon Dried tomatoes, home-made (recipe, page 28) or bottled, cut into fine julienne

1 truffle, about 20 g/ ¾ oz, fresh or preserved

60 g/2 oz flour, plus extra for dusting

1 teaspoon olive oil

100 ml/4 fl oz dry vermouth

eggwash (1 egg yolk beaten with 1 teaspoon water)

20 g/ ¾ oz shallot, finely chopped

coarse salt

fine salt and freshly ground pepper

Illustrated on page 149

PREPARATION

The scallops: Open them by inserting the blade of a rigid knife between the upper and lower shells, pushing the sharp edge upwards towards the inside of the top shell. Pull off the beards from the scallops and thoroughly wash them and the scallops and corals, if any, in cold water to get rid of all the sand. Place the white scallops and corals on a plate and refrigerate. Put the beards in a bowl and keep them for the sauce.

Keep the two best concave shells and lids, scrub well inside and out under cold water and keep at room temperature.

The vegetable julienne: Gently heat 20 g/ ⅔ oz butter in a saucepan and add the carrot and leek julienne. Cook very gently for 3 minutes, without letting them colour. Take the pan off the heat, add the dried tomato julienne, season with salt and pepper, transfer to a bowl and keep at room temperature.

The truffle: If you are using a fresh truffle, brush it gently under a trickle of cold water. Cut 12 good slices out of the fresh or preserved truffle and finely chop all the trimmings and ends. Add these to the vegetable julienne. Place the truffle slices on a plate, cover with well-dampened kitchen paper and keep at room temperature.

The water dough: In a bowl, mix 60 g/2 oz flour with the oil, a pinch of salt and 2 tablespoons water. Work the dough with your fingertips until completely homogenous, with a firm consistency and a little elasticity. Put in a bowl, cover with clingfilm and place in the fridge for a few minutes.

ASSEMBLING THE SCALLOPS

Divide half the vegetable and tomato julienne between the two reserved concave shells. Cut each scallop into 3 good slices. Arrange 6 slices in a rosette on the vegetables in each shell, spreading them out slightly. Melt a little butter and brush it over the truffle slices. Slip a truffle slice between each slice of scallop and put 2 corals (sliced lenthways if they are large) in the centre of each rosette. Season lightly with salt and pepper and partially cover the rosettes with half the remaining vegetable julienne. Pour a few drops of vermouth over each filled shell (not more than 1 teaspoon per shell) and put on the lids, making sure that the edges fit together perfectly snugly.

Divide the water dough into 2 equal pieces. On a lightly floured surface, roll out each piece into a 22 cm/9 in long sausage shape. Brush the outside edges of the scallop shells with eggwash, making a 1.5 cm/$\frac{5}{8}$ in border all round. Gently flatten the dough 'sausages' with the palm of your hand and press the dough round the join of the shells over the eggwash border to make a hermetic seal. Pinch a little dough between your thumb and forefinger to crimp it and glaze the top surface with the remaining eggwash.

The sauce: Melt 20 g/$\frac{3}{4}$ oz butter in a small saucepan. Add the shallots and scallop beards and sweat for 2 minutes, without letting them colour. Add the remaining vermouth and reduce by two-thirds. Add the remaining vegetable julienne and boil for 1 minute. Take the pan off the heat, beat in the rest of the butter, remove the beards and season the sauce with salt and pepper. Keep hot, taking care not to let it boil again.

Preheat the oven to 200°C/400°F/gas 6.

—————————————— BAKING THE SCALLOPS ——————————————

Spread a large handful of coarse salt in the bottom of a roasting pan large enough to hold both the scallop shells. Put the scallops on this bed of salt and bake in the preheated oven for 15 minutes.

—————————————— PRESENTATION ——————————————

Make a bed of coarse salt in 2 deep plates. As soon as the scallops are cooked, place one in each plate, take them to the table and open them by inserting a sharp, rigid knife blade between the shells. Put a plate in the middle of the table for the top shells. Serve the sauce separately, and pour a little on to each scallop.

—————————————— NOTES ——————————————

If the prospect of opening the scallops intimidates you, ask your fishmonger to do it for you when you buy them.

Like so many of the recipes in this book, this one can be prepared in its entirety several hours in advance. Just bake the scallops 15 minutes before serving and reheat the sauce without letting it boil.

OYSTERS ON A BED OF CRISP VEGETABLES WITH REMOULADE SAUCE

Huîtres sur croquants de légumes, sauce remoulade

*O*YSTERS *are at their best during winter — they are not so plump during summer and so are generally unavailable. In this dish, the crisp raw vegetables make an original and agreeable contrast with the rather more slippery oysters.*

PREPARATION TIME
20 minutes

INGREDIENTS

12 medium Colchester or native oysters

2 tablespoons Mayonnaise (recipe, page 30)

1 teaspoon strong Dijon mustard

1 tablespoon capers, very finely chopped

1 tablespoon pickled gherkins, very finely chopped

1 hard-boiled egg, finely chopped

20 small tender celery leaves

60 g/2 oz tender green leek, cut into julienne

60 g/2 oz celeriac, cut into julienne and lightly sprinkled with lemon juice

1 teaspoon horseradish, preferably fresh, grated and lightly sprinkled with lemon juice

½ teaspoon mustard seeds

coarse cooking salt

fine salt and freshly ground pepper

PREPARATION

The oysters: Using an oyster knife, open them over a bowl to catch the sea water inside them, taking care not to splinter the shells. Take the oysters out of their shells and place them in the sea water. Thoroughly wash the concave shells in cold water, place on a plate and refrigerate, together with the oysters in the bowl.

The remoulade sauce: Put the mayonnaise in a mortar or bowl and use a pestle or whisk to mix in the Dijon mustard, chopped capers, gherkins and hard-boiled egg. Finely chop 4 celery leaves and mix them into the sauce. Work until the sauce is perfectly homogenous. Season to taste with salt and pepper.

PRESENTATION

Spread a handful of coarse salt in two large deep plates or oyster dishes and arrange 6 oysters on each plate. Mix half the remoulade sauce into the julienne of leek and celeriac and divide this mixture between the 12 shells. Top with an oyster. Add 1 teaspoon of oyster juice to the remaining sauce and coat the oysters with the sauce. Place a celery leaf on one side of each oyster, a little horseradish on top of the oysters, and make a border of several mustard seeds around the edge. Serve the oysters as soon as they are ready. They should be cold, but not chilled.

Top: Scallops baked in the shell with vegetables and truffle (recipe, page 146);
Bottom: Oysters on a bed of crisp vegetables with remoulade sauce.

WHITING BOATS WITH CREAMED MUSHROOMS
Merlan en bâteau au moelleux de champignons

*T*HIS *dish is particularly good served with a Surprise baked potato (recipe, page 160). Apart from boning the fish, which does require some dexterity, it is very easy to prepare.*

PREPARATION TIME
20 minutes

COOKING TIME
10 minutes

INGREDIENTS

2 whiting, each about 350 g/ 12 oz

100 ml/4 fl oz dry white wine

2 tablespoons snipped celery leaves

150 g/5 oz button mushrooms

60 g/2 oz butter

juice of $\frac{1}{2}$ lemon

1 shallot, about 40 g/1 $\frac{1}{2}$ oz, finely chopped

2 tablespoons double cream

3 tablespoons grated parmesan

salt and freshly ground pepper

PREPARATION

The whiting: Cut off all the fins with scissors and trim off part of the tails. Lay a whiting on its side and, using a filleting knife, cut along the backbone round to the middle of the belly, being careful not to cut the skin of the belly. Turn over the fish and repeat on the other side. Snip the backbone with scissors at the head and tail ends. Snip out the gills and pull out the backbone and guts. Prepare the other fish in the same way.

Carefully rinse the whiting under a trickle of cold water and pat dry with kitchen paper. Open out the fish and lay them in a shallow oval dish. Pour over the white wine, sprinkle with celery leaves and place in the fridge.

The mushrooms: Scrape any grit off the stalks with a sharp knife, then wipe the mushrooms one at a time with a damp cloth. Slice, then chop them. Heat 20 g/$\frac{3}{4}$ oz butter in a frying pan, put in the mushrooms, lemon juice and shallot, and sauté over high heat until all the moisture has evaporated. Add the cream and cook for another minute, then season with salt and pepper to taste, and transfer the contents of the pan to a bowl and leave to cool.

COOKING THE WHITING

Preheat the oven to 220°C/425°F/gas 7.

Using a spoon, spread the cooled mushroom mixture over the whiting and sprinkle with parmesan. Bake in the preheated oven for 10 minutes. Immediately pour the cooking wine and celery into a small saucepan and reduce by half. Take the pan off the heat and whisk in the remaining butter. Season to taste.

PRESENTATION

With a palette knife, slide a whiting on to each hot plate and pour the wine and celery sauce around the edge. Serve at once.

THINLY SLICED SMOKED HADDOCK ON A BED OF SPINACH AND POTATOES

*Tranches fines d'aiglefin fumé sur lit d'épinards
et de pommes de terre*

*T*HIS *dish has the advantage that it can be prepared in advance and quickly reheated, so is
perfect for a snack lunch or dinner. The final heating phase can be done in a microwave
oven, if you prefer, which will give just as good a result as a conventional oven.*

——— PREPARATION ———

The spinach: Wash in cold water and remove the stalks. Quickly heat half the butter
in a frying pan, put in half the spinach, salt lightly and cook until wilted. Drain in
a colander. Cook and drain the remaining spinach in the same way.
The potatoes: Peel and cut into rounds.
The vinaigrette: Mix the olive oil and balsamic or sherry vinegar, season to taste,
then add the chopped shallot.

——— PRESENTATION ———

10 minutes before the meal, preheat the oven to 220°C/425°F/gas 7.

Place the spinach in the bottom of a gratin dish, put in the potato rounds and
grind over a little pepper. Cover with foil and cook for 6 minutes. Remove the foil
and cover the potatoes with slices of smoked haddock. Return the dish to the
oven, uncovered this time, for no more than 2–3 minutes, just to heat the
haddock. Moisten generously with vinaigrette, sprinkle with parsley or chervil
and serve immediately.

PREPARATION TIME
20 minutes

COOKING TIME
8–10 minutes

INGREDIENTS

*150 g/5 oz smoked haddock,
thinly sliced like smoked salmon*

*500 g/1 lb 2 oz spinach, young
shoots if possible*

40 g/1½ oz butter

*200 g/7 oz small potatoes, boiled
in their skins*

6 tablespoons olive oil

*2 tablespoons balsamic or sherry
vinegar*

*1 shallot, about 40 g/1½ oz,
finely chopped*

*leaves from 2 flat-leafed parsley
or chervil stalks*

salt and freshly ground pepper

ROAST PARTRIDGES WITH APPLES AND BLACKBERRIES

Perdreau rôti aux pommes et aux mûres

*P*ARTRIDGES *are the first game birds of the winter season, and they begin to appear in the shops from late September or early October. They taste divine, especially when combined with wild blackberries, chestnuts and apples. All these fruits are at their best in the autumn, and their flavours marry harmoniously with the delicate flesh of the partridge.*

PREPARATION TIME
30 minutes

COOKING TIME
15–20 minutes

INGREDIENTS

2 young partridges, plucked, drawn, trussed and barded (ask your butcher for the necks, gizzards and livers)

1 eating apple, preferably a Cox

juice of ½ lemon

80 g/3 oz butter

a pinch of sugar

10 chestnuts

100 ml/4 fl oz milk

1 celery stalk

100 g/4 oz blackberries

2 tablespoons groundnut oil

2 shallots, total weight about 60 g/2 oz, roughly chopped

1 carrot, about 60 g/2 oz, roughly chopped

1 sprig of thyme

4 button mushrooms, total weight about 80 g/3 oz, thickly sliced

150 ml/5 fl oz red wine

1 bunch of watercress

salt and freshly ground pepper

PREPARATION

Preheat the oven to 240°C/475°F/gas 9.

The apple: Peel and core with an apple corer, brush with lemon juice and cut in half horizontally. Butter a small frying pan and put in the apple halves, rounded side up. Sprinkle with a little sugar, put a nut of butter in the cavities left by the cores and keep at room temperature.

The chestnuts: With a sharp knife, make an incision in the shells and place them on a baking tray. Place in the preheated oven for 2–3 minutes, until the shells burst open, then remove the chestnuts. Lower the oven temperature to 220°C/425°F/gas 7.

Peel the chestnuts with a sharp knife, taking care not to break them. Place in a small saucepan with the milk and add enough water to cover them. Salt lightly, add the celery and poach until tender, over the lowest possible heat, so that the chestnuts do not disintegrate. This will take between 10 and 15 minutes, depending on the size and freshness of the chestnuts. As soon as they are cooked, keep them warm, still in their cooking liquid.

The blackberries: Halve the largest berries (about half the total) down the middle, arrange on a plate and cover with clingfilm. Keep the remainder for the sauce.

COOKING THE PARTRIDGES

Heat the oil in a roasting pan, smear the partridges with some of the butter, season lightly with salt and pepper, and sear in the pan for 2–3 minutes, until golden all over. Arrange the chopped shallot, carrot, thyme, mushrooms and partridge giblets around the birds. Roast in the preheated oven for 15 minutes, turning over the partridges after 10 minutes.

At the same time, roast the apples in the oven, removing them after only 10 minutes. As soon as the partridges are cooked, untruss them, but do not remove the barding fat, and wrap the birds loosely in foil.

The sauce: Pour off the fat from the roasting pan and set over high heat to brown all the vegetables and aromatics. When they are a deep brown, add the blackberries you reserved for the sauce and the red wine, and cook over high heat for 5 minutes. Add 50 ml/2 fl oz water and cook for another 5 minutes. Pass the sauce through a fine conical sieve into a small saucepan. It should be slightly syrupy; if it is not, reduce over medium heat for a few more minutes. Take the pan off the heat and whisk in 30 g/1 oz butter. Season the sauce to taste.

PRESENTATION

Arrange the partridges on an oval platter, and place the apple halves in front of them, flat side down. Pile some of the halved blackberries on to the centre of the apples and arrange the rest around them. Drain the chestnuts, brush them with a little butter and place them beside the partridges. Place a small bouquet of watercress between the feet of each bird and serve the sauce separately, or pour it over the partridges, as you prefer.

NOTE

We like our partridges cooked slightly pink, so 15 minutes roasting is enough. If you prefer them cooked medium, they will need 20 minutes.

CHICKEN LIVERS WITH MUSHROOM SAUCE AND FRESH PASTA

Sauté de foie de volaille aux champignons et pâtes fraîches

*D*ESPITE *the wonderful, creamy sauce, this delicious dish is very light, which makes it easy to eat and digest. It is also very simple to prepare.*

PREPARATION TIME
25 minutes

COOKING TIME
2–3 minutes for the livers

INGREDIENTS

150 g/5 oz chicken livers

100 ml/4 fl oz milk

150 g/5 oz small button mushrooms

50 g/2 oz butter

2 shallots, each about 40 g/ 1½ oz, finely chopped

100 ml/4 fl oz madeira

50 ml/2 fl oz double cream

200 g/7 oz fresh pasta, home-made (recipe, page 32), or bought

3 tablespoons groundnut oil

a pinch of flour

1 tablespoon chopped parsley

salt and freshly ground pepper

PREPARATION

The chicken livers: Leave them whole and soak in the cold milk for 20 minutes. Rinse under a trickle of cold water, then sponge gently. Place on a plate, cover with another plate and refrigerate.

The mushrooms: Trim the stalks, wipe with a damp cloth and slice thickly. Heat 30 g/1 oz butter in a sauté dish and, when it is hot, sweat the mushrooms over medium heat for 2–3 minutes, stirring with a wooden spatula. Add the shallots and cook for another minute, then pour in the madeira and let the mixture bubble for 3 minutes. Add the cream and bubble until the sauce is thick enough to coat the back of a spoon lightly. Adjust the seasoning and keep the sauce hot.

The pasta: Cook in boiling salted water for 3–5 minutes, until done to your taste, adding a spoonful of the oil to prevent the pasta from sticking together. As soon as it is cooked, run a little cold water into the pan to stop further cooking. Drain the pasta, melt the remaining butter and roll the pasta in it. Season to taste.

COOKING THE CHICKEN LIVERS

Heat the remaining oil in a frying pan. Very lightly flour the livers, season and sauté over high heat for 2–3 minutes, until they are done to your liking. Immediately, drain in a colander, then put the livers into the mushroom sauce and simmer gently for 30 seconds.

PRESENTATION

Arrange the pasta in a ribbon around the edge of a shallow dish. Make a space in the middle and pour in the chicken livers and mushrooms. Sprinkle with plenty of parsley and serve very hot.

NOTE

If you cannot find madeira, use port, although the flavour will not be as fine.

TWO-PEPPERED ENTRECOTE STEAKS

Entrecôte minute aux deux poivres

*I*T takes only a minute to cook these peppered steaks, which will awaken the most jaded palate. Serve them with a watercress and chicory salad dressed with a very mustardy vinaigrette.

PREPARATION

Sprinkle one side of the steaks with white peppercorns, and press with the flat of a chef's knife to embed them in the meat. Treat the other side in the same way, using the black peppercorns.

COOKING THE STEAKS

Put the oil in a sauté pan, set over high heat and pan-fry the steaks for 30 seconds on each side if you like them rare, or for 1 minute on each side for medium. A few moments before the steaks are done, pour in the cognac and ignite it with a match. When the flames die down, transfer the steaks to a wire rack. Pour the cream into the pan, bubble for 1 minute, then season with salt.

PRESENTATION

Put the steaks on heated plates. Coat them with the cream and cognac sauce, arrange a few watercress leaves on one side of the steaks and serve at once.

PREPARATION TIME
5 minutes

COOKING TIME
1–2 minutes

INGREDIENTS

*2 entrecote steaks, about 1 cm/
½ in thick, each about 180 g/
6 oz*

*1 teaspoon white peppercorns,
crushed*

*1 teaspoon black peppercorns,
crushed*

1 tablespoon groundnut oil

2 tablespoons cognac

2 tablespoons double cream

1 small bunch of watercress

salt

SPATCHCOCKED POUSSIN WITH SAUCE DIABLE

Poussin crapaudine, sauce diable

*T*HE *most time-consuming and tedious part of this recipe is boning the poussins: preparing and cooking the birds is simplicity itself. The resulting dish has an appetising appearance and melting texture, while the piquant sauce brings out the flavour of the poussins.*

PREPARATION

The poussins: Singe over a gas flame, remove any stubble and carefully wipe with a tea towel. With a sharp, pointed knife, bone the poussins through the back, taking care not to pierce the skin. Remove the carcass, cut out the thigh bones, cut the wing tips at the first joint and cut off the feet. Refrigerate.

The poussin stock: Wash the bones, carcasses and feet in cold water. Chop, place in a saucepan with 500 ml/18 fl oz cold water and bring to the boil over medium heat. Skim, add the carrot and onion and the bouquet garni and cook gently for 30 minutes. Strain through a conical sieve and keep at room temperature.

The lettuces: Remove 2–3 outer leaves if necessary and wash the whole lettuces in cold water. Blanch in salted water for 2 minutes, refresh and drain.

Preheat the oven to 200°C/400°F/gas 6.

COOKING THE POUSSINS

In a large sauté dish, heat the olive oil over direct heat. Season the poussins inside and out and fold the skin over on to itself. Put the poussins into the dish, breast-side down until browned, then turn over the birds and brown the other side.

Place the lardons, half the chopped shallots and the finely diced vegetables around the poussins and sweat gently for 1 minute, stirring continuously. Add the blanched lettuces, the poussin stock and red wine. Place the dish in the oven and cook for 15 minutes. Tuck the baby corn into the lettuces and juices around the poussins and cook for another 10 minutes. Cover and keep warm.

THE SAUCE

In a small saucepan, combine the vinegar, the remaining shallot, bay leaf and thyme, and reduce by three-quarters. Remove the bay leaf and thyme, add the tomato purée, strain in all the cooking juices from the poussins and cook gently until slightly syrupy. Add the Worcestershire sauce and cayenne pepper and season to taste with salt. Keep the sauce hot.

PRESENTATION

Fan out a lettuce on each of 2 large, warmed plates and put a poussin on top. Place a few watercress leaves between the bird's legs, scatter over the baby corn and lardons and pour the sauce over this garnish. Serve immediately.

PREPARATION TIME
40 minutes

COOKING TIME
25 minutes

INGREDIENTS

2 poussins, about 400 g/14 oz each

60 g/2 oz carrot, roughly chopped

60 g/2 oz onion, roughly chopped

1 bouquet garni

2 small hearty lettuces, about 180 g/6 oz each

3 tablespoons olive oil

125 g/4 oz streaky bacon, cut into small lardons and blanched

2 shallots, about 60 g/2 oz total weight, finely chopped

30 g/1 oz carrot, finely diced

30 g/1 oz celery, finely diced

30 g/1 oz tender green leek, finely diced

50 ml/2 fl oz red wine

80 g/3 oz baby corn cobs, preferably fresh

50 ml/2 fl oz red wine vinegar

1 bay leaf

1 sprig of thyme

1 tablespoon tomato purée

¼ teaspoon Worcestershire sauce

a pinch of cayenne pepper

1 small bunch of watercress

salt and freshly ground pepper

HONEY-GLAZED PORK CHOPS WITH WHITE WINE SAUCE
Côtes de porc voilées de miel au vin blanc

*T*HE *perfect dish for a cold winter's day, this needs few ingredients and takes very little time to prepare. Fresh pasta (recipe, page 32) makes an excellent accompaniment.*

PREPARATION TIME
10 minutes, plus 15 minutes marinating

COOKING TIME
10–12 minutes

INGREDIENTS

2 pork chops, each about 250 g/ 9 oz

1 teaspoon black peppercorns, crushed

2 tablespoons runny honey

1 tablespoon groundnut oil

1 shallot, about 40g/1½ oz, finely chopped

50 ml/2 fl oz white wine vinegar

100 ml/4 fl oz dry white wine

½ teaspoon cornflour, mixed with 1 tablespoon white wine

30 g/1 oz pickled gherkins, cut into fine julienne

salt and freshly ground pepper

PREPARATION

Cut off the excess fat from around the chops. Scrape the ends of the bones to remove all the fat and sinews.

Sprinkle both sides of the chops with crushed peppercorns and press them with the flat blade of a large knife so that the pepper sticks to the meat. Place the chops in a dish or on a large plate and pour a veil of honey all over them. Keep at room temperature for 15 minutes before cooking.

Preheat the oven to 140°C/275°F/gas 1, or the grill to medium low.

COOKING THE CHOPS

Heat the oil in a sauté dish set over high heat, and cook the chops for 3 minutes on each side, until amber coloured. Transfer them to a serving plate and place them under the grill or in the preheated oven for 5 minutes to finish cooking while you make the sauce.

The sauce: Off the heat, put the shallot in the sauté dish in which you cooked the chops, stir with a wooden spatula, set over medium heat and immediately deglaze the dish with the vinegar. As soon as this has reduced by half, add the wine and reduce by one-third. Add 100 ml/4 fl oz water, increase the heat to very high and reduce the sauce by two-thirds. Add the cornflour and wine mixture and cook until the sauce is thick enough to coat the back of a soup spoon lightly. Add the gherkins and stop the cooking.

PRESENTATION

Pour the cooking juices from the chops into the sauce, season to taste and pour the hot sauce over the meat. Serve immediately.

GRATIN OF LEEKS IN RED WINE
Poireaux au vin rouge au gratin

*T*HE *beauty of this delicious, simple dish is that it takes only a few minutes to prepare. Another advantage is that you will need very few ingredients.*

───────────── PREPARATION ─────────────

The leeks: Cut off the root and greenest parts. Quarter the leeks lengthways to within 5 cm/2 in of the base and wash in cold water.

───────────── COOKING THE LEEKS ─────────────

Bring a pan of salted water to the boil, put in the leeks and blanch for 5 minutes. Refresh and drain. Return them to the pan with the red wine and onion, and cook gently for 20–30 minutes, depending on their size. Drain, reserving the red wine in a small saucepan. Use half the butter to grease a small gratin dish and put in the leeks, folding some of the green leaves under the white parts.

───────────── PRESENTATION ─────────────

Preheat the grill. Reduce the red wine to a half-syrupy consistency. Take the pan off the heat and beat in the remaining butter. Coat the leeks with this sauce. Sprinkle over the emmenthal and place under the hot grill until the cheese has melted. Serve immediately, straight from the dish.

PREPARATION TIME
10 minutes

COOKING TIME
25–35 minutes

INGREDIENTS
300g/11 oz tender young leeks
250 ml/9 fl oz red wine
1 onion, stuck with 2 cloves
40 g/1 ½ oz butter
2 tablespoons finely grated emmenthal
salt

SURPRISE BAKED POTATOES

Pomme de terre au four en surprise

*A*LTHOUGH *this delicious potato dish can be served as a vegetable accompaniment to a main course, it also makes an excellent winter hors d'oeuvre.*

PREPARATION TIME
20 minutes

COOKING TIME
1½ hours, plus 10 minutes

INGREDIENTS
2 baking potatoes, about 350 g/ 12 oz each

coarse cooking salt

20 g/¾ oz butter

3 egg yolks

1 teaspoon snipped chives

1 teaspoon chopped parsley

70 ml/3 fl oz double cream

1 teaspoon milk

20 g/¾ oz grated gruyère

salt and freshly ground pepper

PREPARATION

Preheat the oven to 200°C/400°F/gas 6.

The potatoes: Wash well in cold water and dry thoroughly. Lay them flat on the work surface and make a 5 mm/¼ in incision all round each potato with the point of a sharp knife.

Spread a large handful of coarse salt in a roasting pan, arrange the potatoes on this bed of salt and bake in the preheated oven for 1½ hours. Push the point of a knife into the centre of the potatoes to check that they are cooked through. Leave the oven turned on.

The herb purée: Halve the potatoes horizontally, following the line of the incisions. Spoon out the potato pulp from the 4 halves, taking care not to damage the skins. Keep the 2 most solid, firm skins to fill with the purée.

Rub the hot potato pulp through a coarse sieve or vegetable mouli and, using a wooden spatula, work in the butter, 2 egg yolks, the herbs and salt and pepper to taste. Keep the purée at room temperature.

The cream: In a small saucepan, reduce by two-thirds, then season lightly.

FILLING THE POTATOES

Heat the grill to high. Fit a piping bag with a ridged 8 mm/⅓ in nozzle, fill with the herb purée and pipe it into the two reserved potato skins. Finish by piping a 1 cm/ ½ in deep border of purée around the edge of the potato shells. Beat the last egg yolk with the milk and brush this eggwash delicately over the borders. Pour the cream inside the borders and sprinkle with gruyère. Place under the hot grill until golden brown, then bake in the preheated oven for 10 minutes.

PRESENTATION

Serve the potatoes very hot on individual plates. A watercress salad enhances the appearance of this simple but delicious dish.

NOTES

The potatoes can be prepared several hours in advance up to the stage of pouring in the cream, which leaves you completely free to entertain your guest.

A small grating of nutmeg added to the herb purée adds to the flavour.

BAKED APPLES WITH HONEY AND PISTACHIOS

Pommes en l'air rôties au miel et pistaches

*A*PPLES *baked in their skins are delicious and easily digestible. The acidity of the apples combined with the sweetness of the honey make for a winter dish full of subtle contrasts.*

--- PREPARATION ---

Preheat the oven to 190°C/375°F/gas 5.

The apples: Wash in cold water. Core with an apple corer. Run the point of a knife to a depth of 1.5 cm/$\frac{5}{8}$ in round the fattest part of the apples to prevent them from bursting. Lightly butter the bottom of two ovenproof dishes just large enough to hold one apple (or use one dish which will hold them both) and put in the apples.

Divide the butter into 2 equal portions and place in the cavities left by the cores. Pour 50 ml/2 fl oz water into each dish, or 100 ml/4 fl oz if both apples are in one dish. Coat each apple with 1 teaspoon honey, sprinkle with sugar and bake in the preheated oven for 35 minutes. To check if they are ready, slide the point of a knife into the thickest part. When the apples are properly cooked, the skins should become the colour of old gold. Keep warm.

The honey sauce: Pour the cooking juices from the apples into a small saucepan and add the honey. Cook over low heat until you have a light-coloured caramel. Add the pistachios, cook for another 20 seconds, remove the pan from the heat, and spoon the sauce generously over the apples.

--- PRESENTATION ---

Serve the apples straight from the dish, so that they remain very hot.

PREPARATION TIME
10 minutes

COOKING TIME
35 minutes

INGREDIENTS

2 Granny Smith apples, about 200 g/7 oz each

40 g/1 $\frac{1}{2}$ oz butter

100 g/4 oz honey, preferably runny

40 g/1 $\frac{1}{2}$ oz caster sugar

20 g/$\frac{3}{4}$ oz freshly shelled pistachios

THAMES SWANS WITH CHOCOLATE SAUCE

Cygnes de la Tamise, sauce chocolat

A charming dessert, which looks and tastes delightful. The swans can be prepared several hours in advance; it takes only 5 minutes to assemble them before serving.

PREPARATION TIME
30 minutes

COOKING TIME
about 24 minutes

INGREDIENTS

200 g/7 oz Choux paste (recipe, page 24)

30 g/1 oz butter

eggwash (1 egg yolk beaten with 1 teaspoon milk), to glaze

300 ml/11 fl oz double cream

50 g/2 oz icing sugar, plus a pinch for decoration

30 g/1 oz bitter chocolate, chopped

PREPARATION

Preheat the oven to 220°C/425°F/gas 7.

Piping the swans' bodies: Fit a piping bag with a plain 1.5 cm/$\frac{5}{8}$ in nozzle and fill with choux paste. Lightly grease a baking sheet and pipe on the paste like a large éclair, about 5 cm/2 in wide at one end and narrowing gradually to finish in a point at the other end. The swan's body should be 6–7 cm/$2\frac{1}{4}$–$2\frac{3}{4}$ in long. Pipe out three more bodies in this way to make four in all. Change the nozzle to a plain 5 mm/$\frac{1}{4}$ in nozzle and pipe four S-shapes (the necks and heads of the swans), 6–7 cm/$2\frac{1}{4}$–$2\frac{3}{4}$ in long.

Brush the bodies, necks and heads with eggwash, and bake in the preheated oven for 12 minutes. Quickly transfer the heads and necks to a wire rack with a palette knife, then bake the bodies for a further 12 minutes. Transfer them to the rack and leave at room temperature.

The chocolate sauce: In a small saucepan set over low heat, melt the chocolate with 70 ml/3 fl oz cream, 30 g/1 oz icing sugar and 30 g/1 oz butter, stirring with a wooden spatula. Boil for 1 minute and leave at room temperature.

The cream sauce: In another small saucepan, reduce 80 ml/3 fl oz cream by half. Add 4 teaspoons icing sugar and keep at room temperature.

The Chantilly cream: In a bowl, whip the remaining cream and icing sugar to a thick ribbon consistency. Fill a piping bag fitted with a ridged 1 cm/$\frac{1}{2}$ in nozzle with this cream and refrigerate.

ASSEMBLING THE SWANS

Using a serrated knife, cut the four bodies horizontally across the middle, then slice the top halves vertically and lengthways to make the wings. Pipe the bottom halves full of Chantilly cream, then place the S-shaped necks and heads in the bodies and attach the wings. Sprinkle the swans with a little icing sugar.

PRESENTATION

Place two swans on each chilled plate. Pour a ribbon of cold cream sauce around each swan, then a little cold chocolate sauce. Use the point of a knife to swirl some of the cream sauce into the chocolate sauce and vice-versa. Put the remaining chocolate sauce in a sauce boat and serve the swans immediately, very cold.

WALNUT TARTLETS

Tartelettes aux noix

A truly regal dessert, wickedly rich and sugary, this is intended for those who avoid counting the calories! Our friend and fellow patissier, Denis Ruffel, created these delectable tartlets and he makes them as a treat for us whenever we visit him in Paris.

PREPARATION

The pastry cases: On a lightly floured marble or wooden surface, roll out the dough to a thickness of about 3 mm/$\frac{1}{8}$ in. Line two 10–12 cm/4–5 in tartlet tins with the dough and leave to rest in the fridge for 20 minutes.

Preheat the oven to 220°C/425°F/gas 7.

BAKING THE PASTRY CASES

Place a circle of greaseproof paper in the bottom of each tartlet tin and fill with dried pulses or baking beans. Bake in the preheated oven for 10 minutes, then remove the pulses or beans and paper, reduce the oven temperature to 200°C/400°F/gas 6 and bake the pastry cases for another 5 minutes.

Leave the cooked cases in the tins for 5 minutes to cool a little, then unmould and place on a wire rack.

THE WALNUT FILLING

Lower the oven temperature to 100°C/200°F/gas $\frac{1}{2}$ and heat the walnuts in the oven for 10 minutes. In a copper or heavy-bottomed saucepan, melt the butter, sugar, honey and glucose over the lowest possible heat, stirring continuously with a wooden spatula. As soon as the mixture begins to bubble, cook without stirring until it becomes a very pale caramel. Take the pan off the heat, pour in the cream and stir with the spatula. Return the pan to the heat and bubble the mixture for 1 more minute, stirring continuously.

Take the pan off the heat, add the walnuts and sultanas. Divide the walnut filling between the pastry cases and leave at room temperature for at least 1 hour before serving.

PRESENTATION

Serve the tartlets on individual plates with no accompanying sauce or coulis.

NOTE

The tartlets can be prepared several hours in advance, but we recommend that in that case you use a sweet shortcrust pastry (recipe, page 22) instead of the shortbread, as it will not soften as quickly once it is filled with the soft caramel. Alas, though, it is less crumbly and delicate than the shortbread.

PREPARATION TIME
15 minutes, plus 20 minutes resting the pastry

COOKING TIME
15 minutes, plus 1 hour cooling

INGREDIENTS
100 g/4 oz Shortbread dough (recipe, page 25)
a pinch of flour
50 g/2 oz shelled walnuts
30 g/1 oz butter
40 g/1 $\frac{1}{2}$ oz caster sugar
1 teaspoon honey
1 teaspoon glucose
50 ml/2 fl oz double cream
15 g/$\frac{1}{2}$ oz sultanas, blanched and macerated in 1 tablespoon rum (the rum is optional)

WINTER DINNERS

Throw yourself wholeheartedly into preparing a winter dinner. Such a feast should be grandiose, divine and rich. If necessary, invent occasions to create a really sumptuous meal at every opportunity.

Dress the table with fine linen and crystal and on it place a basket of fruits scattered with nuts and a few dates. Choose the finest wines and spin out the pleasures of the table. Do not swamp the plates with food; savour and enjoy it and prolong the evening together. We have chosen two winter menus.

For a winter dinner:
Marinated scallops with mussels in a saffron mayonnaise
Pan-fried rib of beef with candied shallots
Mango tartlet Tatin with green peppercorns

Our Christmas menu:
Truffle and potato surprise with coarse salt
Fillets of sole with a potato crust and champagne sauce
Breast of pheasant 'Grand'mère' en papillote
Stilton croûte with pears
Jasmine tea-flavoured creams

TRUFFLE AND POTATO SURPRISE WITH COARSE SALT

Truffe en pomme de terre croque-sel

*T*HE *perfect surprise hors d'oeuvre for a special occasion, such as Christmas. The scent of the truffle as you cut open the potato is sublime, and those who regard potatoes as humble vegetables will see them in a new light. This recipe was given to us by Christian Germain from the Château de Montreuil, who is the supreme master of this gastronomic treat.*

PREPARATION TIME
10 minutes

COOKING TIME
30 minutes

INGREDIENTS

2 attractive oval potatoes, each about 160 g/5 oz

2 truffles, preferably fresh, or preserved, each about 20 g/¾ oz

60 g/2 oz butter, melted

40 g/1½ oz clarified butter

a handful of coarse cooking salt, for serving

fine salt and freshly ground pepper

PREPARATION

The potatoes: Wash in cold water and peel with a sharp knife, shaping them into neat egg-shaped ovals. Halve lengthways and scoop out the insides with a parisienne baller to make a large enough cavity to hold a truffle. Brush the insides of the potatoes with plenty of melted butter and season lightly with salt and pepper. *The truffles:* Wash them if they are fresh. Place a truffle in one potato half and cover with the other half, to restore the potato to its original shape. Tie up with string. Prepare the other potato in the same way.

Cut two 20 cm/8 in squares of foil and brush with the remaining melted butter. Preheat the oven to 220°C/425°F/gas 7.

COOKING THE POTATOES

Heat the clarified butter in a small frying pan, put in the potatoes and cook over high heat until golden brown all over. Wrap the potatoes in the foil squares and place on a baking sheet. Bake in the preheated oven for 30 minutes, turning them over after 15 minutes to brown both sides.

PRESENTATION

Remove the foil from the potatoes and cut off the string. Place the potatoes on two small warmed plates, with a good pinch of coarse salt beside them. Take the potatoes to the table, then, with a very sharp knife, cut them open lengthways, or, if you prefer, slice into thick rounds like a hard-boiled egg.

BAKED EGGS WITH EMMENTHAL
AND WILD MUSHROOMS

Oeufs en cocotte à l'emmenthal et aux champignons sauvages

*I*F, *during the truffle season, luck should guide you to a truffle bed, do not hesitate to replace the wild mushrooms with one of these black diamonds. Truffles belong to the mushroom family and, believe us, they make divine companions for eggs, emmenthal and cream. Hot fingers of toast are as delicious dipped into these baked eggs as they are with boiled eggs.*

PREPARATION TIME
15 minutes

COOKING TIME
5–7 minutes

INGREDIENTS

4 extremely fresh eggs

100 g/4 oz wild mushrooms (eg girolles, ceps, oyster mushrooms)

50 g/2 oz butter

6 tablespoons double cream

60 g/2¼ oz emmenthal, grated

1 tablespoon chopped parsley

salt and freshly ground pepper

PREPARATION

The mushrooms: Wipe gently with a damp cloth and trim the stalks with a sharp knife if necessary. Cut the mushrooms into large dice. Heat half the butter in a frying pan and sauté the mushrooms over high heat for 2–3 minutes, until all their moisture has evaporated. Season lightly and place in a bowl.

Preheat the oven to 220°C/425°F/gas 7.

ASSEMBLING THE COCOTTES

Generously butter the insides of 4 egg dishes or ramekins, about 8 cm/3¼ in diameter, 4 cm/1½ in deep. Mix the cream and grated emmenthal into the cooled mushrooms and divide this mixture between the dishes. Crack an egg into each dish, taking care not to break the yolk, season with pepper to taste and a very little salt, but do not sprinkle any salt on to the yolk. Line a deep ovenproof dish with a sheet of foil and put in the egg dishes.

Pour enough boiling water into the deep dish to come halfway up the sides of the egg dishes and bake in the oven for 5–7 minutes, depending on whether you prefer your eggs just set or a little more cooked. Sprinkle with parsley.

PRESENTATION

Arrange a round doily or pleated napkin on two plates and place two egg dishes on each plate. Serve immediately and eat the eggs with a teaspoon.

JULIENNE DARBLAY

*W*E *have slightly adapted and modified this classic winter soup to our own taste. It is a recipe which we have both enjoyed since our apprentice days. The great advantage of soups is that they can be prepared well in advance and easily reheated just before dinner.*

PREPARATION

The leeks and potato: Peel, wash in cold water and dice finely
The carrot, cabbage and turnip: Peel, wash in cold water and, using a sharp knife, cut into thick matchsticks.

COOKING

Melt 30 g/1 oz butter in a saucepan and very gently sweat the diced leeks and potato for 2 minutes. Add 400 ml/14 fl oz water and the bouquet garni and bubble gently for 12 minutes. Add the vegetable matchsticks and cook for another 3 minutes. Remove the bouquet garni, stir in the remaining butter with a wooden spatula, a little at a time, season to taste and keep hot.

PRESENTATION

Serve piping hot in a tureen and ladle it out at the table into deep soup plates.

PREPARATION TIME
20 minutes

COOKING TIME
15 minutes

INGREDIENTS

200 g/7 oz very white leeks, with tender green leaves

60 g/2 oz potato

30 g/1 oz carrot

30 g/1 oz savoy cabbage

30 g/1 oz turnip

120 g/4 oz butter

1 small bouquet garni

salt and freshly ground pepper

CHEESE SOUFFLE WITH MACARONI AND MUSHROOMS

Soufflé au fromage aux macaronis et champignons

*S*OUFFLES *make wonderfully light dinner dishes. The divine marriage of gruyère, macaroni and mushrooms in this dish is bound to delight every gourmet.*

—————— PREPARATION ——————

The macaroni: Cook for a few minutes in boiling salted water until 'al dente'. Refresh, drain, pat dry and place in a bowl.

The mushrooms: Wipe with a damp cloth. Finely chop 50 g/2 oz and slice the rest.

The soufflé mixture: In a small saucepan, heat 20 g/$\frac{3}{4}$ oz butter, put in the chopped mushrooms and cook over low heat for 2 minutes, then add the flour. Stir with a small whisk and cook gently for another minute. Add the milk and cook at a gentle bubble for 3 minutes, stirring continuously. Take the pan off the heat, stir in the egg yolk, cover the pan with a small plate and keep at room temperature.

The sliced mushrooms: Melt a nut of butter in a small saucepan and sweat the mushrooms for 3–4 minutes, until all their water has evaporated. Add the cream and cook until it is thick enough to coat the back of a spoon lightly. Season to taste and add the chopped parsley. Keep 2 tablespoons of this mixture in a ramekin for the garnish. Mix the rest into the macaroni and keep warm.

Preheat the oven to 200°C/400°F/gas 6.

—————— ASSEMBLING THE SOUFFLES ——————

Liberally grease the inside of two individual soufflé dishes, about 10 cm/4 in diameter, 6 cm/2$\frac{1}{4}$ in deep, with the remaining butter and coat generously with gruyère. Beat the egg whites with a pinch of salt until firm but not too stiff. Using a balloon whisk, carefully fold two-thirds into the soufflé mixture, together with all but 1 tablespoon of the remaining gruyère. Fold in the rest of the egg white with a wooden spoon.

Fill the soufflé dishes two-thirds full with the mixture, divide the macaroni and sliced mushroom mixture between the dishes and fill to the top with soufflé mixture. Smooth the surface of the soufflés with a palette knife and run the point of a knife all round the edge, between the mixture and the dish.

Line the bottom of a bain-marie with greaseproof paper, put in the soufflé dishes and pour in enough boiling water to come halfway up the dishes. Cook in the preheated oven for 8 minutes, then quickly sprinkle the reserved gruyère on top of the soufflés and cook for another 4 minutes.

—————— PRESENTATION ——————

The moment that the soufflés come out of the oven, arrange the reserved 2 tablespoons of sliced mushrooms in the centre and serve at once.

PREPARATION TIME
25 minutes

COOKING TIME
12 minutes

INGREDIENTS

20 g/$\frac{3}{4}$ oz short macaroni, about 1 cm/$\frac{1}{2}$ in long

150 g/5 oz small button mushrooms

50 g/2 oz butter

1 tablespoon flour

50 ml/2 fl oz milk

1 egg yolk

30 ml/1 fl oz double cream

1 teaspoon chopped parsley

4 egg whites

50 g/2 oz gruyère, finely grated

salt and freshly ground pepper

MUSSELS WITH ROQUEFORT AU GRATIN
Moules gratinées au roquefort

*M*USSELS *and roquefort — called by many people 'the King of Cheeses' — make a marvellous combination. We adore this dish, which is simplicity itself to prepare.*

PREPARATION TIME
25 minutes

COOKING TIME
about 4 minutes

INGREDIENTS

1 kg/2¼ lb mussels (about 40)

50 ml/2 fl oz dry white wine

2 shallots, each about 40 g/ 1½ oz, finely chopped

1 small bouquet garni

30 g/1 oz roquefort, crushed with a fork

200 ml/7 fl oz double cream

100 g/4 oz spinach, preferably young and tender

30 g/1 oz butter

a small pinch of nutmeg

salt and freshly ground pepper

PREPARATION

The mussels: Scrub, debeard, wash in several changes of very cold water and drain.

Put the white wine, shallots and bouquet garni in a large saucepan, then add the mussels. Cover the pan and cook the mussels over high heat for about 4 minutes, shaking the pan and stirring every minute until all the mussels have opened. Discard any which have not. Tip the mussels into a colander set over a bowl to catch the cooking juices. Take the mussels out of their shells, place in a bowl and keep at room temperature.

The sauce: Strain the mussel juices through a conical sieve into a small saucepan, add the roquefort and cook over low heat until the sauce is half syrupy. Add 150 ml/5 fl oz cream and cook, still over low heat, until the sauce is thick enough to coat the back of a soup spoon lightly. Season to taste with salt and pepper, cover the pan and keep hot.

Whip the rest of the cream to a ribbon consistency and place in the fridge.

Preheat the grill to hot.

The spinach: Wash in cold water, remove the stalks and pat the leaves dry. Put the butter into a large frying pan and cook until nutty brown. Put in the spinach and cook over high heat for 1½ minutes, stirring continuously with a wooden spatula, then season lightly with nutmeg, salt and pepper and drain in a colander.

PRESENTATION

Arrange the spinach in two heatproof china shell-shaped dishes or deep plates. Drop the mussels into the hot sauce and boil for not more than 5 or 6 seconds, stirring all the time. Take the pan off the heat and carefully fold in the whipped cream with a wooden spatula, then divide the mussel and sauce mixture between the dishes. Place under the grill for 1–2 minutes, until the top of the sauce is a pale golden brown. Serve very hot.

CREAM OF MUSHROOM SOUP TOPPED WITH A CREAMY MOUSSE

Velouté de champignons et sa mousse crémeuse

*T*HE *ribbon of creamy mousse floating on top of this delicious velvety mushroom soup is slightly reminiscent in appearance of the foam on a cappuccino.*

──────────── PREPARATION ────────────

The mushrooms: With a sharp knife, cut off the sandy part of the stalks, wipe the mushrooms with a damp cloth or wash in cold water and slice thinly.
The onion, leek and potato: Peel, wash in cold water and chop roughly.

──────────── COOKING ────────────

Melt the butter in a saucepan, add the chopped vegetables and bouquet garni and sweat gently for 2 minutes. Add the mushrooms and sweat for another 2 minutes, then add the chicken stock or water. Bring to the boil and bubble for 15 minutes. Stir in half the cream, give the soup another bubble, then stop cooking. Remove the bouquet garni, pour the contents of the pan into a blender and blend for 3 minutes. Pass the soup through a conical sieve into a clean saucepan, add salt and pepper to taste and keep hot.

Lightly whip the remaining cream to a ribbon consistency and add the chopped parsley and cognac if you are using it.

──────────── PRESENTATION ────────────

Serve the piping hot soup, preferably in soup bowls, although soup plates will do. Spoon the lightly whipped cream on to the surface and serve at once.

──────────── NOTES ────────────

The chicken stock gives the soup more body, but whether you use stock or water, it is the taste of the mushrooms that should dominate.

A few cooked mushrooms cut into matchsticks and placed in the bottom of the bowls will enhance the presentation of the soup.

PREPARATION TIME
15 minutes

COOKING TIME
about 20 minutes

INGREDIENTS

250 g/9 oz very white button mushrooms

30g/1 oz butter

80 g/3 oz onions

40 g/1 ½ oz white part of leeks

60 g/2 oz potato

1 small bouquet garni

500 ml/18 fl oz Chicken stock (recipe, page 18), or water

100 ml/4 fl oz double cream

leaves from 1 stem of parsley, chopped

1 teaspoon cognac (optional)

salt and freshly ground pepper

MARINATED SCALLOPS WITH MUSSELS IN A SAFFRON MAYONNAISE

*Noix de Saint-Jacques marinées à l'huile d'olive
et moules au safran*

*T*HE *glowing colours and textures which range from creamy to refreshingly sharp make this original dish a great favourite with regular customers at The Waterside Inn. It is simple to prepare, and takes only a few minutes to assemble before the meal.*

PREPARATION

The mussels: Debeard, scrub and wash in cold water. Place in a saucepan with the wine, bouquet garni and crushed peppercorns and put on the lid. Set over high heat and cook, shaking the pan every 2 minutes, until all the mussels have opened. Discard any which have not. Tip the mussels into a colander set over a saucepan to catch the cooking liquid. Shell the mussels, place in a bowl, cover with a plate and leave to cool. When they are cool, refrigerate.

Strain the cooking liquid through a conical sieve into a saucepan and reduce over high heat until you have only about 2 tablespoons of slightly syrupy liquid left. Add the saffron and leave to cool.

Whisk the cooled mussel liquid into the mayonnaise and whipped cream, season to taste with salt and pepper and mix this saffron sauce into the mussels. Keep in the fridge.

The scallops: Debeard, wash thoroughly in cold water to remove all traces of sand, and detach the corals, if any. Cut each scallop into 5 slices, arrange in one layer in a dish with the corals and season with salt and pepper. Mix the olive oil with the lemon juice and pour over the scallops. Sprinkle on the crushed coriander and leave to marinate in the fridge for at least 20 minutes.

PRESENTATION

Divide the mussels between two well-chilled plates. Place the julienne of raw vegetables around the mussels, then arrange the sliced scallops and the corals around the edge like a wreath. Scatter the chervil or parsley over the scallops. This dish should be served cold, but not chilled.

PREPARATION TIME
20 minutes, plus 20 minutes marinating

COOKING TIME
5–6 minutes for the mussels

INGREDIENTS

6 very fresh scallops, about 50 g/ 2 oz each

1 kg/2¼ lb mussels

100 ml/4 fl oz dry white wine

1 bouquet garni

10 peppercorns, crushed

a pinch of saffron threads, or a tiny pinch of powdered saffron

4 tablespoons Mayonnaise (recipe, page 30)

2 tablespoons double cream, whipped to a ribbon consistency

4 tablespoons olive oil

juice of 1 lemon

10 coriander seeds, crushed

20 g/¾ oz raw beetroot, 20 g/¾ oz celeriac and 20 g/¾ oz carrot, all peeled, washed and cut into the finest possible julienne

6 sprigs of chervil, or 6 flat-leafed parsley leaves

salt and freshly ground pepper

FILLETS OF SOLE WITH A POTATO CRUST AND CHAMPAGNE SAUCE

Filets de sole sur paillasson de pommes de terre, sauce champagne

*T*HE *crunchy potatoes contrast divinely with the soft sole fillets and subtle champagne sauce studded with delicate pearls of caviar in this delicious dish, which we adore.*

PREPARATION TIME
30 minutes

COOKING TIME
3–4 minutes

INGREDIENTS

*1 Dover sole, about 500 g/
1 lb 2 oz*

200 g/7 oz potatoes

50 ml/2 fl oz groundnut oil

1 egg yolk

a pinch of flour

30 g/1 oz butter

*2 shallots, total weight about
50 g/2 oz, thinly sliced*

*50 g/2 oz button mushrooms,
thinly sliced*

*150 ml/5 fl oz champagne or dry
sparkling wine*

150 ml/5 fl oz double cream

50 g/2 oz clarified butter

2 teaspoons caviar or lumpfish roe

*8 sprigs of chervil or flat-leafed
parsley, to garnish*

FOR THE FISH STOCK:
100 ml/4 fl oz white wine

1 small leek, shredded

1 small bouquet garni

*50 g/2 oz mushrooms, thinly
sliced*

1 small onion, thinly sliced

*or 150 ml/5 fl oz ready-made
Fish stock (recipe, page 18)*

PREPARATION

The sole: Lift the 4 fillets off the bone with a filleting knife, then remove the skin. Rinse the fillets in cold water, pat dry and cut each fillet diagonally lengthways. Refrigerate the resulting 8 fillets.

The fish stock: Wash the bone of the sole to remove all traces of blood, then chop it. Place in a small saucepan with all the other stock ingredients and 150 ml/5 fl oz water. Bring to the boil, skim, then turn down the heat to low. Simmer for 30 minutes and strain through a conical sieve. You will only need 150 ml/5 fl oz stock for the sauce, so reduce it if necessary.

The potatoes: Peel, wash in cold water and, using a mandoline, cut into fine julienne. Heat the oil in a non-stick frying pan, put in the potato julienne and cook over low heat for 2–3 minutes, stirring continuously so that the potatoes do not colour, but soften and are lightly cooked. Drain in a colander.

Put the drained potatoes in a bowl, add the egg yolk, season with salt and pepper and mix well. Lightly flour the 8 sole fillets, season lightly with salt and pepper and spread a little potato julienne over each fillet. Refrigerate the sole, potato-side up, until ready to cook.

The champagne sauce: In a small saucepan, melt 15 g/½ oz butter, put in the shallots and mushrooms and sweat until soft. Add the champagne and 150 ml/5 fl oz fish stock. Reduce over medium heat until half-syrupy. Add the cream and cook over low heat until the sauce is thick enough to coat the back of a spoon. Take the pan off the heat, stir in the rest of the butter and strain the sauce through a conical sieve. Season to taste, cover and keep warm.

Preheat the oven to 220°C/425°F/gas 7.

COOKING THE SOLE

In a non-stick ovenproof frying pan, quickly heat the clarified butter. Put in the sole fillets, potato-side down, and cook over high heat so that the potatoes on the fish become golden brown. Turn over the fillets and cook in the preheated oven; the 4 thinner fillets will need 3 minutes and the thicker fillets 4 minutes. As soon as they are cooked, lay the fillets potato-side down on kitchen paper.

PRESENTATION

Arrange 4 fillets in the shape of a butterfly on warmed plates, with the potato-covered side upwards. Mix the caviar into the champagne sauce and pour a generous amount of sauce between the fillets. Garnish and serve immediately.

GRILLED SEA BASS STUFFED WITH COUSCOUS AND SAGE, WITH SAUCE VIERGE

Bar de ligne grillé, sauce vierge à la sauge

*T*HIS *imposing-looking dish is perfect for a special occasion, although it is quick to prepare. Serve with leaf spinach or some mange-tout, both make excellent accompaniments.*

PREPARATION

The sea bass: Scrape off the scales with the back of a knife and cut off the fins with scissors. Use the point of the scissors to snip open the gill fins, then clean the fish, pulling out the gut through the gills. Snip a small opening at the base of the stomach and, holding the fish under a trickle of cold running water, wash the inside. Rinse the outside, pat dry with a tea towel and place the bass in the fridge.
The couscous: Heat 3 tablespoons olive oil in a frying pan, put in the onions and sweat for 1 minute, taking care not to let them colour. Add the couscous and cook until golden, stirring with a wooden spatula. Add the fish stock or water and half the lime zest and juice. Cook gently until all the liquid has evaporated. Add half the snipped sage, season to taste, and leave to cool at room temperature.

COOKING THE BASS

Preheat the oven to 200°C/400°F/gas 6 and heat a grill pan until very hot.

Stuff the bass with the cooled couscous through the gills. Brush the fish with 1 tablespoon olive oil, season lightly and place in the heated grill pan. Grill for $1\frac{1}{2}$ minutes, then give the fish a quarter-turn to make an attractive lattice marking, and grill for another $1\frac{1}{2}$ minutes. Turn over the fish and repeat on the other side.

Transfer the bass to a roasting pan, brush with another tablespoon olive oil and cook in the preheated oven for 20 minutes. While the fish is cooking, prepare the sauce vierge.

THE SAUCE VIERGE

Pour the remaining olive oil into a small saucepan, add the tomato lozenges, coriander seeds and the rest of the lime juice and zest, and gently warm the sauce. Season to taste and keep warm.

PRESENTATION

Arrange the bass on a heated oval platter. Halve the lemon, place a sprig of sage on each half and place on either side of the platter. Pour a ribbon of sauce around the fish and serve the rest in a sauce boat.

NOTE

On no account should you serve potatoes or any other starchy vegetable with the bass; the couscous stuffing makes these unnecessary.

PREPARATION TIME
20 minutes

COOKING TIME
about 20 minutes

INGREDIENTS

1 striped sea bass,
650–700 g/about $1\frac{1}{2}$ lb

12 tablespoons olive oil

100 g/4 oz onions, finely chopped

50 g/2 oz couscous

100 ml/4 fl oz Fish stock
(recipe, page 18), or water

juice and zest of 1 lime

2 teaspoons sage leaves, snipped

300 g/11 oz plum tomatoes,
preferably Roma, peeled, deseeded
and cut into lozenge shapes

20 coriander seeds, crushed

1 lemon

2 sprigs of sage

salt and freshly ground pepper

MILLE-FEUILLE OF SALMON AND GREEN CABBAGE WITH A SHERRY SABAYON
Mille-feuille de saumon vert pré au sabayon de sherry

*T*HE *flavours and colours of salmon and green cabbage marry harmoniously in this dish, while the sherry adds a pleasant winter note to the sabayon sauce. As this is a generous and filling dish, preface it with tiny portions of a very light hors d'oeuvre.*

PREPARATION TIME
30 minutes

COOKING TIME
10 minutes

INGREDIENTS

1 medium savoy cabbage

130 g/4½ oz melted butter

100 ml/4 fl oz dry white wine

300 g/11 oz fresh salmon fillet, very thinly sliced into 15–20 long, narrow strips, about 3 mm/⅛ in thick

2 egg yolks

1 tablespoon dry sherry

30 g/1 oz watercress, stalks removed and leaves finely snipped

salt and freshly ground pepper

PREPARATION

Remove any damaged or marked outside cabbage leaves. Pull off the next 10 leaves, taking care not to damage or tear them. Using a 15 cm/6 in pastry cutter, cut a circle out of each cabbage leaf.

Bring a pan of salted water to the boil and cook the cabbage circles for about 8 minutes, until cooked but still a little firm. Refresh and drain each circle individually, carefully pat dry and refrigerate until needed.

Finely shred the trimmings from the leaves and sweat them in 100 g/4 oz butter for 3 minutes, stirring every minute. Add the white wine and cook gently for another 10 minutes, then season, transfer the cabbage to a bowl and leave to cool at room temperature. When the shredded cabbage is cold, squeeze it in a muslin cloth to extract three-quarters of the liquid. Keep this liquid for the sauce.

ASSEMBLING THE SALMON MILLE-FEUILLE

Lay one of the cabbage circles on the work surface. Brush the circle with melted butter, then season lightly with salt and pepper. Put a spoonful of shredded cabbage in the centre, flatten it out slightly, then cover the rest of the circle with thin slices of salmon. Place a cabbage circle on top, and press down lightly. Make 8 more layers in the same way, finishing with the last cabbage circle.

Refrigerate the mille-feuille until you are ready to serve the dish. Keep any remaining shredded cabbage warm.

THE SAUCE

Fifteen minutes before dinner, heat the cabbage juices to lukewarm. Put the egg yolks, sherry and ½ teaspoon of water in a small saucepan or the top of a double boiler. Set over very gentle indirect heat (a pan of hot water or the bottom of the double boiler) and beat the sauce with a wire whisk as for a hollandaise. The temperature of the mixture should be 55°C/130°F. Remove the pan from the heat and whisk in the warmed cabbage juices, a little at a time, whisking continuously. Adjust the seasoning with salt and pepper and keep the sauce in a warm place.

COOKING THE SALMON MILLE-FEUILLE

Ten minutes before dinner, place the mille-feuille on a small round wire rack, if possible, or on a small plate. Prepare a steamer, place the rack or plate in the top, cover and steam for 10 minutes.

PRESENTATION

Carefully lift the mille-feuille out of the steamer and transfer it to a carving board. Using a very sharp knife, cut it vertically through the middle, then slide the two pieces on to a warmed oval platter or large plate, arranging them in a wedge to show off the layers of green cabbage and pink salmon.

Add two-thirds of the chopped watercress to the sabayon sauce and pour the sauce generously over the edges of the mille-feuille. Serve the remaining sauce separately in a sauce boat. Scatter the rest of the watercress over the middle of the mille-feuille and serve immediately. Serve the remains of the shredded cabbage in a separate bowl.

NOTES

The mille-feuille can be prepared several hours in advance, but remember that if it has been kept in the fridge for 6–8 hours, it will be very cold, so it will need an extra 2 minutes' steaming (12 minutes in all).

If you prefer, salmon trout can be substituted for the salmon in this dish; if you do salmon trout, the slices should be fractionally thicker.

FILLET OF COD IN A SALT CRUST, WITH LIGHT WATERCRESS SAUCE

Filet de cabillaud en croûte de sel, nage de cresson

*A*LL *the preparation for this dish can be done well in advance before your guest arrives; it will need only 15 minutes' baking before dinner. The thyme-scented salt crust smells delicious as it cooks, and it imparts a wonderful flavour to the fish. It is essential to break open the crust at the table, so that you can both appreciate the glorious aromas which waft out and fill the room. All in all, it is a truly festive dish for a winter occasion.*

PREPARATION TIME
40 minutes

COOKING TIME
15 minutes

INGREDIENTS

500 g/1 lb 2 oz cod fillet, skinned

2 × 25 cm/10 in Savoury pancakes (recipe, page 30)

30 g/1 oz melted butter

salt and freshly ground pepper

FOR THE SALT CRUST:
220 g/8 oz coarse cooking salt, plus a pinch for decoration

350 g/12 oz flour, plus a pinch for dusting

2 egg whites

20 g/$\frac{3}{4}$ oz thyme, finely chopped

100 ml/4 fl oz cold water

eggwash (1 egg yolk beaten with 1 teaspoon milk)

FOR THE WATERCRESS SAUCE:
60 g/2 oz watercress leaves

1 shallot, about 40 g/1 $\frac{1}{2}$ oz, finely shredded

50 g/2 oz button mushrooms, peeled and thinly sliced

50 ml/2 fl oz white wine vinegar

150 ml/5 fl oz dry white wine

1 tablespoon double cream

100 g/4 oz butter

PREPARATION

The salt crust dough: Put all the salt crust ingredients except the eggwash and pinches of salt and flour into a mixer fitted with dough hooks or a plastic blade, and mix at low speed for 3 minutes, until completely amalgamated. Transfer the dough to a bowl, cover with a plate and leave in the fridge for about 20 minutes.

WRAPPING THE COD IN THE SALT CRUST

While the dough is resting, preheat the oven to 220°C/425°F/gas 7.

Cut the cod fillet into 6 even slices, trim the edges to make neat, regular shapes, and keep the trimmings for the sauce. Season the cod slices with salt and pepper, then pile 3 slices on top of each other to make 2 slabs. Brush these with melted butter, wrap each slab in a pancake and place on a plate.

On a lightly floured marble or wooden surface, roll out the salt crust dough into a 40 × 30 cm/16 × 12 in rectangle, about 5 mm/$\frac{1}{4}$ in thick. Cut this rectangle in half and wrap each pancake-wrapped cod slab in the dough, sealing the joins with eggwash. Put the slabs of cod in their salt crusts on to a baking sheet, brush the tops and sides with eggwash and sprinkle with a little coarse salt. Place in the fridge to rest for 10 minutes.

The light watercress sauce: Finely dice the cod trimmings and put them in a saucepan with the shallot, mushrooms, vinegar and wine. Bubble gently until reduced by two-thirds. Put aside about 20 attractive watercress leaves to add to the sauce at the last moment, add the remainder to the pan together with the cream and bubble for another 3 minutes. Off the heat, whisk in the butter, a little at a time, then purée the sauce in a blender for 2 minutes. Strain through a conical sieve into a small saucepan and season with salt and pepper. Add the reserved watercress leaves, cover the pan with a lid and keep the sauce hot in a bain-marie.

COOKING AND PRESENTATION

Bake the cod in the preheated oven for 15 minutes.

Place the 2 slabs of cod in their salt crusts on a serving platter and bring to the table. Use a sharp knife to cut round the top edge, and lift off the crust. Serve on to heated plates and pour over the watercress sauce.

NOTES

If you have no mixer, the salt crust dough can be made by hand, although it is very stiff and unmalleable. You will be left with an excess of about 20 per cent, since it is difficult to make a successful sheet of dough using smaller quantities.

The pancakes wrapped around the fish in this way help both to keep the fish moist and to prevent it from sticking to the salt crust.

ROAST DUCKLING WITH PEARS POACHED IN CLARET

Caneton rôti aux poires et au vin de Bordeaux

*T*HIS *elegant, grand dinner dish deserves a good wine to accompany it; try a red Graves from Bordeaux, which will complement the subtle aromas and the glorious musky sauce.*

PREPARATION

The pears: Peel, brush lightly with lemon juice, halve lengthways and remove the cores. Keep the peel and cores for the sauce. Put the pears and red wine in a saucepan and poach gently for 10 minutes. Remove from the heat, and keep the pears in the cooking wine at room temperature.

COOKING THE DUCKLING

Preheat the oven to 220°C/425°F/gas 7.

Put the butter in a roasting pan, set over medium heat and cook the duckling until golden all over, sprinkling it with sugar and cinnamon as you turn it. Scatter the pear peelings and cores, the shallot and green peppercorns around the duck and roast in the preheated oven for 25 minutes, turning the duck over half-way through cooking. Take it out of the oven and immediately wrap it in foil. Leave to rest, breast-side down. Keep the oven turned on.

The sauce: Pour off all the excess fat from the roasting pan, then pour in the cooking wine from the pears and the remaining lemon juice, and cook over medium heat until the sauce is thick enough to coat the back of a soup spoon lightly. Strain the sauce through a conical sieve and season with salt and pepper to taste. Put the pear halves in the sauce and keep warm.

PRESENTATION

Cut off the duck legs, place in a small roasting tin and return to the oven for 5 minutes. Carve off the breasts, slice thinly and arrange on heated plates. Remove the pear halves from the sauce and finely lay them in a border around the duck. Pour the hot sauce over the duck and pears. Place a bouquet of watercress on one side of each plate and serve immediately. Serve the duck legs as a second course, either on their own or with a green salad.

PREPARATION TIME
25 minutes

COOKING TIME
25 minutes

INGREDIENTS

1 oven-ready duckling, about 1.4 kg/3 lb

2 very ripe pears, total weight about 200 g/7 oz

juice of 1 lemon

500 ml/18 fl oz red Bordeaux, preferably Graves

30 g/1 oz butter

1 tablespoon caster sugar

a generous pinch of ground cinnamon

1 shallot, about 40 g/1 ½ oz, finely shredded

1 tablespoon soft green peppercorns

1 bunch of watercress, for garnish

salt and freshly ground pepper

BRAISED KNUCKLES OF LAMB WITH CHICORY

Souris d'agneau braisée aux chicons

*T*HE *sweet knuckles of lamb are braised until the meat is falling off the bone and melts in the mouth, while the slightly crunchy and refreshing chicory contrasts with the richness of the sauce. We suggest you use butchers' knives to eat this wonderful winter dish.*

PREPARATION

The knuckles of lamb: Scrape every morsel of meat from the top of the bones with a knife to leave about 5 cm/2 in bare bone.

Preheat the oven to 190°C/375°F/gas 5.

COOKING THE LAMB

In a wide, deep casserole with a lid, quickly heat the clarified butter. Put in the lamb knuckles and cook until dark brown on all sides. Place the diced vegetables around the lamb and cook, still over high heat, for 2–3 minutes, until lightly coloured, stirring continuously with a wooden spatula. Sprinkle the flour on to the vegetables, and, still stirring, cook quickly for 1 minute.

Pour in the red wine, simmer gently for 10 minutes, then add the chicken stock, bouquet garni, garlic and chopped tomatoes and salt lightly. Bring to the boil, cover the casserole and cook in the preheated oven for 2 hours, turning the lamb knuckles in the cooking broth after 1 hour.

The chicory: While the lamb is cooking, wash the chicory in cold water and remove any damaged or marked outer leaves. Trim the core ends slightly and brush the chicory with lemon juice.

Bring a pan of lightly salted water to the boil, blanch the chicory for 2 minutes, drain and pat dry. Halve the chicory lengthways. In a saucepan, heat 25 g/1 oz butter over high heat, put in the chicory and sauté, sprinkling on the sugar, until golden on both sides. Season lightly with salt and pepper, reduce the heat to low, cover the pan with foil and cook for another 5 minutes.

PRESENTATION

Lift the knuckles of lamb out of the cooking broth and place in a small casserole. Arrange the chicory like a crown around the lamb. Strain the cooking broth through a conical sieve into a saucepan and skim the fat off the surface with a soup spoon. Bring the broth back to the boil, then beat in the remaining butter, season to taste and pour the sauce over the lamb and chicory. Cover the casserole and simmer gently for a few minutes. Sprinkle generously with parsley and serve straight from the casserole. Alternatively, if you prefer, put the lamb and chicory on individual plates, with the sauce poured around.

PREPARATION TIME
20 minutes

COOKING TIME
2 hours

INGREDIENTS

2 knuckles from legs of lamb, 600–700 g/1 $\frac{1}{4}$–1 $\frac{1}{2}$ lb each

40 g/1 $\frac{1}{2}$ oz clarified butter

1 carrot, about 150 g/5 oz, diced

1 onion, about 150 g/5 oz, diced

1 celery stalk, diced

1 medium leek, diced

15 g/ $\frac{1}{2}$ oz flour

300 ml/11 fl oz red wine

500 ml/18 fl oz Chicken stock (recipe, page 18)

1 bouquet garni

1 garlic clove, crushed

250 g/9 oz very ripe tomatoes, roughly chopped

4 plump, compact heads of chicory (Belgian endive), not too long, about 70 g/3 oz each

juice of $\frac{1}{2}$ lemon

50 g/2 oz butter

a pinch of caster sugar

1 tablespoon chopped parsley

salt and freshly ground pepper

PAN-FRIED RIB OF BEEF WITH CANDIED SHALLOTS
Côte de boeuf poêlée au confit d'échalotes

*M*AKE *sure the meat you use for this simple dish is of excellent quality, and ask your butcher to give you some beef trimmings for the sauce and to trim the steak for you.*

PREPARATION TIME
25 minutes

COOKING TIME
1 hour for the sauce, about 20 minutes for the beef

INGREDIENTS

1 rib of beef, trimmed and ready to cook, about 800 g/1 ¾ lb

about 300 g/11 oz meat trimmings, including the sinew, fat and a piece of bone

10 shallots, each about 30 g/1 oz

2 bouquets garnis, with plenty of thyme

1 garlic clove, crushed

6 tablespoons groundnut oil

100 g/4 oz carrots, peeled, washed and thinly sliced

200 g/7 oz button mushrooms, peeled, washed and thinly sliced

100 g/4 oz shallots, thinly sliced

FOR THE SAUCE:
500 ml/18 fl oz red wine

2 unpeeled garlic cloves

20 black peppercorns, crushed

1 tablespoon caster sugar

50 ml/2 fl oz red wine vinegar

1 bunch of watercress, for garnish

40 g/1 ½ oz butter

salt and freshly ground pepper

PREPARATION

Preheat the oven to 220°C/425°F/gas 7.

The whole shallots: Peel, arrange on a sheet of foil, add 1 bouquet garni and the crushed garlic and sprinkle with 2 tablespoons oil. Fold up the sides of the foil and seal the edges to make an airtight parcel. Bake in the preheated oven for 45 minutes, then leave the parcel unopened at room temperature.

The sauce: At the same time as you are baking the shallots, place the beef trimmings in a roasting pan and roast for 20 minutes, until browned. Add the sliced vegetables and cook for another 15 minutes. Deglaze the pan with the wine, place on the hob and boil for 10 minutes.

Transfer the contents of the roasting pan to a saucepan, add the second bouquet garni, the unpeeled garlic, peppercorns and 1 litre/1¾ pints water. Simmer gently at about 95°C/195°F for 1 hour, skimming whenever necessary. Strain the sauce through a conical sieve and reduce until half syrupy. Keep warm.

Increase the oven temperature to 230°C/450°F/gas 8.

COOKING THE RIB OF BEEF

Lightly salt the beef. Heat the rest of the oil in a frying pan and fry the beef over high heat for 2 minutes on each side. Cook in the hot oven for 15 minutes, turning the meat over half-way through. The beef should now be rare. If you prefer it medium, cook it for another 5–7 minutes. Transfer the cooked beef from the pan to a wire rack and leave for a few minutes in a warm place.

CANDYING THE SHALLOTS

Drain all the contents of the foil parcel in a colander, then transfer to a frying pan and set over high heat. After a few minutes, remove the bouquet garni, sprinkle the shallots with caster sugar and cook until golden, stirring every 2–3 minutes. When the shallots are well caramelised, deglaze the pan with the wine vinegar and cook for another 2 minutes. Season to taste and keep warm.

PRESENTATION

Place the beef on an oval platter or a carving board. Carve 6 slices diagonally and arrange the shallots around the edge, keeping aside 2–3. Finely slice these and place them on top of the slices of beef. Place a bunch of watercress against the bone. Bring the sauce back to the boil, beat in the butter, adjust the seasoning and serve the sauce separately in a sauceboat. Serve the beef very hot.

CRUNCHY SWEETBREAD WITH ROSEMARY

Noix de ris de veau croquante sur branche de romarin

SURPRISE and delight your guest with this original winter dish, which uses simple
ingredients and is modest in its conception, but full of flavour.

—————— PREPARATION ——————

The sweetbread: Refresh under a trickle of cold running water for 30 minutes.
Blanch in boiling water for 5 minutes, refresh and drain. Remove all traces of fat
and fibres, and pat dry with kitchen paper.

Drain the caul and spread it out on the work surface. Mix the breadcrumbs
with 4 tablespoons parsley and the chopped rosemary and spread this mixture
over the caul. Place the sweetbread on the breadcrumb-encrusted caul and wrap it
in the caul. Thread the rosemary branch through the sweetbread along its length
and secure the two ends of the rosemary with string to prevent the sweetbread
from moving during cooking. Refrigerate.

The purée of potato, celeriac and apple: Peel the vegetables and apple, wash in cold
water, cut into chunks and cook in a pan of lightly salted water for 25 minutes.
Drain the cooked vegetables and apple and rub through a vegetable mouli or
coarse sieve. Put the resulting purée into a saucepan and heat gently, then add the
butter, cream and the remaining spoonful of parsley. Season with salt and pepper
to taste. Keep hot in a bain-marie.

Preheat the oven to 190°C/375°F/gas 5.

—————— COOKING THE SWEETBREAD ——————

Heat the clarified butter or oil in a sauté dish. Lightly season the sweetbread with
salt and pepper, put it in the dish and sear until golden all over. Cook in the
preheated oven for 15 minutes, turning the sweetbread over every 5 minutes.

—————— PRESENTATION ——————

Pipe the hot purée on to a warmed oval dish, using a piping bag with a large ridged
nozzle, or, if you prefer, shape it into quenelles using two soup spoons. Cut the
string off the ends of the rosemary branch and pull out most of the branch to allow
you to carve the sweetbread. Slice the sweetbread into 6 escalopes and arrange
them in the centre of the dish. Serve immediately.

PREPARATION TIME
*45 minutes, plus 30 minutes
refreshing the sweetbread*

COOKING TIME
15 minutes

INGREDIENTS

*1 calf's sweetbread, about 400 g/
14 oz*

*60 g/2 oz caul, soaked in cold
water*

40 g/1½ oz fresh breadcrumbs

5 tablespoons chopped parsley

1 teaspoon finely chopped rosemary

1 attractive branch of rosemary

150 g/5 oz potatoes

200 g/7 oz celeriac

120 g/4 oz dessert apple

30 g/1 oz butter

2 tablespoons double cream

*30 g/1 oz clarified butter,
or 3 tablespoons groundnut oil*

salt and freshly ground pepper

BREASTS OF PHEASANT GRAND'MERE 'EN PAPILLOTE'

Suprêmes de faisan grand'mère en papillote

*T*HIS *delicate dish with a wonderful country flavour is ideal for a Christmas menu, or indeed any special winter occasion. Because so many of the elements can be prepared in advance, it will leave you free to enjoy yourself before the meal.*

PREPARATION TIME
45 minutes

COOKING TIME
about 2 hours 10 minutes for the stock, plus about 15 minutes for the papillotes

INGREDIENTS

1 pheasant, about 1.6 kg/3½ lb, plucked and drawn

150 g/5 oz onions, diced

100 g/4 oz carrot, diced

1 small leek, about 50 g/2 oz, diced

250 ml/9 fl oz red wine

1 garlic clove, crushed

1 bouquet garni, including a stick of celery

1 teaspoon tomato purée

10 peppercorns, crushed

6 raw peeled chestnuts, preferably fresh, or pre-cooked canned or packaged

a nut of butter mashed with 1 teaspoon flour to make a beurre manié

40 g/1½ oz clarified butter

150 g/5 oz small potatoes, peeled and cut into rounds

100 g/4 oz button onions

100 g/4 oz streaky bacon, cut into lardons and blanched

1 teaspoon chopped parsley (optional)

salt and freshly ground pepper

PREPARATION

Preheat the oven to 220°C/425°F/gas 7.

The pheasant: Using a small, very sharp knife, cut out the wishbone and keep it for the stock. Cut off the legs and separate them into thighs and drumsticks. Remove the bones from the thighs. Chop up the drumsticks to use in the stock.

With the same knife, cut off the breasts from the carcass. Remove the wings and keep them for the stock. Place the two breasts and thighs in the fridge.

The stock: Put all the pheasant bones, carcass, drumsticks and wings into a roasting pan and roast in the preheated oven for 20 minutes, until they are a deep brown in colour. Add the diced vegetables and roast for another 15 minutes, stirring with a wooden spatula after 10 minutes.

Take the roasting pan out of the oven and set it over medium heat. Pour in the red wine and boil for 5 minutes, scraping up the sediment from the bottom of the pan. Pour all the contents of the roasting pan into a saucepan.

Add the garlic, bouquet garni, tomato purée, crushed peppercorns and 750 ml/ 1¼ pts water, bring to the boil, then simmer gently at about 95°C/203°F for 1 hour, skimming every 15 minutes.

Strain the stock through a conical sieve into a smaller saucepan, set over low heat, add the fresh raw chestnuts if you are using them, and poach for 15 minutes (pre-cooked chestnuts will need only 3 minutes' poaching). Lift the chestnuts out of the stock with a slotted spoon and keep in a bowl at room temperature. Reduce the stock to only about 200 ml/7 fl oz, then whisk in the beurre manié and cook for another 5 minutes. Season the sauce with salt and pepper, strain it through a conical sieve into a bowl and keep at room temperature.

PRE-COOKING THE PHEASANT AND GARNISH

Quickly heat the clarified butter in a sauté pan. Season the pheasant breasts and thighs with salt and pepper and brown them in the hot butter over high heat, turning them over after 2 minutes until golden all over. Transfer to a plate.

Dry the potato slices thoroughly and put them in the very hot pan. Cook for 1 minute, then put in the button onions and cook for 3–4 minutes, stirring continuously, until golden. Add the lardons of bacon and, still over high heat, cook for another 3 minutes, stirring all the time. Tip all the garnishes into a sieve to drain off the fat. Preheat the oven to 230°C/450°F/gas 8.

continued on page 196

— ASSEMBLING THE PAPILLOTES —

Cut each of the pheasant breasts into 4 escalopes and split the thighs lengthways in two. Prepare two pieces of foil, 60 × 50 cm/24 × 20 in. Lay one piece of foil on a perfectly flat surface and place 4 pheasant escalopes and one split thigh on one half of the foil, leaving the other half completely empty. Arrange half the garnish around the pheasant pieces and add 3 halved chestnuts. Pour over half the sauce. Fold the empty side of the foil over the side containing the pheasant and garnish. Roll over the three edges to seal the papillote securely, taking care not to pierce the foil. Assemble the other papillote in the same way.

— COOKING THE PAPILLOTES —

Place the papillotes on a baking sheet and bake in the preheated oven for 10 minutes, until the foil has puffed up like a small rugby ball.

— PRESENTATION —

Take the baking sheet out of the oven and immediately use a palette knife to slide the papillotes on to large warmed plates. Bring them immediately to the table and snip a cross in the top of the papillotes with scissor tips. Pull back the edges of the foil slightly to allow the scent of this glorious dish to waft out. Sprinkle with parsley if you like.

SPLIT PEAS WITH MUSTARD SAUCE AND CRUNCHY LARDONS

Pois cassiés aux piquants de moutarde et lardons croquants

*T*HIS *winter dish has a touch of piquancy without assaulting the palate. It makes the perfect accompaniment to Crunchy sweetbread with rosemary (recipe, page 193).*

PREPARATION TIME
15 minutes

COOKING TIME
about 1 hour

INGREDIENTS

120 g/4 oz split peas

1 small bouquet garni

2 tablespoons double cream

2 tablespoons Dijon mustard

1 teaspoon groundnut oil

50 g/2 oz streaky bacon, cut into small lardons

salt

— PREPARATION —

The split peas: Rinse in cold water, place in a saucepan and cover with plenty of cold water. Add the bouquet garni and a little salt. Cook over low heat for about 1 hour until tender, and leave to cool in the cooking liquid.
The sauce: Put the cream and mustard in a small saucepan and heat gently for 2–3 minutes. Preheat the oven to 200°C/400°F/gas 6.

— COOKING AND PRESENTATION —

Drain the split peas, which should now be cold or almost cold, and discard the bouquet garni. Put the peas in a small gratin dish, pour over the mustard sauce and cook in the preheated oven for 5 minutes. Two minutes before you take the peas out of the oven, heat the oil in a frying pan, add the lardons and sauté over high heat until crunchy. Drain, sprinkle over the peas and serve immediately.

PAN-FRIED NOISETTES OF VENISON WITH MARRONS GLACÉS AND ARMAGNAC SAUCE

Noisettes de chevreuil poêlées aux marrons glacés à l'armagnac

*T*HE *marrons glacés give this delicate, subtle dish just a touch of sweetness. It takes very little time to prepare, and is perfect for an evening of serious intent . . . .*

———— PREPARATION ————

The venison: Trim off all the sinews and membrane and keep them with the bones or trimmings for the sauce.

The mushrooms: Peel and wipe with a damp cloth. Cut off the stalks and keep them for the sauce. Heat 30 g/1 oz butter in a frying pan, put in the chopped shallot and mushrooms and sauté over a gentle heat until all the moisture has evaporated. Season to taste and keep warm.

The sauce: Put the oil in a shallow pan, set over high heat and sear the venison bones and trimmings. Add the bouquet garni, flame with armagnac, then pour in the chicken stock. Reduce the heat to low and cook for 20 minutes. Add the mushroom stalks, redcurrant jelly and crushed peppercorns, and continue to cook until the sauce is slightly syrupy. Strain the sauce through a conical sieve, then beat in 20 g/¾ oz butter, a little at a time. Season to taste, delicately stir in the marrons glacés and keep the sauce hot.

———— COOKING THE NOISETTES OF VENISON ————

Heat the remaining butter in a frying pan and quickly fry the noisettes for 2–3 minutes on each side, depending on whether you prefer your venison to be served rare or medium. As soon as the noisettes are done, transfer them to a wire rack to rest for a minute or two.

———— PRESENTATION ————

Divide the oyster mushrooms between two heated plates and lay the noisettes of venison on top. Arrange the marrons glacés between the mushrooms and meat and pour the hot sauce over the venison. Serve at once.

PREPARATION TIME
15 minutes

COOKING TIME
4–6 minutes for the venison

INGREDIENTS

4 noisettes of venison, cut from the back of the saddle, total weight about 300 g/11 oz

100 g/4 oz venison bones, chopped, or trimmings

100 g/4 oz oyster mushrooms

70 g/2 oz butter

1 shallot, about 40 g/1½ oz, finely chopped

1 tablespoon groundnut oil

1 bouquet garni

50 ml/2 fl oz armagnac

200 ml/7 fl oz Chicken stock (recipe, page 18)

2 tablespoons redcurrant jelly

10 black peppercorns, crushed

100 g/4 oz marrons glacés

salt and freshly ground pepper

VEGETABLE BLINIS WITH DILL
Blinis de légumes à l'aneth

W E adore these delicate, dill-flavoured blinis, which seem to be popular with everyone. Serve them as a vegetable or with an aperitif; either way, they are a real treat.

──────────────── PREPARATION ────────────────

The leaven: In a bowl, whisk the yeast into the lukewarm milk until dissolved. Mix in 1 tablespoon flour, cover with a plate and leave in a warm place (approximately 24°C/75°C) for 1 hour.

The batter: When the leaven has risen, work in the 40 g/1½ oz flour and the egg yolk with a spatula. Cover with a plate and leave at room temperature to prove for another hour.

The egg white: Beat with a pinch of salt until firm, then gently mix it into the batter, together with two-thirds of the dill fronds. Season lightly with pepper.

The vegetables: Top and tail the beans, peel the carrot and turnip and cut into matchsticks. Blanch in boiling water for 1 minute, refresh and drain well.

──────────────── COOKING THE BLINIS ────────────────

Pour a few drops of oil into a non-stick frying pan. Lay 2 fronds of dill in the pan, then ladle a generous tablespoon of batter on to each frond. Cook for 1 minute, spread a little of the prepared vegetables and a frond of dill over the blinis and cook over high heat for another minute. Turn over the blinis and cook for 1 minute on the other side. Take the two cooked blinis out of the frying pan, add a few more drops of oil and cook another two blinis in the same way.

The sauce: Mix the whipped cream with the lemon juice and chopped dill and season to taste with salt and pepper.

──────────────── PRESENTATION ────────────────

Put one or two blinis, depending on your appetites, on hot plates and serve immediately. Serve the sauce separately in a sauce boat.

MAKES 4 blinis

PREPARATION TIME
15 minutes, plus 2 hours resting

COOKING TIME
3 minutes per blini

INGREDIENTS

FOR THE LEAVEN:
1 teaspoon fresh yeast

80 ml/3 fl oz milk, warmed to blood heat

1 tablespoon wheat flour

FOR THE BATTER:
40 g/1½ oz wheat flour

1 egg, separated

a pinch of salt

1 tablespoon groundnut oil

2 tablespoons dill fronds, stalks removed

20 g/¾ oz french beans

20 g/¾ oz carrot

1 small turnip, about 30 g/1 oz

FOR THE SAUCE:
50 ml/2 fl oz double cream, lightly whipped

1 tablespoon lemon juice

1 tablespoon chopped dill

salt and freshly ground pepper

TEMPURA OF FRENCH BEANS AND COURGETTE STICKS IN A LIGHT BATTER
Haricots verts et doigts de courgette en fine friture

*V*EGETABLES *cooked in this way are light, and retain a delicious crunch. They make a wonderful nibble, especially for an evening spent sitting by the fireside.*

PREPARATION TIME
4 minutes

COOKING TIME
20 minutes

INGREDIENTS

4 small, long courgettes, about 40 g/1½ oz each

80 g/3 oz fine french beans

100 g/4 oz flour

50 ml/2 fl oz white wine vinegar

1 egg

½ teaspoon cumin seeds

½ teaspoon chopped parsley

500 ml/18 fl oz groundnut oil, for deep frying

salt and freshly ground pepper

—————— PREPARATION ——————

The courgettes: Wash in cold water, trim off the ends and cut each courgette into 8 even-sized sticks.

The beans: Top and tail, and wash in cold water.

Pre-cooking the vegetables: Bring a pan of lightly salted water to the boil and cook the courgettes and beans for 2 minutes. Refresh, drain and pat dry.

The tempura batter: In a bowl, whisk together the flour, 100 ml/4 fl oz cold water, the vinegar and egg. Add the cumin and parsley and season with salt and pepper.

—————— COOKING ——————

Heat the frying oil to 180°C/350°F. Dip the courgette sticks and beans into the batter. Use a fork to lift the lightly coated vegetables out of the batter, one at a time, and fry them in the hot oil in 4 batches for 4–5 minutes each batch. Drain in a colander and lay on kitchen paper to absorb excess fat.

—————— PRESENTATION ——————

Line a plate with a paper napkin or doily and heap on the vegetables. They are at their best if served as soon as they are cooked.

STILTON CROUTE WITH PEARS
Croûte de stilton en habit de poires

*S*URPRISE *your palate with the contrast of cold fruit and hot pastry in this unusual cheese course. Its success depends entirely on using the finest quality, perfectly ripened stilton (or fourme d'Ambert, if you prefer) and a ripe pear, bursting with juice and flavour.*

—————— PREPARATION ——————

On a lightly floured marble or wooden surface, roll out half the pastry as thinly as possible into a rectangle one and a half times as large as half the pear. Cut out a pear shape, half as large again as the pear and place on a baking sheet. Repeat with the rest of the pastry. Leave to rest in the fridge for 20 minutes.

Preheat the oven to 220°C/425°F/gas 7.

Baking the pastry pears: Bake in the preheated oven for 12 minutes. Transfer to a wire rack and keep warm.

The pear: Peel, halve lengthways, remove the core and rub the two halves of the pear all over with lemon juice. Lay the pear halves flat-side down and cut long horizontal slices in the fattest half, leaving the top intact. Place on a plate.

—————— PRESENTATION ——————

Preheat the grill for 5 minutes. Gently spread the stilton over the pastry shapes, then place under the grill for 2 minutes, until the stilton melts. Top each pastry shape with a pear half and slightly fan out the bottom half. Place on two cheese plates and serve immediately. A glass of vintage port enhances the flavour.

PREPARATION TIME
15 minutes, plus 20 minutes resting the pastry

COOKING TIME
12 minutes

INGREDIENTS
60 g/2 oz Quick puff pastry (recipe, page 23)

flour for dusting

1 ripe juicy pear, any variety, about 180 g/6 oz

juice of ½ lemon

80 g/3 oz ripe stilton, crushed with a fork

Top: Jasmine tea flavoured creams (recipe, page 204); Bottom: Stilton croûte with pears.

JASMINE TEA FLAVOURED CREAMS
Petit pot de thé au jasmin

*T*HIS *is one of the late Alain Chapel's delectable classic recipes. We often used to treat ourselves to these little creamy pots at his restaurant. The creams are especially delicious served with a slice of freshly grilled brioche (recipe, page 60), sprinkled with a veil of icing sugar. They also make a delicate, light dessert to end a Christmas menu.*

PREPARATION TIME
15 minutes

COOKING TIME
about 50 minutes, plus 3–4 hours chilling

INGREDIENTS

4 egg yolks

75 g/3 oz soft brown sugar

50 ml/2 fl oz milk

375 ml/13 fl oz whipping cream

1½ tablespoons jasmine tea leaves

4 pinches of caster sugar

PREPARATION

Put the egg yolks and soft brown sugar in a bowl, and work together lightly with a wooden spoon for 1 minute.

Pour the milk and 125 ml/4 fl oz of the cream into a small saucepan and bring to the boil. Immediately take the pan off the heat, stir in the tea, cover the pan and leave to infuse for 2 minutes.

Pour the hot infusion on to the egg mixture and mix thoroughly. Add the remaining cream and leave the mixture at room temperature for 30 minutes, skimming the top with a soup spoon occasionally to prevent any bubbles or foam from forming on the surface.

Preheat the oven to 150°C/300°F/gas 2, and put in a baking sheet to warm.

POACHING THE CREAMS

Pass the cream mixture through a conical sieve, then fill two ramekins, about 8 cm/3¼ in diameter, 4 cm/1½ in deep, with the cream. Use a teaspoon to remove any bubbles which rise to the surface.

Line the bottom of a deep ovenproof dish with greaseproof paper and put in the ramekins. Pour in enough water heated to about 70°C/158°F to come halfway up the sides of the ramekins. Place the dish in the preheated oven, covering the ramekins with the warmed baking sheet, and cook for 50 minutes.

Remove the cooked creams from the oven, lift off the baking sheet and leave to cool, uncovered, at room temperature. When the creams are cold, place in the fridge to chill for several hours before serving.

PRESENTATION

Heat the grill. Lightly sprinkle the surface of the creams with caster sugar and glaze the tops under the hot grill for a minute or two. Serve at once.

Illustrated on page 202

MILLE-FEUILLE OF PANCAKES AND VANILLA-FLAVOURED APPLE COMPOTE
Mille-feuille de crêpes à la pomme vanillée

*W*E have a passion for pancakes, and the combination of these with apple makes an ideal winter dessert, which is one of our favourites. It is equally delicious served cold.

PREPARATION

The apple compote: Put all the compote ingredients except the calvados in a thick-bottomed saucepan. Cover the pan and cook gently for 15 minutes. Remove the vanilla pod and pour the contents of the pan into a blender or food processor. Blend for 3–4 minutes, until very smooth. Add the calvados if you are using it, and keep the compote at room temperature.

The pancakes: While the compote is cooking, make fourteen 15 cm/6 in pancakes, following the method on page 30.

ASSEMBLING AND PRESENTING THE MILLE-FEUILLE

Lightly butter a serving plate. Lay a pancake on the plate and spread over a thin layer of warm compote. Top with another pancake, and continue to make layers of pancakes and compote, ending with a pancake. Heat the apricot jam and use it to coat the mille-feuille. Cut it with a very sharp knife and slide a palette knife under each slice to transfer it to the serving plates.

NOTES

The mille-feuille can be prepared and assembled several hours in advance. Just heat it in a microwave for 1–2 minutes, then coat with the glaze.

PREPARATION TIME
20 minutes

COOKING TIME
15 minutes for the apple compote, plus about 15 minutes for the pancakes

INGREDIENTS

FOR THE APPLE COMPOTE:
400 g/14 oz dessert apples, preferably Cox's, peeled and quartered

juice of $\frac{1}{2}$ lemon

50 g/2 oz caster sugar

1 vanilla pod, split

50 g/2 oz butter

100 ml/4 fl oz cold water

2 tablespoons calvados (optional)

quarter quantity Pancake batter (recipe, page 30)

20 g/$\frac{3}{4}$ oz butter, for greasing the pan

60 g/2$\frac{1}{4}$ oz apricot jam, sieved, for the glaze

APPLE SORBET

Sorbet aux pommes

*T*HIS *sorbet looks particularly effective if it is served in an apple shell. Simply scoop out the flesh from two apples and fill with the sorbet just before serving.*

PREPARATION TIME
10 minutes

COOKING TIME
about 20 minutes, plus 15–20 minutes churning

INGREDIENTS

120 g/4 oz green apples (eg. Granny Smith)

50 g/2 oz caster sugar

juice of ½ lemon

1 tablespoon calvados (optional)

PREPARATION

The apples: Wash in cold water, quarter and cut out the cores. Place in a saucepan with 120 ml/4 fl oz water, the sugar and lemon juice. Poach gently for about 20 minutes, until tender. Put the apple segments with the poaching liquid into a blender, and purée for 3 minutes, then pass through a conical sieve. Leave the purée to cool at room temperature. Once it is cold, cover with clingfilm and keep in the fridge until you are ready to churn.

PRESENTATION

Immediately before serving, add the calvados if you are using it, then churn the apple purée in an ice cream maker for 15–20 minutes, depending on the model. Shape the sorbet into large ovals, using two soup spoons, or make one or two balls per person with an ice cream scoop. Serve in deep glass dishes.

NOTES

Two tablespoons of liquid glucose added to the apples during cooking will give the sorbet a smoother texture. In this case use only 40 g/1½ oz sugar.

ROSE PETAL SORBET

Sorbet de roses et candi de pétales

*R*OSES *give this dessert a delicate, scented flavour, full of romance – perfect for an evening spent tête-à-tête. In summer, you could use roses from your own garden to make this delicious sorbet. Try to use purplish-red roses, plus one of another colour.*

PREPARATION TIME
15 minutes, plus 3–4 hours drying the petals and 1–2 hours chilling the syrup

INGREDIENTS

petals from 12 medium scented roses, total weight about 60 g/ 2 oz

220 g/8 oz caster sugar

juice of ½ lemon

PREPARATION

Pull off the rose petals and wash gently in very cold water.
The crystallised petals: Put the sugar in a small saucepan with 150 ml/5 fl oz water and dissolve over low heat, then boil for 2 minutes and skim.

Take the pan off the heat and drop in about ten of the most attractive petals, including a few of a different colour from the red (yellow, for instance). Leave the petals in the syrup until cold, then drain them one by one and spread them out well apart on a wire rack. Leave the petals to drain for 3–4 hours.
The sorbet mixture: Add 150 ml/5 fl oz water to the syrup in which you crystallised

the petals and add the lemon juice. Bring to the boil and drop in all the, by now, lightly crystallised rose petals. Take the pan off the heat and leave to cool at room temperature, then refrigerate for 1–2 hours.

--------------------- CHURNING AND FREEZING THE SORBET ---------------------

Strain the rose petal syrup through a conical sieve, pour into an ice cream-maker and churn for 20–25 minutes, depending on your machine. The texture of the sorbet should be soft and creamy, and the colour divine.

--------------------- PRESENTATION ---------------------

Serve the sorbet as soon as it is ready, if possible in two wide glass dishes, and arrange the crystallised petals around the edge and on the top.

--------------------- NOTE ---------------------

Do not churn the sorbet too long before serving, or it will lose its lightness.

MANGO TARTLETS 'TATIN', WITH GREEN PEPPERCORNS

Tartelettes Tatin à la mangue au poivre vert

*L*IGHT *and fruity, spicy yet sweet — a plethora of flavours meld into one in these unusual tartlets, which can be served with cream, if you like..*

PREPARATION

The caramel: Melt the butter in a small saucepan, add the caster sugar, stir and cook to a pale caramel. Pour this caramel into the bottom of two tartlet tins, about 10 cm/4 in diameter, 3 cm/1¼ in deep.

The mango: Peel with a sharp knife and halve lengthways, cutting round the stone to remove as much flesh as possible. If necessary, trim the ends of each mango half to the same diameter as the tartlet tins. Cut the mango halves diagonally into 5 equal-sized slices. Divide the green peppercorns between the caramel-lined tins, then arrange the mango slices in the tins, with the curved edges on the caramel. Cut the trimmings into large dice and arrange them on the slices.

Preheat the oven to 220°C/425°F/gas 7.

THE ALMOND SPONGE BASE

Separate the egg and put the yolk in one bowl and the white in another. With a small wire whisk, work the yolk with 25 g/1 oz icing sugar until you have a ribbon consistency. Lightly beat the egg white, add the remaining 25 g/1 oz icing sugar and continue to beat until firm.

Using a spatula, carefully fold the egg white into the yolk mixture, at the same time showering in the almond and flour mixture. Take great care not to overwork this delicate mixture. Divide it equally over the mango and immediately bake in the preheated oven for 25 minutes. Leave the cooked tartlets in the baking tins at room temperature for 2–3 minutes before unmoulding.

PRESENTATION

Invert the tartlets on to warmed plates and serve at once. We prefer to eat them plain, without cream so that the flavours are not masked.

PREPARATION TIME
15 minutes

COOKING TIME
25 minutes

INGREDIENTS

1 mango, about 350 g/12 oz

50 g/2 oz butter

80 g/3 oz caster sugar

20 soft green peppercorns

1 egg

50 g/2 oz icing sugar

15 g/½ oz ground almonds sifted together with 15 g/½ oz flour

OUTDOOR EATING

Sailing on the sea, sitting on the beach, walking in the country or the woods or the mountains, fishing on the river bank or simply in your garden at home – all these venues make the perfect setting for outdoor eating tête-à-tête. We love to draw on the memories of the picnics of our childhood, to eat and drink in the open air and to taste the simple serenity which brings such happiness.

Some advice on how to barbecue to perfection:

Choose the right fuel. We prefer wood; vine shoots are best of all. Depending on what food you are cooking, barbecue over intense or medium heat, or over the embers, but never over open flames.

Baste the food with olive oil and some thyme stalks bundled together to make a brush. Have handy a plastic bottle filled with water to damp down any flames which might flare up and burn the food.

Start by cooking the densest foods and those which need intense heat. Sip a glass of wine as you cook and, from time to time, arrange a few mussels at the edge of the barbecue. Eat them as soon as they open!

For a really successful picnic we suggest:

Egg, anchovy and spinach roulade
Grilled salmon tail with tarragon butter
Breast of veal marinated in honey with caramelised lemons
Cold fillet of beef en croûte with horseradish sauce
Meringue hearts for lovers

PASTRY BOATS WITH FLAKED SALMON

Barquettes d'effeuillée de saumon

*T*HIS *is an original and tasty way to use any leftover pieces of salmon you may have. You will need eight 12 cm/5 in barquette moulds to make the pastry boats.*

PREPARATION TIME
25 minutes, plus 30 minutes chilling

COOKING TIME
about 15 minutes

INGREDIENTS

1 salmon steak, about 150 g/ 5 oz, or 120 g/4½ oz cold poached salmon

a pinch of flour

100 g/4 oz Shortcrust pastry (recipe, page 22)

1 sprig of thyme

1 bay leaf

a pinch of salt

1 lemon

4 tablespoons Mayonnaise (recipe, page 30)

60 g/2 oz beansprouts, blanched for 10 seconds and drained

a pinch of curry powder

12 capers

4 fronds of dill

8 cherry tomatoes

salt

—— PREPARATION ——

The pastry boats: On a lightly floured marble or wooden surface, roll out the pastry to a thickness of about 2 mm/$\frac{1}{12}$ in. Line 4 barquette moulds with the pastry and refrigerate for 30 minutes.

Preheat the oven to 190°C/375°F/gas 5.

—— COOKING THE PASTRY BOATS ——

Prick the pastry in 4 or 5 places with the point of a knife. Put a second mould inside each lined mould and press down lightly. Fill with dried pulses or baking beans and bake in the preheated oven for 12 minutes. Remove the empty moulds and bake the pastry cases for another 3–4 minutes, until the pastry is pale golden. Unmould the boats on to a wire rack and keep at room temperature.

—— COOKING THE SALMON ——

Put the salmon steak in a saucepan with the thyme, bay leaf, a pinch of salt and the juice of one-third of the lemon. Cover with water and bring to the boil over moderate heat. Immediately, turn off the heat and leave the salmon in the cooking liquid at room temperature until it is completely cold. Drain the cooled salmon and remove the skin and bones with a knife. Carefully flake the fish into a bowl, cover with clingfilm and refrigerate.

—— PRESENTATION ——

Mix half the mayonnaise with the beansprouts and add the curry powder. Divide the mixture between the pastry boats, then arrange the flaked salmon attractively on top. Cut a cross in the capers and open them up to look like flowers, then decorate each boat with 3 capers. Pipe the remaining mayonnaise decoratively on to the boats and finish with a frond of dill. Arrange 2 boats on each plate, with 4 cherry tomatoes around the edge and a piece of decoratively carved lemon.

—— NOTES ——

These filled boats are rather difficult to transport, so for a picnic, it is best to pack the empty boats in a plastic box, with crumpled foil between them to prevent breakages. The fillings can be prepared the day before and carried separately. It will only take 5 minutes to assemble the boats in situ.

LITTLE PASTRY-WRAPPED
VEGETABLE PURSES
Dômes de friands de légumes

*A*N *original way to serve vegetables out of doors, in the country, at the seaside or in your own garden, these little purses also make an excellent dish for a vegetarian guest.*

PREPARATION TIME
30 minutes

COOKING TIME
15 minutes

INGREDIENTS

8 open cultivated mushrooms, each about 50 g/2 oz

35 g/1 ½ oz butter

50 g/2 oz cauliflower

50 g/2 oz broccoli

1 tablespoon flour, plus a pinch for dusting

100 ml/4 fl oz milk

1 egg yolk

a pinch of nutmeg

1 sprig of thyme, preferably lemon-flavoured, finely chopped

150 g/5 oz Quick puff pastry (recipe, page 23)

eggwash (1 egg yolk beaten with 1 teaspoon milk)

salt and freshly ground black pepper

PREPARATION

The mushrooms: Remove the stalks, scoop out a little of the flesh with a teaspoon and wipe gently all over with a slightly damp cloth. Heat 20 g/¾ oz butter in a frying pan over medium heat, put in the mushroom caps and seal for 30 seconds on each side. Place on a wire rack to drain.

The cauliflower and broccoli: Separate into small florets, wash in cold water and cook separately in two pans of lightly salted boiling water, cooking the cauliflower for 2 minutes and the broccoli for 1 minute. Refresh, drain and place on kitchen paper.

The sauce: In a small saucepan, melt the remaining butter, then add the flour and cook for 1 minute, stirring with a small wire whisk. Add the milk, still stirring, and cook at just below boiling point for 5 minutes. Add the cauliflower and broccoli to the sauce and cook for another minute, stirring with a wooden spatula. Take the pan off the heat and stir in the egg yolk. Season with salt, pepper, nutmeg and thyme. Fill the mushroom caps with this mixture, dividing the cauliflower, broccoli and sauce in equal quantities between them. Keep in a cool place until they are completely cold.

ASSEMBLING THE PASTRY-WRAPPED VEGETABLES

Preheat the oven to 200°C/400°F/gas 6.

On a lightly floured marble or wooden surface, roll out the pastry to a thickness of about 2 mm/1/12 in. Using a plain 10–12 cm/4–5 in pastry cutter, cut out 8 rounds of pastry and place each one in a tartlet tin. Lay a cold filled mushroom in the middle of each round. Brush the borders of the pastry with eggwash. Fold up the edges of the pastry over the mushrooms, twisting and pinching them together to seal the little mushroom purses. Brush the tops with eggwash and leave to rest in the fridge for 10 minutes.

COOKING

Bake in the preheated oven for 15 minutes. Immediately the purses are cooked, take them out of the tartlet tins and place on a wire rack.

PRESENTATION

Serve the little purses cold for a picnic. They can, indoors, be served hot, straight from the oven.

RILLETTES OF RABBIT WITH HAZELNUTS
Rillettes de lapereau aux noisettes

*I*F you have the patience to wait for 24 or 48 hours, these delicious rillettes will taste all the better. For a picnic, serve them with some plain or toasted country bread.

PREPARATION

Using a flexible knife, carefully remove the rind from the barding fat and cut the fat into very small dice.

COOKING

Put the diced fat into a small cast iron cocotte or casserole with all but 4 teaspoons of the wine, 50 ml/2 fl oz water, the pork fillet, bouquet garni and rabbit legs. Cover and cook over very gentle heat (90°C/194°F) for 30 minutes, stirring with a wooden spatula every 10 minutes. Add the carrot, shallot and garlic, lower the heat to about 80°C/176°F and cook, still with the lid on, for a further hour, stirring occasionally, until the rabbit flesh is falling off the bones. Leave the meat in the pan at room temperature.

The hazelnuts: Heat the grill. Place the hazelnuts in the grill pan and grill until the skins begin to come away and the nuts turn golden. Put in a tea towel, fold up the towel and rub the hazelnuts together to remove the skins. With a sharp knife, halve the hazelnuts down the middle.

PRESENTATION

Remove the bouquet garni from the casserole. Use a fork to pull the meat away from the rabbit bones and shred it. Still using the fork, shred the pork fillet. Add the halved hazelnuts, green peppercorns and the remaining 4 teaspoons wine. Mix with a spatula and season to taste.

Spoon the rillettes into two ramekins or a small oval terrine, cover and chill in the fridge for at least 6 hours before serving.

NOTE

Shred a mauve chive flower over the surface of the rillettes just before you serve them to add a soft touch of colour and a very delicate oniony flavour.

PREPARATION TIME
30 minutes

COOKING TIME
1 ½ hours, plus 6 hours chilling

INGREDIENTS
2 rabbit forelegs
120 g/4 oz pork barding fat
120 ml/4 fl oz dry white wine
40 g/1 ½ oz pork fillet
1 small bouquet garni
30 g/1 oz carrot, finely diced
30 g/1 oz shallot, finely chopped
½ garlic clove, crushed
30 g/1 oz hazelnuts
20 soft green peppercorns, drained and crushed
salt and freshly ground pepper

CHAUD-FROID OF STUFFED MUSSELS
Moules farcies en chaud-froid

*T*HIS *festive dish is very simple and inexpensive to prepare, and its glowing colours make it a delight to the eye. It is ideal to serve at an outdoor summer party.*

─────────── PREPARATION ───────────

The mussels: Debeard them, scrub and wash in cold water. Put them in a saucepan with the shallot, thyme, bay leaf, crushed peppercorns and white wine. Cover the pan and set over high heat for 2–3 minutes, until all the mussels have opened. Immediately drain them in a colander set over a bowl to catch the juices.

Remove the mussels from the shells and put them in their cooking juice. Reserve the deeper shell from each mussel for serving, and keep both shells and mussels at room temperature.

The red pepper: Cut away the white membrane and seeds. Peel the pepper with a potato peeler. Cut the flesh into small, even dice and place in the fridge.

The spinach: Remove the stalks, wash the leaves in cold water and drain. Heat the butter in a frying pan until nutty brown, then put in the spinach and cook for 2 minutes, stirring with a fork. Season with salt, nutmeg and a pinch of sugar. Drain and keep in a bowl at room temperature.

─────────── STUFFING THE MUSSELS ───────────

Divide the spinach equally between the 18 shells, and place a well-drained mussel in each shell.

Strain the mussel juices into a saucepan and reduce over high heat to only about 2 tablespoons. Take the pan off the heat and stir in the soaked gelatine with a spoon, then stir the mixture into the mayonnaise. Use a teaspoon to coat each mussel with mayonnaise as neatly as possible. Arrange some diced pepper on one side and the chervil leaves on the other, pressing them down lightly on the mayonnaise. Refrigerate for 30 minutes, until the gelatine has set.

─────────── PRESENTATION ───────────

To transport the mussels, arrange them in a deep dish or on a large plate and cover with clingfilm. Eat them with a small oyster fork or a teaspoon.

PREPARATION TIME
30 minutes, plus 30 minutes chilling

COOKING TIME
2–3 minutes

INGREDIENTS
18 medium mussels, about 500 g/1 lb 2 oz
30 g/1 oz shallot, finely chopped
1 sprig of thyme
1 bay leaf
10 peppercorns, crushed
200 ml/7 floz dry white wine
½ red pepper
150 g/5 oz young spinach shoots
30 g/1 oz butter
a pinch of nutmeg
a pinch of sugar
1 gelatine leaf, soaked in cold water
250 g/9 oz Mayonnaise (recipe, page 30)
18 chervil leaves
salt

MARINATED TUNA PIE WITH ORANGE ZESTS

Tourte au thon mariné aux zestes d'orange

THIS pastoral yet regal dish is a delight to the eye and palate. It is perfect for a grand picnic, since it is easy to transport, and it would be ideal to serve at the seaside.

PREPARATION TIME
40 minutes, plus 4 hours marinating and 30 minutes chilling

COOKING TIME
25 minutes

INGREDIENTS

1 fresh tuna steak, about 300 g/ 11 oz

1 orange

juice of 1 lemon

1 tablespoon chopped savory or lemon thyme

2 tablespoons rum

3 tablespoons olive oil

a pinch of flour

300 g/11 oz Shortcrust pastry (recipe, page 22)

1 teaspoon butter, for greasing

150 g/5 oz fresh broad beans, shelled, cooked until crunchy, then skinned

eggwash (1 egg yolk lightly beaten with 1 teaspoon milk)

200 g/7 oz treviso lettuce, radicchio or mesclun, for serving

salt and freshly ground pepper

PREPARATION

The tuna: Use a filleting knife to cut off the skin and remove the flesh from the bone. Cut the flesh into 2 cm/¾ in cubes, put in a salad bowl and place in the fridge.
The marinade: Pare off half the orange zest with a vegetable peeler. Using a heavy knife, cut into fine julienne strips. Blanch in boiling water for 30 seconds, refresh and drain. Halve the orange and squeeze out the juice. Mix it with the lemon juice, savory, rum and blanched orange zests. Pour this marinade over the cubes of tuna and mix delicately. Pour over all but 1 teaspoon of the olive oil. Cover with clingfilm and refrigerate for at least 4 hours.

ASSEMBLING THE PIE

On a lightly floured marble or wooden surface, roll one-third of the pastry into a 25 × 12 cm/10 × 5 in rectangle, about 3 mm/⅛ in thick. Roll it on to the rolling pin, then unroll it on to a lightly greased baking sheet.

Drain off the excess marinade from the tuna. Season the fish to taste with salt and pepper, then add the remaining olive oil and the broad beans and arrange the mixture on the pastry, leaving a clear 2 cm/¾ in border around the edge. Brush this border with eggwash.

Roll out the remaining pastry into a 30 × 16 cm/12 × 6 in rectangle. Roll it on to the rolling pin, then unroll it over the filled pastry base. Gently press the edges of the pastry together so that they are sealed by the eggwash. Leave the pie to rest in the fridge for at least 30 minutes.

Preheat the oven to 240°C/475°F/gas 9.

COOKING THE PIE

With a small, sharp knife, cut away part of the pastry border to make the shape of a fish. Brush the top of the fish-shaped pie with eggwash and use the knife to decorate it with scales, a head and a tail. Place immediately in the preheated oven and bake for 10 minutes. Reduce the temperature to 220°C/425°F/gas 7 and bake for another 15 minutes. Use a palette knife to slide the baked pie on to a wire rack.

PRESENTATION

Leave the pie to cool and serve at room temperature within 8 hours of cooking. Place it on an oval dish and garnish with a border of a combination of treviso lettuce, radicchio or mesclun dressed with olive oil and lemon.

EGG, ANCHOVY AND SPINACH ROULADE
Roulade d'oeufs aux anchois et aux épinards

*T*HIS *delicious roulade is simple to make, and has the advantage that it can be prepared a day or two before your picnic and kept in the fridge. A simple tomato salad, or, some sliced tomatoes dressed with a drizzle of olive oil, make the perfect accompaniment.*

———— PREPARATION ————

The anchovies: Soak in the milk for 10 minutes, then drain and chop very finely with a chef's knife. Place in a bowl.

The spinach: Wash in cold water, drain and remove the stalks. Heat 20 g/$\frac{3}{4}$ oz butter in a frying pan. When it is very hot, put in the spinach and cook over high heat for 1 minute. Season lightly with salt and pepper. Tip the spinach into a colander until well-drained and almost cold, then mix in half the anchovies.

———— COOKING THE EGGS ————

Break the 4 eggs into a bowl, add the cream, season to taste and beat for 20 seconds. Melt 20 g/$\frac{3}{4}$ oz butter in a saucepan, then pour in half the eggs. Cook over low heat, stirring with a wooden spatula to scramble them. When the eggs are cooked, transfer to a bowl and leave at room temperature for 10 minutes.

Heat the grill.

———— COOKING THE ROULADE ————

Gently mix the scrambled eggs into the raw eggs and stir in the remaining anchovies. Generously grease both sides of a 40 × 30 cm/16 × 12 in sheet of greaseproof paper with the remaining butter and place it on a baking sheet. Spread the roulade mixture over the paper to make a rectangle 15 cm/6 in wide and the full length of the paper. Place under the hot grill for 1–2 minutes, until the egg mixture is cooked but not at all dried out.

As soon as the mixture is cooked, spread the spinach over the roulade and use the greaseproof paper to help you roll it up like a swiss roll. Keep at room temperature until cold, then refrigerate until needed.

———— PRESENTATION ————

Wrap the roulade in greaseproof paper or foil to transport it to your picnic spot. To serve it, remove the wrapping and cut into slices for you and your guest.

PREPARATION TIME
25 minutes

COOKING TIME
4–5 minutes, plus 10 minutes standing

INGREDIENTS
4 eggs, preferably free range
12 anchovy fillets
100 ml/4 fl oz milk
100 g/4 oz small tender spinach leaves
60 g/2 oz butter
1 tablespoon double cream
salt and freshly ground pepper

SMOKED FISH PLATTER

Gourmandise de poissons fumés

*T*HIS *wonderfully simple dish can easily be transported in plastic boxes or greaseproof paper for a picnic, and will delight your companion with its rich blend of subtle flavours.*

PREPARATION TIME
20 minutes

INGREDIENTS

1 small smoked trout, filleted and skinned

50 g/2 oz smoked haddock, thinly sliced

50 g/2 oz smoked salmon, thinly sliced

150 g/5 oz chicory (Belgian endive)

1 small lollo rosso lettuce, or 50 g/2 oz oak leaf lettuce

40 g/1 ½ oz oyster mushrooms

5 tablespoons vinaigrette, made with a good red wine vinegar

20 g/¾ oz shallot, very finely chopped

2 potatoes, each about 50 g/ 2 oz, boiled in their skins

20 g/¾ oz real caviar if possible, otherwise black lumpfish roe

1 tablespoon chervil leaves

salt and freshly ground pepper

PREPARATION

The chicory: Trim, wash and cut into long strips.
The lettuce: Trim, wash and gently pat dry.
The mushrooms: Trim, wipe with a damp cloth and slice thinly. Season with salt and pepper and a spoonful of vinaigrette, then mix in the chopped shallot.
The potatoes: Scoop out two-thirds of the flesh.

PRESENTATION

On a large platter or individual plates, arrange the salads in alternate bunches. Arrange the mushrooms around the edge. Mix the caviar with the vinaigrette and fill the hollowed-out potatoes with some of this mixture. Place in the centre of the plate. Spoon the remaining caviar and vinaigrette over the salad. Arrange the smoked fish attractively on the salad and sprinkle with the chervil leaves.

NOTE

Depending on the time of year, regional availability and your finances, you can substitute other types of smoked fish, such as smoked eel or halibut.

SALAD OF LETTUCE HEART, EGG MIMOSA AND PINE NUTS

Coeur de laitue, mimosa d'oeuf dur et pignons

*T*HIS *salad is a course in itself, to be eaten while your barbecue is sizzling and you are relishing your environment. It is also perfect for serving with simply grilled meats or fish.*

—————————— PREPARATION ——————————

The lettuce: Discard any very green or marked outer leaves, wash the lettuce in cold water and gently shake it dry, taking care not to rub the leaves. With a heavy knife, cut it into quarters, then refrigerate.

The watercress: Wash in cold water, shake dry, pick off the leaves, place them in a bowl and refrigerate.

The egg: Separate the white and yolk. Rub them separately through a wire sieve, or chop finely with a heavy knife. Put the white in one saucer and the yolk in another, and place in the fridge.

The avocado: Halve lengthways and remove the stone. With the small end of a melon baller or a teaspoon, scoop out as many smooth round or oval balls as possible. Roll these in lemon juice, place in a bowl and refrigerate.

The vinaigrette: Mix together all the ingredients and season to taste.

—————————— PRESENTATION ——————————

Arrange the lettuce quarters in a wide, shallow salad bowl or on a large plate. Place a little watercress between each piece. Roll the avocado balls in the mustard seeds and arrange them in the centre of the bowl.

Pour the vinaigrette over all the ingredients and sprinkle the whole salad with alternate lines of egg white, egg yolk and pine nuts for an attractive effect.

—————————— NOTES ——————————

For a picnic, all the ingredients can be prepared the day before and kept separately in the fridge. They can be transported in plastic bowls, and it will take only a few minutes to assemble the salad once you have reached your chosen spot.

PREPARATION TIME
15 minutes

INGREDIENTS

1 small, hearty lettuce, about 150 g/5 oz

1 small bunch of watercress, about 60 g/2 oz

1 hard-boiled egg

1 firm, ripe avocado, about 300 g/11 oz

juice of ½ lemon

1 teaspoon mustard seeds

30 g/1 oz pine nuts, lightly toasted

FOR THE VINAIGRETTE:
6 tablespoons olive oil

2 tablespoons white wine vinegar

1 teaspoon Dijon mustard

salt and freshly ground pepper

GRILLED SCALLOPS WITH A VERMOUTH NAGE

Coquilles Saint-Jacques grillées, nage de vermouth

*T*HIS *delicate dish is perfect for the barbecue, the scallops needing no salad or vegetable accompaniment. It is best eaten with a spoon so that you can enjoy the sauce.*

PREPARATION TIME
20 minutes, plus 3–4 hours marinating

COOKING TIME
3–4 minutes

INGREDIENTS

6 scallops, in their shells if possible

2 tablespoons olive oil

10 white peppercorns, crushed

1 sprig of thyme, preferably lemon thyme

30 g/1 oz shallots, finely chopped

1 carrot, about 50 g/2 oz, finely diced

1 small bouquet garni

100 ml/4 fl oz dry white vermouth

30 g/1 oz butter

1 lemon, decoratively carved, for garnish

salt and freshly ground pepper

PREPARATION

The scallops: Using a knife with a rigid blade, open the scallops, debeard them and separate the white parts and corals from the beards. Rinse the beards very thoroughly in cold water and reserve them. Rinse the white flesh in cold water, pat dry and place in a dish with the olive oil, crushed peppercorns and thyme leaves. Place in the fridge and leave to marinate for several hours. Reserve two of the concave shells, for serving.

The sauce: Combine the shallots, carrot, bouquet garni, vermouth and scallop beards in a small saucepan. Stand it either on the edge of the barbecue or over low heat indoors and reduce by two-thirds. Remove the bouquet garni and scallop beards, then beat the butter into the sauce with a whisk. Season to taste and keep the sauce warm over low heat.

COOKING THE SCALLOPS

Pierce the corals with the point of a knife. Place the scallops and corals on the barbecue or in a grill pan over high, but not excessive heat. Turn them after 1 minute, then cook until they are attractively patterned and done to your liking. A 50 g/2 oz scallop will need 4 minutes to be cooked *à point* (medium).

PRESENTATION

Place the white flesh and corals in the two reserved shells or, if you prefer, in a deep dish and leave in a fairly warm place for 1–2 minutes. Just before serving, pour the warm sauce over or around the scallops. Garnish each shell with a decoratively carved lemon half and serve immediately.

GRILLED SALMON TAIL WITH TARRAGON BUTTER

Queue de saumon grillé au beurre d'estragon

*T*HIS *is a grand dish which will impress your guest who will wonder why they have never eaten salmon in this way before. The aroma of salmon cooking with the wafts of tarragon could only be enhanced by a chilled glass of white wine to quieten your rumbling appetites.*

PREPARATION

Descale the salmon. Trim off a little of the tail and rinse the fish in cold water.

Starting from the back of the salmon, use a filleting knife to lift the flesh away from the bones as though you were going to fillet the fish, but stop 1 cm/½ in before the backbone. Turn the fish over and repeat the operation on the other side. Prepare the belly of the fish in the same way; this will release the four fillets from the side bones, while leaving them still attached to the backbone. Finally, make a slash along the length of both sides of the fish to ensure that it cooks evenly.

Mix the tarragon into the butter and season with a little salt and plenty of pepper. Use a spoon or palette knife to spread the tarragon butter between the fillets and the bone. Keep about 2 tablespoons of the butter to use later. Reshape the salmon tail and tie it (not too tightly) in three places with the strips of salmon skin or kitchen string.

Place the salmon on a plate, cover with a damp tea towel or clingfilm and refrigerate for 2–3 hours.

COOKING

Heat a barbecue or grill pan until red hot. Brush the salmon tail all over with oil, sprinkle with a little coarse salt and place it on the barbecue grid or in the pan, taking care to put the thickest part of the fish in the hottest place. Cook for approximately 8 minutes (depending on your taste and the heat of the barbecue), then turn the salmon over and cook in the same way for another 8 minutes. Move the fish from the centre of the barbecue to the side, over less intense heat, or lower the heat under the grill pan and cook for a further 2 minutes.

PRESENTATION

Place the salmon tail on a platter or dish. If you used string, remove it. Brush the salmon with the remaining tarragon butter, cover with the lemon slices and leave to rest for 1 minute. Serve one fillet at a time. Since the fish is still partly attached to the bone, it will keep warmer and moister if you leave the lemon slices in position until you serve it. The thicker part should be pink near the bone, while the rest of the tail will be a little more cooked. Serve with a french bean salad.

PREPARATION TIME
20 minutes, plus 2–3 hours chilling

COOKING TIME
18 minutes

INGREDIENTS

1 salmon tail piece, about 600 g/ 1¼ lb

1 piece of salmon skin, cut into long strips (optional)

15 g/½ oz tarragon, snipped

2 tablespoons groundnut oil

80 g/3 oz softened butter

1 lemon, cut into rounds

coarse cooking salt

freshly ground pepper

COLD FILLET OF BEEF EN CROUTE WITH HORSERADISH SAUCE

Filet de boeuf en croûte froid, sauce raifort

*T*OO *often, we see rare roast beef in summer time served in its simple glory. With such a small amount of extra effort you can create a dish to be remembered and talked about until the next picnic . . . and if beef is on your menu, we know how you will serve it!*

PREPARATION TIME
35 minutes, plus 30 minutes chilling

COOKING TIME
28 minutes

INGREDIENTS

1 centre-cut fillet of beef, trimmed, about 400 g/14 oz

200 g/7 oz button mushrooms

30 g/1 oz butter

juice of 1 lemon

40 g/1 ½ oz shallots, finely chopped

1 tablespoon chopped parsley

2 tablespoons groundnut oil

a pinch of flour

300 g/11 oz Brioche dough (recipe, page 60)

eggwash (1 egg yolk lightly beaten with 1 teaspoon milk)

100 ml/4 fl oz double cream or plain yoghurt

1 tablespoon snipped chives

1 tablespoon grated fresh horseradish, or 2 tablespoons bottled horseradish

salt and freshly ground pepper

PREPARATION

The mushroom duxelles: Trim the mushroom stalks with a sharp knife. Wipe the caps with a damp cloth or wash them in cold water if necessary. Place on a chopping board and chop finely with a heavy knife.

Heat the butter in a frying pan and fry the mushrooms with one-third of the lemon juice over high heat. When all the moisture has evaporated, add the shallots and cook for another minute. Add the chopped parsley, season to taste with salt and pepper, then put the duxelles into a bowl and keep in a cool place.

PRE-COOKING THE FILLET OF BEEF

Salt the meat lightly. Heat the oil in a frying pan, then fry the beef over medium heat, turning it until it is pale golden all over; this will take about 8 minutes. Transfer it to a wire rack and leave in a cool place until completely cold.

WRAPPING THE BEEF IN THE PASTRY

On a lightly floured marble or wooden board, roll out the brioche dough into a rectangle about 25 × 18 cm/10 × 7 in and 5 mm/¼ in thick. Spread one-third of the duxelles over the centre of the dough to precisely the size of the fillet of beef.

Lay the beef on this soft bed of mushrooms and use a palette knife to spread the rest of the duxelles over the meat. Brush the edges of the dough with eggwash. Fold one of the long sides over the beef, brush the dough with eggwash, then fold the other long side over the first. Brush the ends of the dough with eggwash, fold them over the beef to wrap it completely, and seal. Use a large palette knife to transfer it to a baking sheet. Chill in the fridge for 30 minutes.

Preheat the oven to 220°C/425°F/gas 7.

COOKING

Brush the pastry-wrapped beef all over with eggwash and decorate it by scoring lines with the point of a knife to make a lattice, or cut flowers from the leftover pastry, or what you will. With a sharp knife, cut a small hole, no bigger than 1 cm/ ½ in diameter, in the top of the pastry so that the steam can escape. Bake in the preheated oven for 20 minutes, then slide the cooked fillet on to a wire rack and leave at room temperature until completely cold.

Lightly whip the cream. Add the remaining lemon juice, the chives and horseradish and season to taste. You can substitute yoghurt for all or some of the cream, in which case, do not whip it. Of course, the sauce will not be as unctuous.

PRESENTATION

Place the beef on a plain dish and slice it as you serve it wherever you are – at the table, on the grass, on the beach. . . . Serve the sauce separately in a sauceboat.

NOTES

Do not keep the beef in the fridge after it is cooked, or the pastry will soften and the meat will lose its flavour; this tends to happen anyway after 2 or 3 hours. Thin pancakes are often laid between the pastry and the meat or fish en croûte to prevent the pastry from becoming soggy. For this marriage of beef, mushrooms and brioche dough served cold, however, we prefer not to use pancakes.

Plainly cooked green peas served cold as a salad, dressed with a light olive oil and lemon vinaigrette and garnished with a few snipped fresh mint leaves make a delicious accompaniment to this classic picnic dish.

CURRY-MARINATED LAMB CHOPS
Côtes d'agneau découvertes grillées au parfum de curry

*I*DEALLY, *you should use the first or second chops from the côte découverte for this dish (this may be hard to find in Britain; the nearest most suitable equivalent is middle neck), as these contain a higher proportion of fat and are therefore more succulent when grilled on a barbecue. The curry marinade gives the lamb a surprising flavour.*

PREPARATION

Place the chops in a deep dish. Wash the lemon and cut into thin rounds. Grill, skin and finely chop the peanuts. In a separate bowl, mix the lemon, oil, peanuts, curry and a pinch of salt and pepper, to taste, and pour the mixture over the chops. Leave to marinate for at least 12 hours.

GRILLING THE CHOPS

Place the chops on a hot barbecue and grill to taste for 2–3 minutes on each side.

PRESENTATION

Serve 2 chops per person, accompanied by an aubergine purée with olive oil (recipe, page 242) or, if you prefer, cucumber salad with a lemon dressing.

PREPARATION TIME
10 minutes, plus 12 hours marinating

COOKING TIME
4–6 minutes

INGREDIENTS
4 middle neck lamb chops, each about 100 g/4 oz

1 lemon

2 tablespoons groundnut oil

20 g/$\frac{3}{4}$ oz peanuts

1 tablespoon mild Madras curry

salt and freshly ground pepper

BREAST OF VEAL MARINATED IN HONEY, WITH CARAMELISED LEMONS

Tendron de veau mariné au miel et son citron confit

*T*HIS *is a deliciously refreshing summer dish, full of flavour. It is also very good made with chicken pieces; either can be cooked on the barbecue or under the grill.*

PREPARATION

The marinade and veal: Heat the honey in a saucepan. Add the lemon juice, crushed peppercorns and paprika and bring to the boil. Immediately draw the pan off the heat and put in a cool place. When the honey marinade is almost cold, brush it all over the veal and place the meat in a dish. Cover with clingfilm and place in the fridge for at least 4 hours.

The lemons: Wash in cold water and prick each one in about 20 places with a trussing needle or the fine point of a knife. Put the sugar in a small saucepan with 250 ml/9 fl oz water and bring to the boil. As soon as the syrup boils, put in the lemons and cover them with a piece of greaseproof paper. Lower the heat and poach gently at about 80°C/176°F for 30 minutes. Leave the lemons to cool in the syrup for at least 4 hours. When they have completely cooled, poach them again at the same temperature for 15 minutes, then leave them in their syrup at room temperature. When the lemons have cooled again, they are ready to be grilled.

COOKING

Brush the breast of veal with groundnut oil, sprinkle with a little coarse salt and put the slices on the barbecue or in a hot grill pan, together with the candied lemons. Keep turning the lemons every minute for 5 minutes. Grill the veal for 2½ minutes on each side. It is ready to serve when the meat is amber-coloured and the lemons are lightly caramelised.

PRESENTATION

Place the veal in a shallow dish. Halve the lemons lengthways and put them with the meat. Serve piping hot. You will need very sharp knives.

NOTES

Dip each piece of veal into a lemon half as you eat it; you can also eat the skins.

The lemons can be candied and kept in their syrup a day or two before your picnic, if you prefer. Use the syrup to make a cocktail, or in a fruit salad.

PREPARATION TIME
20 minutes, plus 4 hours marinating

COOKING TIME
4 minutes

INGREDIENTS
2 slices of breast of veal, taken from the front, about 250 g/9 oz each

2 tablespoons clear honey

juice of ½ lemon

10 peppercorns, crushed

1 teaspoon sweet paprika

225 g/8 oz caster sugar

2 lemons

1 tablespoon groundnut oil

coarse cooking salt

GRILLED VEAL KIDNEY WITH SWEET AND SOUR SAUCE
Rouelles de rognon grillé à l'aigre-doux

*K*IDNEYS *have a strong, distinctive taste, and tender veal kidneys, in particular, are wonderful when cooked on a barbecue. Give your tastebuds a treat with this simple dish.*

PREPARATION TIME
20 minutes, plus 8 hours marinating

COOKING TIME
4–6 minutes

INGREDIENTS
1 veal kidney, about 450 g/1 lb, trimmed of its fat

100 ml/4 fl oz olive oil

2 good sprigs of thyme, finely chopped

2 garlic cloves, finely sliced

30 g/1 oz butter

50 g/2 oz soft brown sugar

2 slices of pineapple, about 150 g/ 5 oz, peeled and finely diced

80 ml/3 fl oz red wine vinegar

200 ml/7 fl oz Chicken stock (recipe, page 18)

1 teaspoon tomato paste

1 teaspoon cornflour

salt and freshly ground pepper

PREPARATION

The kidney: Cut into 8 even slices about 1 cm/$\frac{1}{2}$ in thick. Place in a bowl with the olive oil, half the thyme and half the garlic. Place in the fridge and leave to marinate for at least 8 hours.

The sauce: In a saucepan, heat the butter, add the sugar and cook gently, stirring with a wooden spatula, until the mixture turns a deep caramel colour. Add the diced pineapple and cook for 3 minutes. Pour in the vinegar, add the remaining thyme and garlic and reduce by one-third. Add the chicken stock and tomato paste and cook over medium heat until reduced by half. Mix the cornflour to a paste with 2 tablespoons cold water, then pour this into the sauce, whisking as you do so. Season to taste. Pass the sauce through a conical sieve and keep hot.

COOKING THE KIDNEYS

Heat a grill pan or the barbecue. Drain some of the marinade from the kidney rounds and put them into the hot pan. After 1 minute, give them a quarter-turn to make an attractive lattice pattern, and cook for another minute. Turn the rounds over and cook the other side in the same way. If you prefer your kidneys *à point* (medium), then leave them in the grill pan or on the barbecue for an extra minute or two.

PRESENTATION

Arrange the kidney rounds on warmed plates and pour over the sauce.

NOTES

An advantage of this dish is that the sauce can be prepared the day before for taking on a picnic. Reheat it in a small pan set at the edge of the barbecue.

SALAD OF LAMBS' TONGUES WITH SHALLOTS AND MUSTARD VINAIGRETTE
Langue d'agneau à l'échalote et vinaigrette de moutarde

*L*AMBS' *tongues are among the most delicate, tender and highly prized offal. They are especially popular in France and Italy, where they are often sold at exorbitant prices. This dish can be served as an hors d'oeuvre or main course, depending on your appetites.*

PREPARATION

The tongues: Refresh under cold running water for 1 hour. Prick them in about a dozen places with the point of a knife and place in a saucepan with the carrot, bouquet garni and onion. Cover with plenty of water and bring to the boil. Reduce the heat and simmer gently for 1¼ hours. Leave the cooked tongues in the cooking broth, then, when they have cooled slightly, carefully peel off the skin with the point of a sharp knife. Reserve the broth.

The beans and cauliflower: Top and tail the beans, wash and cook in a pan of boiling salted water until still firm, but not crunchy. Refresh and drain.

Cut the cauliflower into small florets and cook in the same way as the beans. Refresh, drain and place in a bowl with the beans.

The vinaigrette: Reduce half the reserved cooking broth until you have 2 tablespoons liquid. Leave until almost cold, then mix in the mustard, vinegar and olive oil, and season to taste with salt and pepper.

PRESENTATION

Mix the vinaigrette into the cauliflower and beans and arrange in a deep dish. Slice each tongue lengthways into four, lay them on the bed of vegetables and sprinkle with the chopped shallots and tarragon. Serve at room temperature.

NOTE

This dish is ideal for a picnic; just serve it in a shallow round plastic bowl.

PREPARATION TIME
20 minutes, plus 1 hour soaking the tongues

COOKING TIME
1½ hours

INGREDIENTS

4 lambs' tongues, trimmed, total weight about 350 g/12 oz

1 carrot, about 80 g/3 oz

1 medium bouquet garni

1 onion, stuck with 1 clove

100 g/4 oz fine French beans

100 g/4 oz cauliflower

2 tablespoons very strong Dijon mustard

1 tablespoon red wine vinegar

4 tablespoons olive oil

2 shallots, finely chopped

1 tablespoon snipped tarragon

salt and freshly ground pepper

Globe

ARTICHOKE AND OLIVE PIE

Tourte aux artichauts et olives

*D*O not stand in awe of this seemingly difficult dish: the method is simple and the result will fill you with pride and delight your guest. The subtle combination of ingredients is quite delicious and it will soon become a regular dish in your repertoire.

PREPARATION TIME
40 minutes, plus 30 minutes chilling

COOKING TIME
30 minutes

INGREDIENTS

2 artichokes, each about 350 g/ 12 oz

$\frac{1}{2}$ lemon

2 tablespoons olive oil

10 coriander seeds, crushed

1 small garlic clove, crushed

1 sprig of thyme

a pinch of flour

250 g/9 oz Quick puff pastry (recipe, page 23)

2 hard-boiled eggs, coarsely chopped

1 tomato, about 100 g/4 oz, skinned, deseeded and chopped

30 g/1 oz black olives, stoned and halved

6 anchovy fillets, very finely diced

6 basil leaves, snipped

eggwash (1 egg yolk, lightly beaten with 1 teaspoon milk)

salt and freshly ground black pepper

PREPARATION

The artichokes: Wash in cold water. Snap off the stems, then pare off all the leaves with a small, sharp knife to leave only the neatly shaped bases. Use a soup spoon to scoop out the chokes which are firmly attached to the bases. Rub the bases all over with the cut lemon.

Cut each base into 12 pieces and place in a small saucepan with the olive oil, coriander seeds, garlic, thyme and a tablespoon of water. Cover and cook over very low heat for at least 10 minutes, until the artichokes are tender and melting and no longer crunchy. Discard the thyme, tip the artichokes into a bowl, cover with clingfilm and leave in a cool place.

ASSEMBLING THE PIE

On a lightly floured marble or wooden surface, roll out 40% of the pastry into a 15 cm/6 in circle, 3 mm/$\frac{1}{8}$ in thick. Place this on a baking sheet.

Gently mix the eggs, tomato, olives, anchovies and basil into the artichokes and season to taste. Put this mixture into the centre of the pastry base. Roll out the remaining pastry into a 16–17 cm/$6\frac{1}{2}$–$6\frac{3}{4}$ in circle of the same thickness as the first. Brush the outer edge of the first circle with eggwash. Roll the second circle on to the rolling pin, then unroll it over the filled circle. Press the edges of the pie together to rest in the fridge for at least 30 minutes.

Preheat the oven to 240°C/475°F/gas 9.

COOKING

Use the point of a knife to trim off the excess pastry to leave a neat, regular base. Glaze the top of the pie with eggwash and score patterns (eg: half-moons or lattices) with the point of the knife. Cut a small hole (about 1 cm/$\frac{1}{2}$ in diameter) in the top for the steam to escape, and bake the pie in the preheated oven for 10 minutes. Reduce the temperature to 220°C/425°F/gas 7 and bake for another 20 minutes. Slide the cooked pie on to a wire rack and keep at room temperature.

PRESENTATION

Serve the pie whole on a plate and cut it just when you are ready to eat it.

NOTES

This dish is best eaten at room temperature within 24 hours of cooking. Serve with a simple green salad, or as a vegetable or hors d'oeuvre.

SWEETCORN AND PEA GALETTES

Galettes de maïs et petits pois

*T*HESE *refreshing galettes are equally tasty hot or cold. They can be cooked the day before and kept in the fridge, and are easy to transport; just wrap in greaseproof paper and stack.*

PREPARATION

Put the flour, 1 tablespoon oil, egg yolk and white into a bowl and mix with a spoon. Add the milk, whisking with a wire whisk until the mixture is smooth and homogenous. With a spoon, carefully fold in the sorrel, sweetcorn and peas. Season with salt and refrigerate for at least 1 hour.

COOKING

Heat a little oil in a 12 cm/5 in frying pan. Pour one-quarter of the mixture into the pan and cook a galette over medium heat, for $1\frac{1}{2}$ minutes on each side, until golden brown. Add a little more oil and cook a second galette in the same way. Make 4 galettes altogether, adding a little more oil and always stirring the mixture with a spoon before pouring it into the pan. You should have enough mixture to make 4 8 cm/$3\frac{1}{4}$ in galettes. As each galette is cooked, place it on a plate.

PRESENTATION

The galettes can be eaten cold at a picnic as an accompaniment to meat or fish. If you prefer them warm, heat on the barbecue for 30 seconds just before serving.

NOTE

Use the remains of the tin of sweetcorn either in a salad or for a delicious soup.

PREPARATION TIME
10 minutes, plus 1 hour chilling

COOKING TIME
3 minutes for each galette

INGREDIENTS
30 g/1 oz flour
3 tablespoons groundnut oil
1 egg yolk
$\frac{1}{2}$ egg white
85 ml/3 fl oz milk
3 sorrel leaves, snipped
40 g/1$\frac{1}{2}$ oz tinned sweetcorn
2 tablespoons cooked frozen or tinned petits pois, about 20 g/$\frac{3}{4}$ oz
salt and freshly ground pepper

ORIENTAL GRILLED QUAILS
Canoe de caille grille l'oriental

*W*E adore quails; even the farmed birds are delicious. The smell of the marinated quails as they cook on the barbecue is sublime; it is well worth staying near the cooking area as they grill. This is a wonderful dish, whose spiciness does not assault the palate.

PREPARATION TIME
20 minutes, plus 24 hours
marinating

COOKING TIME
6–9 minutes

INGREDIENTS

2 fresh quails

2 spring onions, snipped

1 teaspoon finely chopped orange
zest

20 g/¾ oz fresh ginger, peeled
and finely chopped

1 teaspoon Szechuan peppercorns,
roasted and ground

1 teaspoon freshly ground black
pepper

1 teaspoon fine salt

1 tablespoon runny honey

1 tablespoon groundnut oil

a small pinch of cayenne pepper

1 teaspoon lemon juice

PREPARATION

The quails: Using poultry shears, split the quails along the back, then bone out the rib cage with a boning knife. Spatchcock the quails by laying them out flat and threading one wooden skewer through the legs and another through the wings. Put the quails in a deep dish.

The marinade: Place the spring onions, orange zest, ginger, Szechuan and black peppers and the salt in a blender and process to a smooth paste.

In a small saucepan, gently heat the honey, oil, cayenne and lemon juice. Add the soft paste from the blender, mix with a spoon and take off the heat. Pour the marinade over the quails and rub it in with your fingertips. Place the dish in the fridge and leave to marinate for 24 hours, turning over the quails after 12 hours.

COOKING THE QUAILS

Grill on a hot barbecue for 3 minutes on each side if you like your quails pink. For medium, add another 1–1½ minutes to the total cooking time.

PRESENTATION

Arrange the quails on a single plate and and eat them with your fingers. It is perfectly acceptable to suck the bones to remove every morsel of meat.

NOTES

If the quails are very small (about 120 g/4 oz), it is advisable to allow two per person. Ideally, each quail should weigh 160–200 g/5–7 oz.

JANNY'S SWEET PEPPERS IN OLIVE OIL
Poivrons doux confits à l'huile, de Janny

*T*HIS *is one of the dishes which Janny Barranco from Gassin cooks divinely well, and which Michel often enjoys at her house. When she has a barbecue, she lays whole, lightly oiled peppers on the dying embers and when the skins puff up and burn, she can peel them off without using a vegetable peeler. The peppers taste even better done this way.*

PREPARATION

Halve the peppers lengthways. Cut out the hard greenish cores, seeds and white membranes. Cut the peppers lengthways into strips about 1 cm/½ in wide. Lay them skin-side up on a flat surface and peel with a vegetable peeler.

COOKING

Put the olive oil, bouquet garni, garlic and peppers in a saucepan and salt lightly. Cook gently for 25–30 minutes, until you can easily crush the peppers with the back of a spoon. Transfer to a bowl and leave to cool. When the peppers are cold, remove the bouquet garni and garlic, then cover the bowl with clingfilm.

PRESENTATION

Serve the peppers in a pot or bowl, take to the table and spread like jam on to slices of country bread.

NOTE

If you prefer, the cooked peppers will keep for several days in the fridge.

PREPARATION TIME
15 minutes

COOKING TIME
25 minutes

INGREDIENTS

1 yellow pepper, about 100 g/ 4 oz

1 red pepper, about 100 g/4 oz

1 green pepper, about 100 g/ 4 oz

50 ml/2 fl oz extra virgin olive oil

1 small bouquet garni

1 garlic clove, crushed

salt

10 crushed peppercorns

CELERIAC AND BEETROOT CRISPS
Chips de céleri-rave et betterave rouge

*T*HE *flavour and colour of these crisps are delightful, and your guests will be surprised to find that not all crisps are made from potatoes. We love to munch them with an aperitif.*

PREPARATION TIME
20 minutes

COOKING TIME
about 3 minutes

INGREDIENTS

1 small celeriac, about 500 g/ 1 lb 2 oz

4 raw beetroot, each about 60 g/ 2 oz

1 litre/1 $\frac{3}{4}$ pts groundnut oil

salt

─────────── PREPARATION ───────────

Wash the celeriac and beetroot and cut off the roots and leaves. With a small sharp knife, cut the celeriac down the middle, then pare the two halves into oval, almost cylindrical shapes. Using a mandoline or heavy knife, cut them into the finest possible slivers (about 1 mm/$\frac{1}{24}$ in) to make crisps.

Pare the beetroot with a sharp knife and cut into slivers like the celeriac.

─────────── COOKING ───────────

Heat the oil in a deep saucepan until a very light heat haze rises from the surface. Lower the heat and carefully drop in the celeriac crisps, one by one. As soon as they rise to the surface and turn a very light golden brown, lift them out with the slotted spoon or strainer, drain well and spread them out on kitchen paper. Fry the celeriac crisps in this way in two batches.

Fry the beetroot crisps in the same way, reheating the oil between batches, as it cools very quickly.

Place the crisps in a warm, very dry place, such as an airing cupboard or in a very low oven (40°C/100°F/the lowest possible gas) and leave for an hour until the crisps are very dry and crunchy. Leave to cool, then place in a greaseproof bag or airtight tin and keep in a dry place.

─────────── PRESENTATION ───────────

Sprinkle the crisps lightly with salt and serve in a bowl or dish. Alternatively, if you prefer, these crisps can be used to garnish a meat dish.

From top: Strawberry tart with preserved ginger Mont-Ventoux (recipe, page 248); Marinated tuna pie with orange zest (recipe, page 218); Cold fillet of beef en croûte with horseradish sauce (recipe, page 228); Celeriac and beetroot crisps (recipe, opposite); Janny's sweet peppers in olive oil (recipe, page 239).

AUBERGINE PUREE WITH OLIVE OIL
Purée d'aubergines à l'huile d'olive

*T*HIS *purée is delicious spread on toasted country bread. It can be reheated on the barbecue in a small foil container and makes the perfect accompaniment to Oriental grilled quails (page 238) and Curry-marinated lamb chops (page 229).*

(page 238) and Curry-marinated lamb chops (page 229).

PREPARATION TIME
5 minutes

COOKING TIME
45 minutes

INGREDIENTS
1 aubergine, about 400 g/14 oz
a handful of coarse cooking salt
100 ml/4 fl oz olive oil
fine salt and freshly ground pepper

PREPARATION

Preheat the oven to 220°C/425°F/gas 7.

Wash the aubergine in cold water, wipe dry and prick in about 10 places with the point of a knife. Make a shallow incision in the skin all round the middle of the aubergine. Spread the coarse salt over the bottom of a small roasting pan, lay the aubergine on the salt and cook in the preheated oven for 45 minutes.

Halve the aubergine following the line of the incision and scrape out the flesh with a soup spoon. Put the flesh in a blender with the olive oil, and purée for 3 minutes, until very smooth. Season to taste and put the purée in a bowl.

PRESENTATION

Serve the purée hot or cold, either at a picnic or barbecue, or at home.

SANDWICHES

*H*ERE *are some suggestions for sandwiches made with different fillings and a variety of breads. Vary the quantities of the binding ingredients (mayonnaise, butter, oil, and so on) and main fillings, such as ham, to suit your own taste. Where butter is used, try flavouring it with fresh snipped herbs, or use fromage blanc.*

Here are some of our favourite sandwiches. Adapt them to create your own specialities.

PRAWNS

Thinly sliced rye bread, peeled prawns, diced cucumber and mayonnaise flavoured to taste with Madras curry.

ROQUEFORT

Thinly sliced rye bread, a mixture of half-and-half softened butter and roquefort cheese, chopped walnuts and grated apple.

CARROT AND COCONUT

Thinly sliced rye bread, grated carrot, blanched currants, grated fresh coconut, seasoned with lemon juice, salt and pepper to taste.

FROMAGE BLANC

Thick slices of country bread, fromage blanc, snipped chives, thin slices of black radish, if possible, or thickly sliced red radish, seasoned with salt and pepper.

AVOCADO

Thick slices of country bread, sliced avocado, mustard seeds, crisply fried diced bacon, seasoned with lemon juice, salt and pepper.

TOMATO AND OLIVE

A baguette split lengthways, brushed with olive oil, rounds of marmande tomato, tapénade (olive paste), shavings of parmesan cheese, and shredded basil leaves, seasoned with salt and pepper.

COLD SCRAMBLED EGGS

3 slices of white bread, 1 layer of scrambled eggs with flat-leafed parsley, 1 layer of crisp, grilled bacon rashers, diced, peeled and deseeded tomatoes, salt and pepper.

COLD ROAST BEEF

2 slices of lightly buttered rye bread sprinkled with grated horseradish, shredded tender savoy cabbage leaves, thin slices of cold roast beef, salt and pepper.

ASPARAGUS AND SMOKED SALMON

A baguette split lengthways, generously spread with mayonnaise, blanched asparagus tips, and thick strips of smoked salmon, seasoned with plenty of pepper.

SARDINES

2 thin slices of country bread, boned sardines mashed with a fork and mixed with some finely chopped shallot. Spread the bread with a mixture of two-thirds softened butter and one-third Dijon mustard, fill with the sardines and season to taste with lemon juice, salt and pepper.

HARD-BOILED EGG AND TUNA

2 slices of rye bread, coarsely chopped hard-boiled egg, drained flaked tuna and a few capers, bound with mayonnaise, diced segments of grapefruit, and seasoned with paprika.

HAM AND WATERCRESS

White bread spread with a mixture of lightly whipped double cream, Dijon mustard and finely diced pineapple, filled with thinly sliced ham and shredded watercress.

BARBECUED GOAT'S CHEESE WRAPPED IN VINE LEAVES

Fromage de chèvre en feuilles de vigne au barbecue

*T*HE *apple takes the sharpness off these little goat's cheeses and adds a delicious soft texture. A green salad makes the perfect accompaniment to this dish, which is one we adore. Do take care as you eat not to burn your tongue on the hot cheese.*

PREPARATION TIME
10 minutes, plus 3 hours marinating

COOKING TIME
12 minutes

INGREDIENTS
120 g/4 oz English goat's cheese (preferably Burndell or Ribblesdale), in one piece, or 2 small semi-dried French goat's cheeses

8 vine leaves preserved in brine

½ eating apple (preferably a Cox)

FOR THE MARINADE:
10 white peppercorns

10 soft green peppercorns

3 basil leaves, snipped

leaves from a sprig of thyme

1 teaspoon lemon juice

a pinch of salt

50 ml/2 fl oz olive oil

PREPARATION

The cheeses: If you are using English cheese, cut the piece in half.
The marinade: Put all the marinade ingredients except the oil in a small mortar and crush with a pestle. Put the 2 pieces of goat's cheese in a bowl. Add the olive oil to the crushed marinade ingredients, then pour the marinade over the cheese. Cover with clingfilm and leave to marinate for at least 3 hours.
The vine leaves: Blanch in a pan of boiling water for 5 minutes, then refresh, drain and remove the stems.
The apple: Peel, core and grate as finely as possible.

WRAPPING THE CHEESES

On a tea towel, lay 4 vine leaves side by side, overlapping them slightly so as not to leave any gaps between them. Spoon one-quarter of the marinade over the vine leaves, add one-quarter of the grated apple, then a piece of cheese. Place another quarter of the apple on the cheese and fold up the vine leaves so that the cheese is completely enclosed.

Assemble the second piece of cheese in the same way.

COOKING

Place the wrapped cheeses on a hot, but not searing, barbecue or in a grill pan and cook for 6 minutes on each side.

PRESENTATION

Serve the cheeses on individual plates as soon as they are cooked. Pull away the vine leaves with a spoon and fork and enjoy the contents.

NOTES

The English cheeses suggested in the ingredients taste quite delicious prepared and served in this way, particularly the Burndell.

CINNAMON-FLAVOURED BANANAS AND PEARS 'EN PAPILLOTE'
Bananes et poires à la canelle en papillote

A delectable dish for late summer or early autumn. Michel loves to prepare this dessert at his shepherd's cottage in Provence, where he serves it with a fine kirsch.

PREPARATION

Put the orange and lemon juices and the apricot jam in the pan and cook over low heat for 3 minutes, until slightly syrupy. Pour into a bowl and keep in a cool place.
  Preheat the oven to 220°C/425°F/gas 7, if using.

THE PAPILLOTE

Peel the pears and bananas. Cut the pears into 1 cm/½ in slices and the bananas into 1 cm/½ in rounds. Mix into the cooled fruit syrup and add a pinch of cinnamon. Make a double thickness 40 × 30 cm/16 × 12 in rectangle of foil, brush the centre of the foil with butter and pour the fruit mixture into the middle. Fold up the open sides of the foil and roll over the edges to make a completely airtight parcel.

COOKING

Place the parcel on a very hot barbecue or, if you prefer, in the preheated oven for 4 minutes, until the foil papillote has puffed up.

PRESENTATION

Pierce the papillote with the point of a knife so that it keeps its puffy shape. Slide it on to a plate and cut it open with scissors only at the moment of serving. The most delicious aromas will waft out. Sprinkle the fruit with kirsch if you are using it, and serve with a spoon or a small ladle.

NOTES

The filled papillote can be kept in the fridge for 8–10 hours before cooking. Do not keep it for longer, or the fruits will soften and lose their savour.

PREPARATION TIME
10 minutes

COOKING TIME
4 minutes

INGREDIENTS

2 pears
2 bananas
juice of ½ medium orange
juice of ½ lemon
2 teaspoons apricot jam
a pinch of ground cinnamon
20 g/¾ oz softened butter
4 teaspoons kirsch (optional)

MERINGUE HEART FOR LOVERS

Coeur de meringue pour nous deux

*W*ITH *this delicious meringue heart filled with a selection of colourful and juicy summer fruits, you can declare or reaffirm your love to your dearest companion.*

PREPARATION TIME
25 minutes

COOKING TIME
1 ½ hours

INGREDIENTS

French meringue made with 2 egg whites (recipe, page 29)

1 teaspoon butter

a pinch of flour

100 ml/4 fl oz double cream

2 teaspoons icing sugar

the seeds from ¼ vanilla pod, or a few drops of vanilla essence

30 g/1 oz small strawberries

30 g/1 oz raspberries

30 g/1 oz redcurrants

30 g/1 oz blueberries

2 sprigs of mint (optional)

PREPARATION

The meringue hearts: On a sheet of greaseproof paper, use a pencil to draw 4 hearts, 12 cm/5 in wide and 11 cm/4½ in high. Lightly butter the paper and dust with a pinch of flour. Put the prepared meringue into a piping bag fitted with a plain 8 mm/⅓ in nozzle and pipe out the meringue, following the outline of the hearts. Inside one of the hearts, continue to pipe more hearts, until the whole shape is filled with meringue.

Preheat the oven to 130°C/250°F/gas 1.

COOKING

Leave the meringue to dry out in the preheated oven for 1½ hours, then carefully remove the filled heart and the outlines from the paper and place them on a wire rack in a very dry place.

Chantilly cream: In a bowl, whip the cream with the sugar and vanilla until fairly stiff. Place in the fridge.

The fruits: Wash, remove the stalks or hull as appropriate. Place in the fridge.

PRESENTATION

Fill a piping bag fitted with the same nozzle as before with the Chantilly cream. Pipe a little cream on to the edge of the filled heart, then place a heart outline on top. Repeat with more cream and another heart outline. (The extra outline should be kept as a spare in case of breakages.) Pipe in more cream to fill the heart-shaped case, then arrange the fruits attractively in concentric rows, with a little mound of blueberries in the centre. Decorate with mint sprigs if you like.

NOTES

To make successful meringue, you must use at least 2 egg whites. Any excess mixture can be piped out into small meringues, cooked and enjoyed as petits fours with coffee. Although I have suggested making an extra outline as a precaution, if it is not needed, you can, of course, eat it as well!

The filled heart can be transported quite easily, provided that you do not drop it, but it does not take kindly to very hot weather.

STRAWBERRY TART WITH PRESERVED GINGER 'MONT-VENTOUX'
Tarte aux fraises Mont-Ventoux

*W*E have never been able to say 'No' to fruit tarts. As children, they were always a favourite and our love of them has stayed with us. The ginger in the cream in this tart is a delicious surprise for your unsuspecting guest.

PREPARATION TIME
20 minutes, plus 30 minutes chilling

COOKING TIME
30 minutes

INGREDIENTS
120 g/4 oz Sweet shortcrust pastry (recipe, page 22)

a pinch of flour

butter, for greasing the flan ring

100 ml/4 fl oz double cream

30 g/1 oz preserved ginger, grated

250 g/9 oz strawberries

2 tablespoons redcurrant jelly, melted and cooled

1 tablespoon flaked almonds, toasted

PREPARATION

The pastry case: On a lightly floured surface, roll out the pastry into a circle about 3 mm/$\frac{1}{8}$ in thick. Use it to line a buttered 12 cm/5 in flan ring, 2 cm/$\frac{3}{4}$ in deep, and place on a baking sheet. Leave to rest in the fridge for 30 minutes.
   Preheat the oven to 220°C/425°F/gas 7.

COOKING THE PASTRY CASE

Prick the base in about 10 places with the point of a knife. Line the pastry with a 16 cm/$6\frac{1}{2}$ in circle of greaseproof paper and fill with baking beans or pulses. Bake for 25 minutes. Remove the baking beans with a spoon, then remove the paper and return the pastry case to the oven for 5 minutes. Transfer the pastry case to a wire rack, remove the flan ring and leave to cool at room temperature.

FILLING THE TART

Whip the cream with the ginger to a ribbon consistency, then put it into the cooled pastry case. Wash the strawberries if necessary, drain and hull them, and arrange them in the pastry case, heaping them up in the centre to form a 'mountain'. Brush the strawberries with the cooled redcurrant jelly and scatter the toasted flaked almonds on top.

PRESENTATION

Serve the tart on a plate and slice it when you and your guest are ready to eat it.

NOTES

The pastry case can be baked the day before, if you prefer, but do not fill it more than 6 hours in advance, or the pastry will start to become soggy. A shortbread dough base (recipe, page 25) is perfect for this tart if you are not intending to transport it, but is too fragile to be carried to a picnic.

APRICOT MERINGUE PILLOWS WITH RASPBERRY COULIS

Les oreillons d'abricots meringués au coulis de framboise

*T*HIS *delicate dessert is particularly good at the height of the season when apricots are at their ripest and most tender and raspberries their juiciest.*

PREPARATION

The apricots: Put 200 g/7 oz sugar in a saucepan with 400 ml/14 fl oz water and slowly bring to the boil. Halve the apricots across the middle, remove the stones and drop the apricot halves into the syrup. Add the lemon juice and gently poach the apricots for 3 minutes. Take the pan off the heat and leave the fruit to cool in the syrup at room temperature.

The raspberry coulis: Put the raspberries in a blender with 40 g/1½ oz sugar and 2 tablespoons of the poaching syrup from the apricots. Purée for 2 minutes, then rub the coulis through a conical sieve into the bottom of a gratin dish.

Preheat the oven to 170°C/325°F/gas 3.

ASSEMBLING THE MERINGUE 'PILLOWS'

Thoroughly drain the apricots and lay them on the raspberry coulis in the gratin dish. Put 300 ml/11 fl oz poaching syrup in a saucepan and reduce over high heat until very thick.

Beat the egg whites until stiff, then gently pour on the thick boiling syrup, whisking continuously. Whisk for 5 minutes, until the meringue has cooled slightly. Fill a piping bag fitted with a ridged 1 cm/½ in nozzle with the meringue and pipe it all over the apricots to cover them completely and attractively. Bake in the preheated oven for 30 minutes. Immediately the meringues are cooked, scatter over the flaked almonds, and keep at room temperature.

PRESENTATION

This dessert should be served either tepid or cold, straight from the dish.

NOTES

As the meringue is delicate and will begin to soften if left too long, this dessert is best eaten within 24 hours. To take it to a picnic, stretch a piece of clingfilm very tautly over the gratin dish, taking great care not to let it touch the meringue.

PREPARATION TIME
30 minutes

COOKING TIME
30 minutes

INGREDIENTS

6 very ripe fresh apricots, total weight about 400 g/14 oz

250 g/9 oz caster sugar

juice of ½ lemon

120 g/4 oz very ripe raspberries

2 egg whites

1 tablespoon flaked almonds, lightly toasted

GRAND CHOCOLATE CHOUX BUN

Grand chou au cacao

*T*HIS *wonderful chocolate, cream-filled dessert is made for sharing. You must both sink your teeth in; it is essential to enjoy it without undue politeness!*

PREPARATION TIME
10 minutes

COOKING TIME
35 minutes

INGREDIENTS

120 g/4 oz Choux paste (recipe, page 24)

30 g/1 oz bitter dark dessert chocolate, melted

50 ml/2 fl oz double cream, whipped to a ribbon consistency

1 tablespoon kirsch (optional)

70 g/2½ oz Pastry cream (recipe, page 29)

1 tablespoon cocoa powder

1 teaspoon icing sugar

PREPARATION

Fill a piping bag fitted with a plain nozzle with the choux paste. On a small baking sheet, pipe out a huge choux bun, 8–9 cm/3¼–3½ in in diameter. Dip the prongs of a fork into a little cold water and lightly press the top of the choux bun twice with the back of the prongs to make an attractive pattern.

Preheat the oven to 230°C/450°F/gas 8.

COOKING

Cook the bun in the preheated oven for 25 minutes, then lower the temperature to 190°C/375°F/gas 5 and cook for another 10 minutes. Place the cooked choux bun on a wire rack and keep at room temperature.

FILLING THE BUN

Using a serrated knife, cut across the bun two-thirds up from the base. Generously brush the inside of the base and lid with tepid melted chocolate. Leave at room temperature for a few minutes, until the chocolate has set.

Mix the whipped cream and kirsch, if you are using it, into the pastry cream. Spoon this mixture into the choux bun and replace the lid.

PRESENTATION

Using a sugar caster or fine sieve, generously dust the top of the bun with cocoa, then with a little icing sugar to make an attractive pattern.

NOTES

To make successful choux paste, it is necessary to make more than you need for this recipe. Any extra can be used to make little cheesy buns which you can sprinkle with gruyère or parmesan to serve with an aperitif. Alternatively, since choux paste freezes well, freeze the extra for later use.

This choux bun travels quite well. Remember to take along your caster so that you can sprinkle on the cocoa and icing sugar at the last moment.

INDEX

Page references in italic refer to photographs